SHARIA COMPLIANT

Sharia Compliant

A User's Guide to Hacking Islamic Law

Rumee Ahmed

STANFORD UNIVERSITY PRESS
Stanford, California

Stanford University Press
Stanford, California

© 2018 by the Board of Trustees of the Leland Stanford Junior University.
All rights reserved.

No part of this book may be reproduced or transmitted in any form or by any means, electronic or mechanical, including photocopying and recording, or in any information storage or retrieval system without the prior written permission of Stanford University Press.

Printed in the United States of America on acid-free, archival-quality paper

Library of Congress Cataloging-in-Publication Data is available upon request.

ISBN 9780804794015 (cloth)
ISBN 9781503605701 (paperback)
ISBN 9781503605718 (electronic)

Cover design: Angela Moody
Typeset by Motto Publishing Services in 11.5/16 Adobe Caslon Pro

For Dr. A. S. Bear, now and always

Contents

A Letter to My Muslim Readers

Something's wrong. Something's *very* wrong. But you already knew that. Every Friday *khutba*, every lecture, every dinner discussion about the plight of Muslims today seems to center on this foundational truth of our modern existence: something's wrong. The evidence is clear to anyone who's looking; from feckless leaders to systematic disempowerment to regressive institutions, we regularly and readily acknowledge amongst ourselves that something is deeply wrong with the current state of the Muslim community.

It's true; something is indeed wrong, but that fact doesn't bother me much. If there's one thing we've learned from increased connectivity and globalization, it's that every community's got something wrong with it. No community is free from violent factions, corruption, misogyny, racism, homophobia, and any number of other vices that pervade corners of our community, and no community is safe from being manipulated for political and economic gain. These are the hallmarks of most every community today, and Muslims are no exception.

No, what bothers me is not so much the *fact* that something is wrong, but the *reason* that our religious leaders most often give for why something is wrong. Across different countries and contexts, I consistently hear the same diagnosis given for the problems plaguing the Muslim community: we are not practicing Islam properly, and we are not following Islamic law. If we were to follow Islamic law correctly, we are told, all of the community's problems would instantly disappear.

For over a generation, I've heard that line repeated by scholars and community leaders the world over, and I'm disheartened to see a new generation of scholars repeating it to a new generation of Muslims with no end in sight. One would think that our leaders, after decades of delivering the same line with no demonstrable results, would try a different approach. After all, repeating the same thing over and over again but expecting different results is, as the saying goes, the very definition of insanity.

I don't believe in the line that our religious leaders constantly repeat to us—that we, the Muslim community, are the cause of all our problems because we are deficient believers with a substandard relationship to Islamic law. Our Prophet taught us to always give the community the benefit of the doubt and to put our trust in its collective wisdom, assuring us that "my community will not agree upon error." I believe that our community is always bent toward justice and that when we make our collective voices heard, we cannot be wrong. I believe this in all matters, including Islamic law. If our religious leaders have a problem with the Muslim majority's relationship with Islamic law, then the problem does not lie with us but with them.

We are taught to side with the community whenever we can and to have a healthy skepticism of institutionalized religious leadership. As a community, we do not recognize any official clerical hierarchy, and therefore no one person can officially say what is or is not Islamic law. That means that the entire community collectively owns Islamic law and that each one of us, as community members, has equal ownership rights. That is part of the beauty of our tradition; we all own the law together, no one can judge another's religious practice, and you never really know whose interpretation of the law is objectively right. This is a tradition of which we should be proud; it models a kind of radical egalitarianism in which all humans have equal standing and in which legal pluralism is a central feature.

This is perhaps the defining aspect of the Islamic tradition, yet it often goes unmentioned by our religious leaders. That is because our leaders are, by and large, invested in giving the impression that they alone have exclusive knowledge of Islamic law. Many of them have made it their business to make you feel unworthy, unentitled, and unqualified to weigh in on Islamic law, regardless of whether you have engaged in careful textual study or not. Instead, they say that you ought to listen to their opinions without question. Many religious leaders—especially those who are also legal scholars—would have you believe that you must obey them in all things and that questioning them is tantamount to heresy, apostasy, and treason.

This authoritarian approach to Islamic law, built on shaming the community into compliance, violates the Islamic spirit and, perhaps more importantly, hides the fact that Muslim legal scholars, even those who are well-known, do not represent the will and wisdom of the community. Numerous studies and surveys have demonstrated a significant divide between Islamic legal scholars and the larger Muslim community that they claim to represent, and poll numbers suggest that most Muslims neither attend mosques nor listen to, or even respect, the opinions of legal scholars.

Having spent years studying in seminaries around the world, I have experienced firsthand the disconnect between legal scholars and the rest of the community. Seminaries tend to function like safe havens from the chaos of the modern world, and Islamic law can be discussed inside a seminary without reference to social and political realities. The result is that seminaries can become a parallel universe. People tend to think differently in seminaries and to hold beliefs that make little sense outside of them. They even speak in a particular dialect, one that uses lots of old-fashioned words and turns of phrase.

The scholars in these seminaries are demonstrably out of sync with the broader Muslim community, often clinging to outmoded ideas like gold-standard economics and Aristotelian physics. I've found myself in arguments with seminarians about gravitational pull, the existence of birth-control pills, and whether schizophrenia is caused by jinn possession. More importantly, I've seen the profound disconnect between the worldviews of most Islamic legal scholars and the majority of Muslims on foundational religious, social, and political issues. This disconnect is not so much because legal scholars reject the views of the Muslim community as that they don't even know about them to begin with.

I remember a seminary class on tax law, taught in Classical Arabic, in which our American-born, Pakistani-educated teacher read aloud from a thirteenth-century text about the different tax levies assessed on various types of jewelry: bangles, tiaras, anklets, earrings, broaches, necklaces, and much, much more. The student body was entirely male, as is the case with most seminaries, and this particular tax class was, from our perspective, entirely pointless. We didn't own any jewelry ourselves, but even if we had, we would have paid our taxes based on state law, not on the thirteenth-century text we were studying. At one point, the teacher looked up from his book and saw that we had clearly checked out. He hit the table and said, "You need to pay attention! You have to know this so that you can teach it to your mothers and sisters and wives."

One student, fighting boredom, chimed in, "Or to a guy with an earring."

Our American-born teacher, in genuine disbelief, asked, "Why would a guy have an earring?"

While legal scholars have been studying in seminaries and parsing medieval texts, the Muslim community has moved on. Whereas legal scholars continue to argue about whether men and women can work in the same space, Muslim-majority states have created quotas to ensure female representation in their parliaments. As legal scholars debate whether democracy is "Islamic," most Muslims have chosen democratic rule for themselves and report that they believe democracy to be the ideal system of governance.

Some of our religious leaders have embraced the community's changing beliefs and practices, but many more have not. Most have responded by saying that the Muslim community is doing things wrong, that it is on a dangerous path, and that Muslims must repent and change their ways if they hope to attain salvation. But if we believe in the collective wisdom of the community, then it is not the community that is wrong but the disconnected religious scholars who oppose the community. If the community cannot agree upon error, then, to determine correct practice, we as community members have to make clear what we *actually* agree upon rather than rely on a small group of people to tell us what we *ought to* agree upon.

That will require us to speak back to the religious elite and to ourselves articulate Islamic laws that better represent our beliefs and aspirations. To do that, we will first have to become literate in Islamic law and become comfortable speaking its language. That will require familiarizing ourselves with the foundations of Islamic legal thought and becoming skilled in an ancient Islamic legal practice, called in this book "hacking."

Hacking is a modern term that describes the process of using existing tools to make something work better or more efficiently. Whenever someone comes up with a new use for an existing product or combines previously unrelated things to solve a problem, we call that a hack. Essentially, hacks are ways to solve problems using no new tools. Businesses now encourage hacking cultures, and institutions run hack-a-thons that bring together teams of unrelated individuals to solve thorny problems. Many universities, including my own, teach courses on ethical hacking to teach students how to come up with ingenious solutions to social problems without causing unintended harm.

Hacking is about working within a system, using its existing tools to make it work better without bringing the whole thing down.

I use the term *hacking* in that sense, and in that sense, hacking is a time-honored Islamic legal tradition. From the earliest times, Muslim scholars wrote legal codes that they claimed reflected values and ideals sanctioned by the community. Whenever the community's values and ideals shifted, scholars would adjust laws, not by rewriting legal codes from scratch but by hacking existing codes so that they changed specific, targeted groups of laws while leaving the underlying legal structure intact. They did this to, for example, abolish slavery, embrace religious pluralism, and develop "sharia-compliant" financial vehicles, among many other things. Each time, rather than reject or replace old laws, Muslim legal scholars hacked them, making them work differently and better in new contexts. As you will see in this book, almost any law can be hacked in this way to better reflect the evolving collective wisdom of the community.

Muslims have been hacking Islamic law for centuries using highly intricate and sophisticated methods. These methods are tried and true and can be learned by anyone with the requisite interest and dedication. That is fortunate, because we need more Muslims to engage in hacking if Islamic law today is to reflect the beliefs of the larger Muslim community. Islamic law has divine sanction only when it reflects the beliefs of the community, and to get to that point, we need community members to express their beliefs about Islamic law.

Hearteningly, Muslims around the world—in Nigeria and Indonesia and Iran and India and North America—are using newfound modes of connectivity to express their deeply held beliefs in the language of Islamic law. Millions of Muslims are now hacking Islamic law free from the watchful eye of the state and the religious establishment. Their hacks challenge common assumptions about Islam and Muslims promoted by powerful religious and political actors. They openly and unreservedly embrace values like human rights, gender egalitarianism, and religious liberty—values that polls suggest most Muslims today support. Importantly, these modern hacks are carefully argued and thoroughly researched, drawing on over a thousand years of Islamic thought, and are expressed in a language that respects an ancient Islamic legal tradition without compromising contemporary ideals.

More Muslims need to take part in hacking to express the collective will of the community and to put pressure on our leaders to take our ideas seriously, fully engage with them, and ultimately adopt them as the truest expressions of Islamic law. This book is designed to help you do that. It will introduce you to the hacking conversation so that you too can express yourself as a community member using the language of Islamic law. Your voice will help us get one step closer to having Islamic law reflect the beliefs of the Muslim community and serve as a forward-looking force for good in this world.

Your voice is also your right; as members of a radically egalitarian community, each one of us has just as much right to Islamic law as anyone else. And in this day and age, in which our thoughts can be shared and amplified without going through official channels, it is our responsibility to make our voices heard and our views known. The fact is, something is wrong. But we are not the problem. We are the solution.

SHARIA COMPLIANT

CHAPTER 1

What Is Sharia? What Is Islamic Law?
What Is Hacking?

IN THIS BOOK, we're going to learn the ins and outs of an ancient Islamic legal practice that I call hacking. Before we start, however, we'll have to answer some basic questions, like, What is sharia? I'd love to say that there's a quick answer to that, but sharia has become so politicized in recent years that defining the term itself is now a political act. People from different ends of the political spectrum want you to believe that sharia is one particular thing or the other. Some say that sharia is the ancient, unchanging law of Islam and Muslims; others counter that it is just an ideal for good living that can never be reduced to specific laws. Some warn that sharia will be the downfall of civilized society; others insist that it will usher in peace and justice. Some describe sharia as oppressive; others say it is liberating. Some say it should be incorporated into state laws; others caution that it should be kept as far away from the state as possible. Some say it is central to every Muslim's life; others say it is peripheral. Sharia is backward; sharia is progressive.

How can we tell which sharia is the real one? They can't all be true at the same time, so how do we distinguish fact from hype? To answer that, we might try to identify some objective source of knowledge that will give us a straightforward, unbiased take on sharia. There are two sources that are commonly called on to provide objective information about the sharia: Islamic legal texts and Muslim beliefs and practices.

Some people argue that looking at texts written by Muslim scholars will give us an inside look at sharia that's free from spin and political correctness. Others argue that we should instead look to Muslim beliefs and practices to see how everyday Muslims understand and implement sharia in their daily lives. Beliefs and practices, in that way of thinking, should show us how sharia functions regardless of what elite Muslim scholars wrote in their texts. These presumably objective sources—texts, beliefs, and practices—should move us beyond punditry and give us a clear picture of what the sharia really is and how it works.

Unfortunately for us, these sources do not help us determine a single, objective definition of the sharia because texts, beliefs, and practices can all say opposite and conflicting things. These "objective" sources can be used to "prove" that the sharia is static and unchanging, but they can also be used to "prove" that it is highly flexible and dynamic. They can show us that sharia is central to Muslim life, and they can also show us that most Muslims couldn't care less about sharia. That might sound ridiculous: after all, how can the same sources be used to prove opposite points?

Let's take the example of Islamic legal texts. We might think that by reading what Muslim scholars wrote about sharia, we will get an unmediated look at what sharia is supposed to be. Even though most of the world's 1.6 billion Muslims don't read Islamic legal texts any more than they read local zoning codes, legal texts might still help us get a basic definition for the sharia. That makes sense, except that different Islamic legal texts say different things about sharia. Take, for example, the following text from the renowned legal scholar Ibn Taymiyya (d. 1328). In his view, sharia is a law that was devised many centuries ago, one that is unchanging and totalizing:

> No statement or action or intention is worth anything unless
> it agrees with [Muhammad's] Prophetic practice. That is the
> sharia, and it is what God and Muhammad commanded. State-

ments and actions and intentions that do not agree with Prophetic practice are innovations, and God does not love them or accept them.

Ibn Taymiyya's message is pretty clear: follow the sharia, which is contained in Muhammad's practices, and don't act otherwise or else God will be unhappy. Ibn Taymiyya makes sharia sound like an ancient, unchanging law laid down by the Prophet for all Muslims to follow in all times and places. But Ibn Taymiyya is just one voice among many. If we turn our attention to a different legal text, this one written by Ibn Taymiyya's star student, Ibn al-Qayyim (d. 1350), we find the exact opposite:

> Indeed, the sharia is founded upon wisdom and welfare for worshippers in this life and the afterlife. In its entirety it is justice, mercy, welfare, and wisdom. Any matter that abandons justice for tyranny, mercy for cruelty, welfare for corruption, and wisdom for foolishness cannot be part of the sharia.

Ibn al-Qayyim described the sharia as elastic; it is defined not by set practices but by "justice, mercy, benefit, and wisdom." Just to be clear, Ibn al-Qayyim added that

> Allah the Exalted has made clear in the sharia that the objective is the establishment of justice between worshippers and fairness among the people, so whichever part leads to justice and fairness is part of the religion and can never oppose it.

For Ibn Taymiyya, sharia is fixed and never changes, but for his student, Ibn al-Qayyim, the sharia always changes to meet the demands of justice and fairness. This kind of divergent thinking is common. Muslim legal scholars throughout history have offered up different and conflicting versions of the sharia, and their diversity of thought is captured in their legal texts. So, it seems that Islamic legal texts will not help us come up with a single definition for the sharia.

Since texts don't give us a definitive answer, some have turned to Muslim beliefs and practices. Maybe everyday Muslims could tell us what they think about sharia, especially since most of them don't read Islamic legal texts anyway. Do Muslims believe that sharia is central to Muslim life or that it is peripheral? Is it fixed, or does it change? Several polls have been taken over the last decade to answer exactly these kinds of questions. A recent Pew poll, for example, asked approximately thirty thousand Muslims around the world about their opinions on sharia law. About 70 percent thought that sharia should be the law of the land. That figure seems pretty clear. One could reasonably conclude that sharia is incredibly important to Muslim life and practice, so much so that it should be the official state law and, like most official laws, should be a fixed entity that is very difficult to change.

A trip to almost any Muslim-majority country, however, will challenge that conclusion. Mosques mostly sit empty; Islamic laws are rarely, if ever, enforced; and Muslims do not seem engaged or even interested in sharia law. When asked, the majority of Muslims in that same Pew poll admitted that they do not pray even once a week (let alone five times a day), that they prefer democracy as a system of government, and that religious freedom is a good thing. So, while they support sharia as the law of the land, they also support democracy and religious freedom and do not follow sharia in their daily lives. If you were to ask your average Muslim about sharia, they would likely tell you that it's a good thing but would be unable to provide any specifics about what sharia actually is. They would likely say that it is incredibly important but not important enough to do anything about.

We quickly see a recurring problem with probing either legal texts or Muslim public opinion to understand sharia: different Muslims have different definitions for and different relationships with sharia. What's more, a single individual might use the term *sharia* differently in different contexts. In legal texts, for instance, the same author might refer to sharia as a specific legal system in one chapter and as an ambiguous moral code in another. If you're not reading carefully, it's easy to get confused. Similarly, when Muslims talk about the importance of sharia, they are sometimes referring to a system of justice and other times referring to a personal law that is between them and God; still other times, they are referring to a system of religious governance. And sometimes, the term *sharia* has nothing to do with laws or governance at all.

Even people who study sharia for a living have a complicated relationship with it. A friend told me about taking his father, a Muslim legal scholar, to meet his new daughter-in-law. When they got to her house, she let them in, seated them, and then left the room. My friend's father was incensed:

"What kind of girl is this?" he demanded. "She didn't even offer us tea!"

"Well," my friend reminded him, "according to the sharia, she doesn't have to give us tea."

His father, the scholar, thundered, "Well, the sharia can go to hell!"

The man wanted his tea.

In the lives of Muslims around the world, sharia means and represents many things. It is all the more peculiar, then, that popular discourse about sharia today narrows it into a kind of law that might or might not apply on a state level. Muslims and non-Muslims alike appear on television and write books that debate whether to adopt sharia as state law, effectively ignoring all the other ways in which Muslims understand the sharia. This is largely because over the last century, sharia has taken on an increasingly important and very specific role in many Muslim-majority states. Some states now tout the fact that they implement sharia on the state level. Many Muslim activists and reformers object to that and insist that sharia should be kept out of statecraft. Some Muslims say state-based sharia is not so bad, whereas other Muslims say it is an abomination.

This very specific debate tends to take up all the airtime devoted to sharia, and we hear about sharia only when people are insisting that it will either nurture or destroy civilization. As a result, we think about sharia only as related to law, and we overlook the fluid and dynamic ways in which most Muslims interact with it. Here, we need to stop and understand how we got to this place. That is, how did it come to be that sharia, if it is so expansive and diverse, is now spoken about in only narrow, purely legalistic terms? There are two connected topics that we will need to examine to answer that; the first has to do with recent Muslim history, and the second has to do with persistent myths about Islam and Muslims.

We should look at recent Muslim history first, because it feeds into the myths about Islam and Muslims that we have today. To do that, we'll have to quickly review the development of Islamic law over the last six hundred years. Through a recap of modern world history, we'll see that the experiences of colonialism and anticolonialism and the rise of Muslim nation-states have skewed the conversation about sharia into one that is obsessed with state practice and law, even as Muslims around the world continue to have varied and complex relationships to sharia.

The Last Few Centuries: A Quick Review

After the Prophet Muhammad died in 632, the small Muslim community that he founded in Arabia expanded very quickly, and within a few hundred years Muslim groups were ruling large swaths of North Africa, southeast Europe, the Middle East, and South Asia. The collective fortune of the Muslim community steadily increased, and by the mid-1400s, Muslims controlled Mecca, Cairo,

Constantinople, Cordova, Fes, Isfahan, Samarqand, Timbuktu, and many other major cities. When you read Islamic texts from that era, it's clear that Muslims thought they ruled the world. Never mind that these places were ruled by different dynasties that often hated one another; all that mattered for Muslims writing in that time was that the most important places in the world—the Arabian Peninsula, Anatolia, Andalusia (for a long time), India (not all of it), Palestine (more or less), Persia, and key parts of the Silk Road (kind of)—were ruled by Muslims. Muslim writers took great pride in that fact. They occasionally mentioned pale barbarians in the Northwest and uneducated marauders to the east, but on the whole, those groups were treated as curiosities. All the action was in Muslim lands, and Muslim writers assumed that everyone wanted to be there.

That started to change with European colonialism, which was aided by a leap in European military technology and a papal bull. In the 1450s, Pope Nicholas V decreed that God had granted Christians command over all the earth. The church thereafter deputized Catholic countries to claim for themselves newly discovered lands in the name of Christendom, allowing them to enslave local populations, especially Muslims, pagans, and anyone else they deemed to be "infidels." With church sanction, several European countries raced to colonize these lands, especially those that had vast natural resources, poor defenses, and weak central governments. Colonizers found many such lands in Africa and the Americas, and so they concentrated much of their early efforts there.

As Catholics were colonizing and enslaving, the Protestant Reformation was gaining steam in Europe, undermining the theological and political authority of the Catholic Church. Protestants battled Catholics for power throughout Europe; each group condemned the other for various heresies, and Protestants began to establish colonies of their own to challenge the hegemony of the Catholic Church and to augment state coffers. With the aid of guns and germs, Catholic and Protestant powers vied with one another to colonize newly discovered lands. When lands were not so easily colonized—as was the case with Egypt, China, India, and Indonesia, which all had relatively strong central governments and armies—Europeans would set up coastal outposts that funneled resources out for international trade.

Except for the relatively rare case in which people fled to a colonized region in search of religious freedom, the colonial enterprise was primarily about control over Europe. Catholics and Protestants fought with one another across Europe, and the colonial enterprise funded their bloody, protracted, and expensive wars. Oftentimes, colonies served as sites for proxy wars between European nations, where colonial powers would engage in increasingly costly battles over trade routes.

To dominate trade routes that were now moving vast amounts of wealth, European countries initiated a naval arms race. In 1588, the English navy, representing Protestant interests, won a decisive victory over Catholic Spain's Armada. The Protestant Dutch, too, scored several victories over the Catholic Portuguese in Southeast Asia, allowing them to set up ports there and reap enormous profits. The reverberations of these military victories were felt throughout the world as Protestant nations became far more confident in their dominance over trade routes. They began to consolidate their power in coastal ports, assuming full control over several port towns, establishing army outposts therein, and asserting colonial jurisdiction over nearby cities and towns. Many Muslim polities at the time found that, despite having Muslim figureheads as rulers, their economic output was increasingly being controlled by Europe.

By consolidating coastal port towns and putting them fully under colonial control, colonial powers intended to boost returns on trade without having to actually conquer the land. They did not wish to absorb the colonized country altogether; the messy process of governing a new land would divert precious resources away from trade. Colonial powers had a vested interest in limited governance that maximized production while minimizing investment. Much of the work of governance was outsourced to the private sector through agencies such as the British East India Company and the Dutch East India Company. These companies worked with their respective Crowns to establish a system of vicegerency in which the company would enforce certain criminal laws and economic policies to ensure economic dominance without interfering with the local customs of colonial subjects. In this system, criminal cases (involving crimes like murder and embezzlement) would be adjudicated by colonial law, and civil cases (involving interpersonal issues like marriage and divorce) would be adjudicated by local, often religious, laws in local courts by local judges.

Colonial powers figured that it would be simple enough to develop a criminal code based in colonial law, which they did through a mash-up of the Law of England, the Napoleonic Code, and, oddly enough, the Louisiana Civil Code of 1825. They then set about developing a separate civil code that would be wholly based on local religious laws. The problem was that, in Muslim lands, as in most colonized lands, there was no such thing as a set of "local, religious laws." Instead, there were many different laws, some of which were based in local practices and others that were contained in thousands of various Islamic legal texts. These legal texts were not really codes of law; they were highly theoretical works that often contained multiple rulings on a single subject. Plus, different legal texts often disagreed with one another.

To complicate matters further, these legal texts were not legally binding and were not enforced by authorities. Judges, for instance, were not bound to rule based on any of these texts, and although judges might have personally preferred one legal text over another, they were ultimately free to rule based on their own discretion. Theoretically, a Muslim living in India could have gone to a court in Delhi and gotten one ruling and then gone to a court in Agra and gotten a completely different ruling on the same case. This was not a problem for the Muslims of India; it was just how things were done.

This system, however, was anathema to colonists. Based on their understanding of law and justice, they thought that only one law ought to apply equally to all cases within a colony. To correct what they saw as legal anarchy, vicegerents in different colonies commissioned European scholars to work with local populations to develop a single, codified civil law. Each major colony would have its own codified civil law based on its particular history and the beliefs, practices, and customs of its inhabitants. But as noted above, there was no single law that governed all Muslims; instead, there were legal scholars who would argue about the law through theoretical legal texts and judges who would apply the law at their discretion.

Colonists could have borrowed from the then popular Muslim practice of collecting a range of acceptable legal opinions from various legal texts and presenting them as options that judges could choose from when adjudicating civil cases. That would have been laborious and time-consuming but would have better captured how Islamic law functioned in Muslim society. They decided not to do that. Instead, they simply singled out some popular precolonial Islamic legal texts and proclaimed that they contained "the sharia." Colonial officials and scholars then translated those books, edited them, and imported whatever was related to civil law into official codes that would thereafter apply to all Muslims in the colony. This was a bizarre move, because even a cursory look at precolonial Islamic legal texts will reveal that they were never intended for that purpose; they were written not as state laws but as theoretical arguments. They were not law books in the modern sense; they were full of hypotheticals and counterfactuals, and they opined about laws with the understanding that judges might refer to them but would rule using their discretion.

For colonists looking to fill out a legal code, though, these precolonial Islamic legal texts looked perfect. They were full of what looked like laws, and they proved useful for creating official civil codes. In India, for instance, long passages from the twelfth-century legal text *al-Hidaya* were simply lifted and inserted into the colonial civil code, with predictably disastrous consequences, some of which we will see later in this book. Once these civil codes were in place, if someone wanted to obtain a divorce in Heliopolis, she would theoretically go through the same process and get the same ruling as she would have in Cairo, all based on the musings of a man who wrote a legal text in the medieval period. Judges were no longer supposed to use their discretion when deciding cases; they were instead instructed to stick to the letter of the precolonial civil laws codified by colonists. With codification, judges did not even have to be Muslim to rule based on the new Islamic code, and in many cases, they were not. Muslim legal scholars were effectively sidelined; with the law already codified, they were no longer needed to make theoretical arguments about the nature and content of the law.

Colonists did all this in the name of religious accommodation. They claimed that by codifying law in this way, they were incorporating sharia into the civil code and therefore respecting the Islamic legal tradition. The fact that they broke from that tradition by codifying laws that were never meant to be codified seems not to have occurred to them. Many colonial writings suggest that they thought they were doing Muslims a favor and that they were giving the sharia its proper due.

An interesting thing happened when the new civil code was implemented: some Muslims started to believe that the sharia was *supposed* to be a codified set of laws implemented on a state level. Some Muslim scholars echoed the colonists' way of thinking and argued that the sharia was, in fact, found in precolonial Islamic legal texts. Some began to think of sharia as a book, complete with all the laws that God and Muhammad laid down centuries ago. And even though colonists had codified only civil laws up to that point, some Muslims started to argue that *all* laws should be codified and that codified sharia should be used in both civil and criminal courts.

I should note that, although the colonial codification project certainly advanced this way of thinking, codification was not an entirely colonial invention. Muslims had been slowly moving toward a kind of codification anyway, most notably in South Asia and in the Ottoman Empire. But previous attempts at codification had still given judges a good amount of discretionary power, providing a range of possible judgments from which they could choose and acknowledging that different rulings might apply in different times and places. The particularly colonial innovation was to decree that only one law would be applied in all courts across the land in the interest of justice and fairness. By equating that single codified law with sharia, colonists wittingly or unwittingly encouraged the idea that the sharia is a fixed legal entity that is just and fair precisely because it does not change.

Not everyone was on board with this way of thinking about sharia, and many Muslims objected. Critics of the codified-sharia model argued that the sharia is not a set of rules that can be written down in a book but rather a method of decision-making that privileges ideas and values found in the Qur'an and in the practice of Muhammad and thus always leads toward justice. The individual laws that result from this decision-making method might therefore change based on time, place, and conceptions of fairness. These two factions—one arguing that sharia should be codified and the other saying that it could never be codified—argued and debated with each other in academic forums. For the most part, no one other than Muslim scholars took part in or even cared about this debate. But then several colonial powers embarked on economic experiments in their colonies that would give the codified-sharia crowd a huge boost.

Unlike colonial legal policies, which at least incorporated some input from locals, colonial economic policies were completely un-concerned with the thoughts and well-being of colonized peoples. When it came to economic policy, colonists tested horribly immoral theories that would have been impossible to deploy at home. The most notorious of these was the use of Malthusian economics in many parts of the British Empire. Malthusian economics is named after Thomas Malthus, who identified a persistent problem with agrarian economies: in order to work the land and create more out-put, families need many children. But more children mean more mouths to feed, requiring that agricultural output be diverted away from trade and toward feeding children. Trade, Malthus concluded, suffers when the population increases. For Malthus, nature pro-vided a tidy solution to this problem in the form of natural disasters like droughts, monsoons, and plagues. When such natural disasters occur, he reasoned, the state should not intervene and should let the population die down naturally. The result would be fewer mouths to feed and thus more agricultural output going toward trade.

The British, along with several other colonial powers, embraced Malthusian economic theory in the latter half of the nineteenth cen-tury and well into the twentieth century. During that time, espe-cially in the last decade of the nineteenth century, regular El Niño and La Niña cycles led to widespread flooding, drought, and pesti-lence throughout the colonized world. The British saw this as an op-portunity to experiment with Malthusian economics, and they re-fused to intervene, instead setting up concentration camps in which they fed already malnourished subjects less than they needed to sur-vive, ensuring that they would slowly starve to death. Between 1875 and 1902, an estimated thirty to sixty million colonized people died in the service of Malthusian economic theory, a time that historian Mike Davis calls the "Late Victorian Holocausts." Amid this un-fathomable level of famine and death, grain exports from the col-onies tripled. The colonies were exporting crops in record num-bers, all while colonized people died of starvation. The desperation among colonized people reached a fever pitch in the early part of the twentieth century, as they looked for any and all means to repel the colonists as a matter of life and death.

Muslim anticolonialists found a rallying cry in the sharia, which was seen as a panacea that would replace the tyranny of colonialism with, in the words of Ibn al-Qayyim, "justice, mercy, benefit, and wisdom." Many Muslims believed that the sharia held the key to social, political, and economic justice and that if the sharia were implemented properly, injustice would disappear. Muslims who supported the codification of civil law started arguing that if sharia had also been codified into the criminal code and had been implemented on the political and economic levels, the Late Victorian Holocausts would have never occurred. They reasoned that since sharia enshrines justice, applying it to all levels of society would have prevented the death and destruction wrought by the colonists. This reasoning tapped into the growing Muslim interest in a codified sharia and the growing existential anxiety about colonial economic policies. A popular sentiment emerged that establishing sharia as the codified law of the land in all legal codes and implementing sharia on all levels of society would bring political and economic justice for all, Muslim and non-Muslim. This sentiment grew so popular that even many non-Muslim anticolonialists supported sharia; it became synonymous with self-determination and social justice, and it galvanized large swaths of the populace against the colonizers.

During the mid-1900s, after mass agitation and even more atrocities, colonial powers began gradually withdrawing from the colonies. They left behind nation-states with new borders and little capacity for governance. These nation-states were forced to quickly create governing bodies, institutions, and legal codes or risk devolving into anarchy. They threw together constitutions—usually modeled on existing European constitutions—that would serve as founding documents for their new countries. Ideologues, plutocrats, and the military vied for power in the vacuum created by the colonial retreat, and many states experimented with various forms of dictatorship, socialism, and democracy. As these nations struggled with internal corruption and external exploitation, the religious elite repeated the rhetoric popularized by the anticolonial movement: justice will be served when sharia is established at all levels of society. This message was repeated in Friday sermons, in print media, and on TV programs around the world. The failures of a Muslim nation, the rhetoric contended, could be traced back to that nation's failure to recognize sharia as the ultimate source of law. Tens—if not hundreds—of millions of Muslims were told on a regular basis that establishing sharia was the cure for all of society's ills.

In the second half of the twentieth century, movements popped up in different nation-states demanding that sharia be the constitutionally recognized law of the land. Again, this was a very modern idea; Muslim nation-states with constitutions did not exist prior to the twentieth century. But the paradigm had shifted, and Muslims had a new and sincere view that sharia must have a central role in state governance. Several Muslim-majority countries responded by injecting language into their constitutions that reflected the primacy of sharia. There are two types of constitutional provisions that countries adopted; one is called a sharia source law, and the other is called a sharia guarantee/repugnancy law. A sharia source law means that sharia will be the ultimate source of all laws in that country. A sharia guarantee/repugnancy law ensures that no law is passed that violates the sharia. Today, about thirty Muslim-majority countries have adopted these constitutional clauses, and the governments of those countries thereby claim to have established sharia.

Of course, none of these countries say exactly how they define sharia or who determines whether something is in line with or violates the sharia. They do not specify which sources of law the sharia is based on or, perhaps more importantly, whose interpretations of those sources count. Several countries have tried to institutionalize sharia through ministries or councils stocked with state-sponsored legal scholars who tell the populace what is and what is not sharia. In this way, ruling regimes can claim that they have established the sharia and that citizens should therefore obey them. As an added bonus for rulers, whenever citizens agitate for greater rights, ruling regimes can say that those agitators are acting contrary to sharia and should be denounced on religious grounds. Many states now regularly use sharia to claim religious legitimacy for state policies and to stifle criticism of the regime.

Muslim citizens, for their part, seem unimpressed with these clumsy attempts to codify and institutionalize the sharia. Polls suggest that despite rhetoric from ruling regimes and their adoption of sharia source laws, most Muslims believe that their governments do not abide by sharia. That is because codified sharia captures only one part of the revolutionary spirit and rhetoric of the anticolonial movements and their appeals to sharia. The anticolonialists promised that applying sharia at the state level would bring about justice and equality. That spirit of justice and equality can never be captured in a law or in a constitutional clause. Rather, it lives in the souls of people who wish for a better society. For them, sharia represents an ideal that must always be worked toward, and it is never realized until there is absolute justice and equality on Earth. Sharia, in that sense, is always in the future tense; it is always just on the horizon, and believers must continually strive for it. Sharia is God's promise for true believers who struggle and sacrifice for the greater good. This religious aspect of sharia can never be reduced to a set of laws.

The Redemptive Power of Sharia

From a religious perspective, sharia describes a utopia in which everything is right and good. Ask religious Muslims what a sharia state looks like, and they will say things like, "There is free electricity," "No one goes hungry," and "Everyone is equal before the law." Sharia is aspirational, symbolizing everything that humanity can be but isn't yet. In an interview, a British citizen advocating for sharia law was asked what a sharia state would offer. He responded that sharia guarantees a slew of social-welfare programs, such as free health care. When reminded that health care is already free in Britain, he responded, "Not really. Some procedures aren't covered, such as vision."

When sharia is established, there will be free vision care. There will be full employment; children will take care of their parents; crime will be nonexistent; political corruption will disappear; all potholes will be filled. These are all claims that I have heard first-hand, including the one about potholes. It is part of a religious mind-set in which the world can always be better, and God's help will come when Muslims work to make the world a better place. This is part of the aspirational logic of Abrahamic religions, in that they look toward a brighter future. For many Muslims, *sharia* is the word that expresses that aspiration. The moment it is codified and implemented in some way, it loses that aspiration; it must always be in the future if it is to be religiously fulfilling. The details are less important and can always be figured out later.

I am intimately aware of sharia's aspirational power, because, before becoming a scholar of Islam, I spent many years in an international organization that was trying to establish sharia law on the state level. For me and my compatriots, sharia represented social and spiritual justice. Without knowing any of the details, I was sure that, if implemented properly, sharia would fix all of society's problems, from boom-and-bust economic cycles to psychological depression. I would preach this to whomever would listen, and, if pressed for details, I asked the person to trust that God would step in if we all worked toward establishing sharia. Religious—or magical, depending on your point of view—reasoning sometimes means that you trust in things without understanding exactly what they are.

Sometimes, people I was trying to convince were concerned that implementing sharia might result in extreme forms of punishment, such as stoning adulterers or executing apostates. I would reply with something like this:

> That might have been true at one point, but Muslim scholars have dealt with all that so that, in practice, no one will actually get hurt. I mean, such laws were operative at one point, and they still are now, but not really. And there's, like, a loophole or a caveat so that adulterers and apostates get forgiven, or pardoned, or something. In fact, I think that in Muslim history, no one really got stoned or killed, and that was because, under sharia, everyone was so happy that they didn't want to commit adultery or leave Islam. Or wait, maybe it did happen once or twice, but that was because people weren't applying sharia properly. Look, sharia used to be applied in the Muslim world before colonialism, and everything was great. God wants us to work to reestablish sharia, and if we don't, we will be responsible for our own misfortunes. Everything will be great once again when we reapply sharia, because when we do, God's mercy will rain down upon us. Trust me."

My infatuation with sharia as humanity's only hope might sound silly and incredibly naive, but it's no sillier than the "sharia will be the death of us all" camp. Both assume that correct Muslim belief and practice center on a certain version of sharia. Both require good Muslims to be homogeneous automatons who dance only to the rhythm of sharia. Most importantly for our purposes, both discourses try to pinpoint a specific thing that is sharia, toward which all Muslims must work.

But sharia's power is precisely that it never *is* something but always *will be* something. It is an idea that is always just coming into being. Whenever someone makes a claim about what sharia *is*, that claim is inherently suspect, because claims about what the sharia *is* automatically lose the power of something that *will be*. For most

Muslims, sharia lives in the future, and claims about it in the past or present will therefore always be contested. So even though we hear lots of noise about sharia and its potential implementation at the state level, that is not how sharia is discussed and experienced in the day-to-day lives of most Muslims. The far more important function of sharia is in positing a religious utopia that awaits all those who work toward it. For some, that utopia looks like a representative democracy; for others, it looks like a theocracy; and for still others, it is a community in which everything is shared. Utopias are unique to each believer, and that is exactly the power of sharia. It offers hope and promises a form of justice that reflects the needs and beliefs of each individual. The more injustices fill daily life, the more sharia can grant redemption.

It is only within this redemptive framework that Islamic legal conversations make any sense, and it certainly the only way that Islamic legal hacking makes any sense, as we will see. Outside of the context of redemption, sharia conversations are sterile, uninteresting, inaccurate, and unhelpful. Yet we find that most analysts, scholars, and observers discuss sharia not in terms of redemption but in terms of a legal code. That is partly because of the historical events recounted earlier and partly because those events brought with them a series of myths about sharia, Islam, and Muslims. These myths are persistent and deep-seated in our collective consciousness, and they oversimplify the debate on sharia. In order to engage with the sharia as a dynamic source of redemption and to enter into the hacking conversation, we will need to dispel these myths.

There are five major myths that are most in need of debunking, and they are that: (1) there is only one official sharia; (2) the sharia never changes; (3) only learned scholars may discuss the sharia; (4) Islamic law is found in the Qur'an and in the sayings of Muhammad; and (5) all Muslims live according to Islamic law. These myths work together to sterilize conversations about sharia. They are championed by those who would demonize the sharia as well as by Muslim elites who claim a monopoly on sharia. Addressing these myths is an essential first step to unlocking the sharia's potential as a source of redemption for Muslims today. Let's start with the first myth.

MYTH #1: THERE IS ONLY ONE, OFFICIAL SHARIA

Debate is a constant feature of the Islamic intellectual tradition, and Muslims have always debated the nature and content of the sharia. Some believe that sharia is nothing more than the moral imperative to do good in the world and that it does not have any fixed content. Others believe that it can be pinned down with careful study. Some Muslim scholars have tried to capture the sharia using legal language. When they do so, they tend to use a particular discourse known as either "Islamic law" (*fiqh*) or, rarely, "sharia law" (*ahkam al-shar'iyya*). *Fiqh* is an attempt to determine how God wants human beings to live in order to achieve salvation. Using a series of interpretive methods, some Muslim scholars have tried to describe exactly how Muslims should behave, in everything from paying taxes to drinking water to getting married. Scholars refer to these as laws, but each law is highly debatable—there are, for example, many different theories about the right way to pay taxes. As a result, there are innumerable interpretations of sharia that are made using the language of Islamic law.

These different interpretations are found in thousands of books that Muslim scholars have written on Islamic law. The authors of these books each claim to have captured the one true sharia. It is as though each author is saying, "Even though there are thousands of books claiming to capture the sharia in legal language, I've actually done it!" But that is only a claim. Obviously all the books on Islamic law can't all be right; some books might be right about some laws and wrong about others. Since God stopped speaking directly to humans over 1,400 years ago, we can never really know for sure which books, if any, are right and which are wrong. To gain some measure of uniformity, some Muslims count themselves members of larger groups with internal hierarchies. Twelver Shiʿas and Ismaʿilis, for instance, have leadership structures that can tell you which laws are right and which are wrong. Sunni Muslims developed more fluid hierarchies, providing Sunnis with multiple versions of Islamic law from which to choose. Even among Twelver Shiʿas and Ismaʿilis there are subgroups with different leaders who advocate different laws; and, of course, a Sunni can always become a Shiʿa and vice versa. The upshot is that there are many different versions of Islamic law, each one claiming to capture the sharia, and Muslims pick and choose the ones that serve them best.

There is, therefore, no one set of laws that authoritatively comprises the sharia. Instead, there are multiple versions of Islamic law that each claim to represent the sharia. This, in fact, must be the case. Recall that sharia always lives in the future; it always *will be*, and once you make a claim about what the sharia *is*, it loses its aspirational power and becomes Islamic law. By definition, the sharia can never be a single thing, and it will never be agreed upon.

In light of this fact, Anver Emon calls sharia a "claim-space," which is a very helpful way to think about it. People make claims about the sharia, and they argue for the relative authority of their claims. Some might say, for instance, that stoning adulterers is part of the sharia, but others will say that stoning has no place in the sharia. Both of these are claims about sharia that can be made using the language of Islamic law. But we should not confuse the claim, which is Islamic law, with the aspirational ideal that always lives in the future, which is sharia. Equating sharia with a specific book of Islamic law is a bit like saying that Adam Smith's *Wealth of Nations* is economics. *Wealth of Nations* is a book that makes claims about economics, but it is not economics itself.

Of course, when people make claims about the sharia, they don't say, "I am making a claim about sharia, which lives in the future and can never be captured in the language of Islamic law." Instead, they say, "What I am claiming is the sharia." That's the way religious arguments are made. Strong language is rewarded, and besides, no one wants to believe that their version of Islamic law *might* lead them to heaven; they want to believe that it *will* lead them to heaven. Muslims regularly make claims about the sharia as though their claims are the truth. They tend to understand that these strong claims are rhetorical rather than coercive, since, especially among Sunnis, there is no clerical hierarchy and people are free to follow whatever version of Islamic law they deem fit.

This idea of sharia as a claim-space is important to keep in mind, particularly when we consider modern nation-states with sharia source laws. Many states have used sharia source laws to come up with their own versions of Islamic law, each state claiming that its version accurately captures the sharia. To hear these states tell it, there is only one version of sharia, and it is the state's version. It is in the interest of the state to say that its version of sharia is the correct, official version, but we should know better than to take such a claim at face value. Just because someone claims to rule according to the one true sharia does not mean that they are actually doing so. Regimes use the term *sharia* to demand obedience from their citizens, insisting that those disputing the law or the regime are actually disputing God. In giving themselves exclusive rights to the sharia, states are claiming to officially represent God on Earth. That's an enormous claim, and we should take it with an equally enormous grain of salt, as we do with most state rhetoric. We do not, after all, think that North Korea is a democracy simply because its official name is the Democratic People's Republic of Korea.

We can easily dismiss state claims to rule by the one true sharia by pointing out that different countries with sharia source laws implement different versions of Islamic law. For example, the minimum age to marry without parental consent is nineteen in Algeria, eighteen in Egypt, and fifteen in Yemen. All of these countries have sharia source laws, and all claim that their marriage ages are based in the sharia. So, which one is it: nineteen, eighteen, or fifteen? It can't possibly be all of them if there is only one sharia. But it is all of them, because sharia is a claim-space that different parties appeal to in order to give their claims religious legitimacy. The laws themselves are not the sharia; they are claims made about the sharia in the language of Islamic law.

Muslim legal scholars historically recognized that they could never pin down the sharia and that they could only ever attempt to approximate it in the language of Islamic law. This, they said, was the nature of religion: one is always trying to figure out God's will but can never be sure to have gotten it right. There is a common refrain among scholars, based on a reported saying of Muhammad, that when you come up with an Islamic law that is actually in accordance with the sharia, God will reward you twice. If you come up with an Islamic law that does not fully accord with the sharia, God will reward you once. Either way, you get rewarded. Legal scholars understood that they were not expected to come up with the actual sharia; that's impossible. Instead, they tried to come close through Islamic laws.

The difference between sharia and Islamic law should always be kept in mind. In shorthand, sharia is the divine ideal, and Islamic law is a human attempt to capture the ideal. The distinction is crucial.

MYTH #2: THE SHARIA NEVER CHANGES

The sharia looks different to every person, since we all have different ideas about what the world is supposed to look like. Some people think the sharia should have a strong public presence, whereas others think that it should be restricted to personal life. Muslims who believe in the importance of sharia can champion a theocracy, a secular democracy, or anything in between. The sharia is unique to each individual and therefore is always changing.

The interesting question for us, then, is not whether sharia changes, but how those changes are expressed in the language of Islamic law. In chapter 2, we will learn about a paradox that underpins all discussions of Islamic law: the law must be ancient and contemporary at the same time. That is, the law has to be rooted in a historical past for it to have authority, but it also has to be relevant to new times and circumstances.

Muslim scholars navigate this paradox when making legal claims about the sharia, and they have developed rather sophisticated methods for doing so. I discuss these methods in chapters 4 and 5, especially two methods that I call patching and hacking. *Patching* is when historical laws are modified to account for some urgent need. *Hacking* is a term that refers to finding a solution to a problem by working within an existing system. Patching can provide temporary fixes, but lasting changes require hacks.

In the computing world, hacking is when a programmer wants to change a piece of computer code in order to make a system work differently. To do so, the programmer must work within the existing computer language to change one part of the code without affecting the entire system. A good hack will make the system work better without anyone even noticing that a hack was made. A bad hack will result in bugs so that one part of the system works well but other parts lag. A really bad hack will bring the whole system down.

Hacking used to refer only to some kind of malicious activity, such as when someone would break into a computer system for nefarious purposes. Today, hacking is used more broadly in everyday language to describe ingenious solutions to persistent problems. Websites and magazines regularly propose life hacks, travel hacks, study hacks, and the like. Whenever a problem is solved or a process made more efficient using only existing tools, we now call that a hack. That is how we will use the term in this book with respect to Islamic law. The sharia can never be hacked, since it lives in the future and exists in the present only as a claim-space, but Muslim scholars hack Islamic law all the time to accommodate changing claims about the sharia. When a good hack is made and historical circumstances make it advantageous, the hack changes prevailing conceptions of Islamic law in lasting and abiding ways.

Chapter 6 gives several examples in which social, political, and economic circumstances lead Muslims to adopt or discard hacks. We will see that Muslim scholars are remarkably adept at hacking even deeply entrenched laws to accommodate for changing times. Actions that were previously thought unquestionably forbidden— for example, using money not backed by precious metals, studying in a mixed-gender classroom, and abolishing slavery—are now widely accepted. We will learn how Muslim scholars made hacks like these, and in chapter 7, we will learn how similar hacks can be made in the future.

MYTH #3: ONLY LEARNED SCHOLARS MAY DISCUSS THE SHARIA

The sharia belongs to every Muslim. From a purely religious perspective, every individual has her own personal relationship with the sharia and must answer to God for herself. One might take guidance from a particular religious leader, but one is encouraged to learn and make decisions about sharia for oneself whenever possible. In previous generations, such personal study was nearly impossible, because literacy was low and centers of learning were few and far between. Now, literacy is widespread and knowledge centers are an internet connection away. As we will see in chapter 3, many, many Muslims now meet or exceed the minimum requirements for deriving and interpreting Islamic law for themselves. Islamic law, therefore, is no longer in the hands of an educated elite but is now the property of most Muslims around the world.

From a political perspective, this is now doubly true with the introduction of sharia source laws. Something deeply ironic happened when these source laws were instituted: by putting sharia clauses into democratic constitutions, regimes unwittingly gave all citizens the right to debate sharia laws. Democratic nations, in which the majority of Muslims live, require citizens to ratify their constitutions. Citizens, therefore, technically vote on whether to have sharia laws. They could, ostensibly, vote to have sharia taken off the books or to have it expressed in different ways. This means that, at least in theory, every citizen has a say in sharia and its workings.

Sharia source laws have, in a sense, ended up democratizing sharia and have led to the rise of groups and individuals who are looking into sharia on their own and are coming up with new and interesting interpretations of sharia using the language of Islamic law. Perhaps the most visible and timely of these are Muslim feminists, who are using their constitutional right to interpret the sharia and to voice their own interpretations of what sharia should be. As citizens of the state, they are allowed—just like anyone else—to express their opinions on sharia, and they are interpreting it to empower women. This may not have been the intention of those who were advocating sharia source laws, but it certainly is the consequence. In the words of Dr. Ziba Mir-Hosseini, "Islamic feminism is the unwanted child of political Islam." In the modern era, every citizen has the constitutional right to discuss sharia, despite state claims to exclusive authority over its content.

MYTH #4: ISLAMIC LAW IS FOUND IN THE
QUR'AN AND THE SAYINGS OF MUHAMMAD

In fact, very little of Islamic law is found in the Qur'an and the sayings of Muhammad (*hadith*). The Qur'an focuses on three main topics: monotheism, social justice, and life after death; it is mostly comprised of stories of prophets, calls for acting justly, and vivid descriptions of the life hereafter. Less than 10 percent of the Qur'an has anything to do with what we might call laws, and those, too, are often general exhortations to act righteously and avoid doing evil.

The sayings of Muhammad, known as *hadith*, are similarly composed mostly of stories and wise sayings. There is a great deal of controversy over which sayings of Muhammad are trustworthy and which are dubious, as we will see later in this book, and Muslim scholars devised different methods for determining whether hadiths were authentic or not. Scholars famously disagree about which hadiths are more authentic than others, how they should be interpreted, and whether they are applicable in law.

Most laws are based not in the Qur'an or in hadith, but in the opinions of Muslim scholars living in the early generations after Muhammad, who themselves often disagreed with one another. When legal texts do reference the Qur'an and hadith, they are usually cited only to justify the opinion of one of those early Muslims over another. We will learn more in the next chapter, but for now it suffices to say that although the Qur'an and hadith form the moral and intellectual backdrop for Islamic legal discussions, they are neither the source for most laws nor the source to which most Muslims turn to learn Islamic law. The Qur'an and the hadith are ever-relevant, foundational sources whose various interpretations can provide guidance in different times and places, but they are not themselves books of law, and one will not understand Islamic law and Islamic legal debates by going directly to the Qur'an and hadith.

MYTH #5: ALL MUSLIMS LIVE
ACCORDING TO ISLAMIC LAW

This myth is part of a larger idea—a racist one—that all Muslims think and act as one. In this myth, Muslims get their marching orders from Islamic legal scholars who themselves follow the Qur'an and the hadith word-for-word. Muslims then try to order their societies according to Islamic law and cannot abide any separation between church and state. Secularism as a project is itself inconceivable to the "Muslim mind," and Muslims all want to live in an Islamic state that enforces medieval Islamic laws. These broad generalizations about Islam and Muslims are so pervasive that they are found in academic scholarship, media reports, political analysis, and even some modern Muslim rhetoric.

It should go without saying—but unfortunately doesn't—that the term *Muslim* describes a diverse group of 1.6 billion individuals who have complex and varied relationships with their religion. Some are deeply religious, while others are not. For some, Islam is a way of viewing the world, whereas for others, it is more of an identity marker. The term *Muslim* tells us next to nothing about a person's beliefs and orientation. Nowhere is this more apparent and easily observed than with the topic of sharia. People have widely differing conceptions of sharia, some of which have nothing to do with Islamic law, and there is a huge gap between rhetoric and practice.

It's fascinating that while polls suggest that Muslims tend to support the implementation of sharia on a state level, those same polls show that most Muslims don't actually abide by Islamic law. As mentioned earlier, polls suggest that most Muslims don't pray five times a day and that only a minority go to the mosque for Friday prayers. The Friday prayer is performed in congregation, and while all prayers are important, Friday prayer is considered especially so; missing it is a big sin. Yet, despite businesses being closed during prayer time and many countries taking Friday off, Muslims, for the most part, find other things to do. Attend a Friday prayer in most Muslim-majority cities, and you'll hear sounds of life outside the mosque—honking, trading, laughing—going on as usual.

Poll numbers aside, there's simply no way that most Muslims attend Friday prayer, if only because there is not enough mosque space to accommodate them all. In the United States, for instance, there are about 2,100 mosques, which simply cannot hold the country's 3.5 million Muslims. The average US mosque has a Friday-prayer attendance of 353 congregants, confirming estimates that only about 25 percent of US Muslims attend Friday prayer.

And it's not just the United States. Dubai, for instance, has 507 mosques that offer Friday prayer for their 1.6 million Muslims.

To accommodate them all, each mosque would have to hold over 3,000 worshippers. But the largest mosque in Dubai, the Khalifa al-Tajer, can hold only 3,500 people, and the second largest, the Blue Mosque, can hold only 2,000. They just get smaller from there. We can reasonably conclude that most of Dubai's Muslims are not attending Friday prayer.

We can play this numbers game with any country that has reliable mosque and population records to get a sense of how many more Muslims there are than mosques. Malaysia's 5,000 mosques must somehow accommodate its 18 million Muslims. Singapore's 70 mosques must cater to its 600,000 Muslims. The Muslim populations of these countries cannot fit into their mosques, which means that most Muslims simply aren't praying the Friday prayer. And it is important to note that infrastructure reflects demand. If Muslims were to complain that they did not have enough space to pray, then governments would likely comply by encouraging mosque construction. But the demand simply isn't there.

We don't have reliable numbers for mosque attendance outside of Friday prayer, but those of us who have lived in Muslim-majority countries can attest that mosques generally lie empty. In Damascus, I would pray my dawn prayers at the mosque of one of the most famous scholars in the Middle East, the late Sa'id Ramadan al-Buti. Every morning I would shuffle in late to the mosque's smaller prayer room in which the dawn prayers were held, and every morning I would pray in the front row. That's because the front row never got filled with worshippers, as most people were sound asleep or getting ready for the day. While studying in Yemen, I would take breaks to pray the noon and afternoon prayers in the nearby thousand-year-old mosque. We averaged about eight worshippers per prayer.

In Karachi, the mosque near my relatives' home could accommodate about two hundred worshippers. There were never more than twenty for the sunset prayer, which is normally the best-attended prayer of the day. For me, these experiences were always remarkable not so much for the poor attendance but for the ease with which most Muslims missed their prayers. As a mosque regular, locals viewed me with curiosity: a weird, gangly foreigner always going off to pray. They probably thought I was a dunce or a spy or an extremist, and they would poke fun at me as I walked down the narrow alleyways toward the local mosque, passing by their cricket and soccer games. They would shout, "Pray for Faisal to learn how to pass the ball," or "Give heaven our fondest regards," or "Tell God to do something about the drones!"

It somehow always shocked me to see Muslims all over the world treating prayer with such nonchalance. Prayer is one of the five pillars of Islam, and one would think that it would be central to almost any version of Islamic law. Yet most Muslims don't feel compelled to pray. We see the same thing with another pillar of Islam, the hajj pilgrimage. Every Muslim is commanded to go to Mecca for hajj at least once in her life if she can afford it. And every year, two million Muslims descend on Mecca to fulfill this religious obligation. Hajj is a singular experience: a crush of humanity seeking God's bounty and blessings, all trying to fulfill a central requirement of the faith. But only 2 million Muslims attend each year, which is a tiny fraction of the world's 1.6 billion Muslims; in fact, it's about one-tenth of 1 percent. If we do the math, we see that no more than 10 percent of Muslims will go on the hajj pilgrimage in their lifetimes. That's not because 90 percent of Muslims cannot afford to go. It's because many choose not to go.

Most Muslims do not live their lives according to some strict version of Islamic law. That does not mean that they are bad Muslims, just that they have different conceptions of Islam and sharia. I cannot count the number of people who have told me that God is found in the heart and that they do not feel the need for rituals. Others have said that they focus on being truthful and generous and that the most important Islamic law is the one demanding good character. Many people have advised me that the core of the sharia is love, not law.

There are innumerable ways to be Muslim, and devotion to the law is but one of them. Muslims who adhere closely to the law are a subgroup of the larger whole. The historian Marshall Hodgson called this group "sharia-minded," and since we are focusing on Islamic law (*fiqh*) in this book, I will call Muslims who hold Islamic law to be an important part of their lives "*fiqh*-minded." The numbers cited in the preceding paragraphs suggest that fiqh-minded Muslims are only a sizeable minority and that most Muslims believe it is unnecessary to follow Islamic laws closely in order to attain salvation.

Yet the perception persists that good Muslims are slaves to the law and that only law-abiding Muslims are true followers of Islam. We hear this from Muslim religious leaders, and we see it in popular Western depictions of Islam and Muslims. That is chiefly the result of a larger myth that has been centuries in the making.

Known as Orientalism, this is a myth that humans create about their societies by casting outsiders as polar opposites. In this case, there is a myth that "the West" and "westerners" are diametrically opposed to values held by those in "the East," including Muslims. From this perspective of the myth, westerners are sophisticated, and Muslims are brutish; westerners are enlightened, Muslims are benighted; westerners are rational, Muslims are irrational; and so on. It is largely for this reason that Muslims are regularly portrayed in Western media as mindless automatons who worship the law and will do anything in its name while those in the West are portrayed as people who follow the ideals and spirit of the law rather than simply the letter of the law.

Muslim-majority countries have their own versions of this myth: Muslims are moral, westerners are immoral; Muslims are besieged, westerners are invaders; Muslims value community, westerners are individualistic. But, of course, there is no actual dichotomy between westerners and Muslims beyond the one that we create in our minds. Muslims live in the West, and many people whom we would call western are Muslim. There is no one individual who personifies "western values," just as there is no one individual who personifies "Muslim values." There are people living in the West who believe in theocracies, and there are religious Muslims who champion secularism. And we all interact with our laws in ways that are varied, complicated, and often irrational.

The reality is that all of us—Muslim or not—have nuanced and, at times, hypocritical relationships with law. We are somehow able to tout the law's importance and flout it at the same time; we can follow the law in some ways and disobey it in others and still consider ourselves good citizens. The next time you catch yourself texting while driving, think of a Muslim scholar who enjoys an occasional drink, of which there are many, believe me. A complicated relationship with the law is a fact of life in all societies. Understanding that fiqh-minded Muslims, like everyone else, have varied relationships with the law is key to understanding how Islamic law functions in Muslim life.

This understanding will help us see that conversations about sharia and Islamic law are deeply human enterprises and not the exclusive purview of a select group of religious, disconnected, irrational actors. Conversations about sharia mirror conversations about any value that people hold dear, and we will see that there are many analogues to Islamic law in purportedly secular legal systems. We all have values that we believe in, and some of us try to express those values in legal language. Often those attempts are messy and inconsistent, requiring us to speak from within an existing legal framework in order to have authority. Similarly, sharia is a value that many Muslims hold dear, and fiqh-minded Muslims try to express that value in the language of Islamic law. When they do, they have to work within an existing legal framework if their expressions are to have authority, and it sometimes gets messy.

This book is designed, therefore, not only to introduce you to the internal language of Islamic law but also to immerse you in the ways in which Islamic law is used to express changing and competing conceptions of the sharia. We will learn about the basic requirements for engaging in legal debates and about how legal arguments must be presented in order to gain authority. We will learn how Muslim legal scholars have historically worked within an existing Islamic legal tradition to hack laws so that they reflect changing times, mores, and beliefs about the sharia while staying true to ancient, historical roots. We will look at instances in which hacks are accepted and in which they are rejected so that we can appreciate how social, political, and economic interests can determine a hack's success or failure. Finally, once we understand how hacking worked in the past and how it works in the present, we will examine how laws can be hacked in the future.

None of this is possible, however, unless we are able to entertain complex notions about Muslims, sharia, and Islamic law. It will be tempting to equate sharia with Islamic law or to fall back on one of the myths discussed earlier. Doing so will return us to a polarized situation in which we can only speak *about* Islamic law instead of speaking *within* Islamic law. In other words, we will be able only to describe Islamic law; we will not be able to hack it. So, throughout this book, please keep in mind that sharia is a claim-space, that Islamic law is an attempt to capture the sharia in legal language, and that Muslims . . . well, Muslims are complicated people, just like everyone else. If you do, by the end of this book you will be able to hack Islamic law to express your own claims about the sharia and harness its power as a redemptive force in the world.

CHAPTER 2

Why Does Islamic Law Get Hacked?

THE FIRST STEP to hacking Islamic law is developing a thorough understanding of why it gets hacked in the first place. Islamic law gets hacked because it attempts to capture the sharia, and the sharia, as we saw in chapter 1, is unique to every individual, reflecting her or his personal outlook on the world and ideas about a perfect future. As times and contexts change, so do people's visions of sharia. Some people's visions embrace capitalism, while other people's visions embrace communism; some advocate theocracy, while others advocate secularism. Each vision claims to have an Islamic foundation, and each claims to represent the will of God. Some people cite the Qur'an to justify their visions, whereas others use logic, science, or history. Some express their visions through stories or songs or pious practices, like meditation and even dancing. Those whom we are calling *fiqh*-minded use the language of Islamic law (*fiqh*) to capture and express their personal visions of sharia.

Fiqh-minded Muslims argue that Islamic law is the best way to express the sharia and that Islamic law is fully capable of accommodating contemporary ideas like international finance, universal human rights, democratic pluralism, and more. Of course, those ideas only came into being over the last few centuries, but to hear the fiqh-minded tell it, they have always been part and parcel of Islamic law. The fiqh-minded argue that although we assume that ideas such as, say, environmentalism, are thoroughly modern, they have in fact always been present in Islamic law, just not by the same names. To show exactly how that is the case, the fiqh-minded tend to use two methods that I call "patching" and "hacking." They can thereby demonstrate how environmentalism is and always has been an integral part of Islamic law, and they can do the same to fully integrate any new or evolving idea into the Islamic legal tradition.

Patching occurs when a specific law is temporarily changed or suspended because of some pressing need. Laws may be suspended, extended, or shifted when they create injustice or fail to serve the needs of the community. Patching is a time-honored method of changing old laws and accommodating new ones, and Muslim scholars speak about it openly and often. But as we will see in chapter 4, its uses are limited. A more far-reaching, effective, and comprehensive way to capture changing conceptions of sharia in the language of Islamic law involves hacking.

Hacking means working within an existing system to bring about some desired change. In order to do this, you first need to learn the system's language; then you can use its existing code to create something different or new. This is a process that reflects a deep religious commitment; when Muslims hack the sharia, they are respecting an age-old tradition and working within it to better understand and apply the law in changing times.

Hacking is not about dismantling the foundations of Islamic law but about interpreting them anew. During this process of hacking, the foundational sources of Islamic law—the Qur'an and the sayings of the Prophet Muhammad—never change. Those sources remain constant; the interpretations that fiqh-minded Muslims provide for them, however, change to reflect new and different circumstances. These new interpretations yield new laws, some of which sit comfortably beside old laws and some of which go against over a thousand years of Islamic scholarly consensus. Hacks are necessary for the fiqh-minded community to adapt and grow and to fully participate in a changing world while adhering to the Islamic legal tradition.

Muslim legal scholars have been hacking Islamic law since the earliest days. After the Prophet Muhammad died, his young Muslim community struggled to honor his example as they encountered new and changing circumstances. As the community grew, it faced new challenges and had to adapt; sometimes they fine-tuned Muhammad's practice, and other times they came up with entirely new laws that had no precedent. Whenever fiqh-minded scholars in this young community engaged in hacking—whether they fine-tuned old laws or came up with new ones—they had to confront a tricky problem: religious laws are supposed to come directly from God and God's messengers, not from flawed humans, no matter how pious. Thus, even as they came up with new laws to address new circumstances, scholars had to ensure that their laws were directly rooted in revelation and the practice of Muhammad, with as little human intervention as possible.

Of course, this is impossible. The Qur'an and the reported sayings of Muhammad do not account for all situations in which laws are required. The early community therefore had to confront a problem that still exists today: the foundational sources of Islamic law do not explicitly address cars, retirement accounts, or Twitter. Yet fiqh-minded Muslims want Islamic laws instructing them on the "Islamic" way to drive, invest, and tweet that somehow is in accordance with the foundational sources. Early fiqh-minded scholars, much like scholars today, had to come up with new laws to address new problems, but they had to do it in a way that ensured that those laws would be seen as direct extensions of the Qur'an and the practice of Muhammad. In essence, the challenge that scholars have is this: they have to come up with new laws that make Islamic law relevant to changing conceptions of sharia, but they have to make sure that those new laws are part of an ancient legal tradition that goes all the way back to the Prophet Muhammad. Thus, Islamic laws have to be part of a historical legacy yet also responsive to new times and circumstances. They have to be simultaneously static *and* dynamic, ancient *and* contemporary.

This paradox is, in one sense, characteristic of all major religions and legal systems. Religions and legal systems are based on foundational sources and practices of a historical community; at the same time, they claim that the values found in those historical sources and practices are relevant today. Whenever someone tries to reinterpret those foundational sources or change those early practices, that person risks corrupting the values contained therein and thus changing the very fabric of the community. It is therefore fully understandable that any proposal to change law—whether religious or not—is often met with skepticism, if not fear.

For example, whenever Americans propose new laws or programs that require reinterpreting the US Constitution, some group always crops up to denounce those new laws or programs as un-American. Surely the US Constitution allows for the production of new and progressive laws to accommodate new circumstances; but even when the Constitution itself and the principles found within it are confirmed to last in perpetuity, new interpretations that result in new or changed laws always invite controversy.

Take the principle that "all men are created equal" in the Preamble of the US Constitution. We now assume that clause to grant all citizens equal rights, but it was not always so. With respect to voting rights, for instance, the clause was initially interpreted to give full voting rights only to property-owning white males. Over time, white males who did not own property argued that the Constitution gave them the right to vote too. They eventually received those rights, but only after a hard and protracted fight against landowners who claimed that the Constitution did not give them that right. The same drama played out when black men demanded voting rights and again when women demanded them. In each of these battles, the Constitution was never discarded or impugned. Rather, it was reinterpreted to support new laws, and every reinterpretation was subject to bitter dispute. Whenever new laws are proposed to reflect new visions of gun ownership or abortion rights or access to education, the US Constitution is always affirmed and its interpretation debated. And there is a battle over whether and how much the law can stretch to accommodate new demands while staying true to its original intent.

The same is true for any set of laws built on foundational sources. Of course, the analogy between US law and Islamic law goes only so far, because for fiqh-minded Muslims, Islamic law is a *religious* law. Imagine that every law not only determined the boundaries of acceptable behavior but also claimed to be (1) commanded by God and (2) necessary for salvation. In that case, the stakes are much higher for getting the law right and for making sure it reflects the desire of the Law Giver. Fiqh-minded scholars, therefore, have the added burden of proving that their laws not only flow directly from foundational sources but also will lead to salvation. It's not enough to just pontificate about the sharia; one should have an iron-clad reason for claiming that a new Islamic law flows directly from God's will.

To assure people that legal claims about the sharia are true to Islam's foundational sources, Muslim legal scholars came up with a story about how all Islamic laws, new or old, are derived. Scholars are at the center of this story; in it, they carefully study the foundational sources and stick to them as closely as possible. They derive law from these sources using a hierarchical method that minimizes human error. This method ensures that laws are derived without personal prejudice or ulterior motives. The method became known as the principles of Islamic law (*usul al-fiqh*), and it describes a scientific, if mythic, way that laws are mechanically derived from foundational sources to ensure their authenticity.

Sunnis are particularly adamant about following principles when deriving law. That is because there is no clerical hierarchy in Sunni

Islam, and so no Sunni can officially say which laws are "right" and which are "wrong" for all Muslims. Sunnis therefore need some sort of objective method that can give their laws authority, and so they identified principles that would ensure some form of authenticity. Without these principles, Sunni scholars claimed, Islamic law would be derived based only on personal whims and desires. Over time, and especially after the eighteenth century, even Shi'a legal scholars, who historically tried to limit Islamic law to whatever is contained in the reported sayings of the Prophet, his family, and his chosen descendants, began to regularly argue that Islamic laws must be derived according to principles if they are to have authority.

Yet, despite this strong rhetoric about needing to follow principles, legal scholars, whether Shi'a or Sunni, do not actually use principles to derive Islamic laws. We will see later in this chapter how legal scholars do derive laws, but for now let's look at the rhetorical story they tell about how they do it. This story is important when hacking the law, because hacks must be presented within the rhetorical story whenever they are made. That will prove that hacks accord with a scientific, objective method rather than with personal whims. The rhetorical story gives us a narrative into which all successful hacks should fit.

Rhetoric: The Principles of Islamic Law (Usul al-Fiqh)

The principles of Islamic law model sets up a hierarchy of sources from which Islamic laws are derived. The first and most authoritative source in the hierarchy is the Qur'an, which was revealed to the Prophet Muhammad in seventh-century Arabia. The Qur'an is commonly understood to be a timeless text that was revealed by God to guide all humanity. The Qur'an contains some verses in which God commands believers to do certain things, and we might call these "laws." Some scholars have estimated that legal verses make up about 10 percent of the Qur'an, but how you calculate the percentage depends on how you define the term *legal*. The 10 percent number includes all commands, both those that are more general (such as commands to believe in God, treat one another with kindness, and always tell the truth) and those that are very specific (such as the command for a man to apportion his mother a one-third inheritance share if he leaves behind no children or brothers). The Qur'an is mostly composed of poetic discourses about the majesty of God, chronicles of God's prophets, and exhortations to live a good life. So, although in theory you can't go wrong if you base all your laws on the Qur'an, in reality it is incredibly difficult to do that since the Qur'an contains precious few laws, each of which can be interpreted in many different ways. As a result, the Qur'an is rarely used in legal argumentation, and almost never as a proof in and of itself.

The second-most authoritative source of Islamic law is the reported sayings of Muhammad, known as *hadith*. If the Qur'an does not directly address an issue, scholars turn to Muhammad's sayings for guidance. His sayings were originally passed down through word of mouth over several generations until they were eventually collected and written down. As you can imagine, word of mouth often results in inaccurate reporting, especially over several generations, and many different, contradictory versions of the same story are common. When they were finally written down over one hundred years after Muhammad's death, hundreds of thousands of hadiths were in circulation, some of which might have been more accurate and some less so. Many hadiths were proved to be outright forgeries, fabricated by both well-intentioned and malicious individuals. Finding out which hadiths were reliable was a huge but necessary task for early Muslim scholars, especially since hadiths are such an important source of law.

In response to this problem, many Muslim scholars took it upon themselves to separate out weak and fabricated hadiths from strong, highly authentic (*sahih*) ones. Still, these scholars disagreed about which hadiths were authentic and which were not. The more authoritative books of hadith include anywhere from a few thousand to almost thirty thousand sayings attributed to Muhammad. It is not possible for Muhammad to have uttered all of these hadiths, some of which contradict others. Even authors of the most selective collections admit to having included weak hadiths in their books. These books also regularly include sayings of Muhammad's family members and companions, the thinking being that their statements are the next best things to sayings of the Prophet himself. Their inclusion requires yet another layer of scrutiny to determine the accuracy and authenticity of hadiths.

But hadiths are the only way to access prophetic statements, and even some of the most stalwart opponents of hadith, who question their authenticity and reliability, concede that they are the second-most authoritative source of law. Yet, like the Qur'an, hadiths are rarely used in legal argumentation. They might be marshaled to support one legal position or another, but more often they are not. Since there are so many hadiths, it's easy to find one that supports almost any position, and citing one hadith to prove a point usually results in someone else citing another to prove the opposite point. To deal with this overabundance of hadiths, legal scholars turn to the third-most authoritative source of Islamic law, Consensus.

Whenever there are conflicting opinions about the law, and when the Qur'an and hadiths are not clear on some subject, scholars turn to the Consensus of historical Muslim scholars. They believe that when scholars of the past agreed on something, it must have been right. That belief is supported by a hadith in which Muhammad is reported to have said, "My community will never agree upon error." That effectively means that if the community agrees on something, it cannot be wrong. Consensus is self-justifying and totalizing: since the community cannot agree on error, no law or belief that is agreed on by Consensus can be wrong or subverted. Consider, for instance, that the aforementioned hadith, "My community will never agree upon error," is not considered a highly authentic saying of the Prophet, which means there is a good chance that Muhammad never said it to begin with. Nevertheless, because scholars agree with its message by Consensus, that hadith is considered authoritative. Consensus can determine how verses of the Qur'an are to be read and which hadiths are important, regardless of their authenticity. Likewise, readings of the Qur'an and hadith that go against Consensus are often dismissed out of hand in favor of readings that scholars mostly agree on. Ironically, there is disagreement about what constitutes a Consensus—whether it is all Muslims, all Muslim scholars, most Muslim scholars, or certain Muslim scholars—but the general idea is that whenever the majority of Muslim scholars agree, they are probably on to something.

When the Qur'an, hadith, and Consensus all fail to directly address a problem, legal scholars then call on a process known as Analogy (*qiyas*) to derive laws. Analogy concerns finding new laws for legal cases on which there is no scholarly Consensus, such as, say, illegally downloading an e-book. To come up with a law about illegal downloads, scholars can compare the issue to similar ones found in the Qur'an, the hadith, or Consensus. To make the Analogy, scholars might compare illegal downloading to stealing physical property and identify connections to property laws. They can then argue for legal opinions about illegal downloads that are analogous to laws found in the foundational sources, thereby determining whether digital pirating is wrong and what punishment, if any, should be prescribed.

According to the principles model outlined above, all Islamic laws supposedly derive first from the Qur'an, then from the hadith, then from Consensus, and finally from Analogy. Using this principled approach to law, one could theoretically derive unprejudiced laws for every conceivable circumstance. Those laws would be considered Islamic because they were derived according to a rigorous methodology that allows Islamic foundational sources to speak for themselves and that minimizes human intervention.

*Practice: Normative Jurisprudence (*Fiqh*)*

In practice, Islamic law does not work like this at all. Muslims, with few exceptions, did not and do not derive laws according to a hierarchy of sources. There is a small and vocal minority that claims to derive law this way, but the majority does not. Rather than being based on principles, Muslim legal scholarship is based on historical books of Islamic law (*fiqh*) that contain the legal opinions of scholars living in the early centuries of Islam. In a fiqh-minded seminary, you study books of fiqh right away, so that the legal opinions contained therein form the bedrock of all future studies. One first learns right actions contained in those books—eating with the right hand, blessing the prophet's name whenever it is mentioned, removing shoes before entering the mosque—and trusts that there is some hierarchy of Islamic sources that justifies those actions. There are thousands of dense books of fiqh that each contain thousands upon thousands of rules; sometimes these books cite sources that justify those rules, but far more often they do not. That is okay because for fiqh-minded Muslims the most important thing is to know *how* to act, not necessarily *why* to act.

It's tempting to make a leap here and conclude that in order to truly understand Muslim beliefs and behavior, we should study these books of fiqh. But that is not the case, for at least three reasons. The first is that, as mentioned in the previous chapter, fiqh-minded Muslims are a minority in the Muslim community. Muslims do not, in general, attend seminaries or read fiqh books. At best, looking at books of fiqh might give us insight into a small subgroup of Muslims.

The second reason is that fiqh books do not contain "laws" as we understand them today. These books were written as religious texts about how Muslims should ideally act in order to be saved on the Day of Judgment. Thus, legal texts did not say, "This is legal," or "That is illegal." Instead, they categorized actions based on whether those actions would lead to salvation or perdition. In their books of fiqh, scholars assigned religious descriptors to different acts: an act could thus be obligatory (*fard*), recommended (*mandub*), permissible (*ja'iz*), reprehensible (*makruh*), or forbidden (*haram*). In a book of fiqh, you would read about how it is recommended to enter the bathroom with your left foot, it is obligatory to show kindness to your parents, and it is forbidden to pray when the sun is at its zenith. But these are rules for living a pious life; they are not state laws. Taken together, these rules reflect what a legal scholar thinks will lead the reader to salvation and describe how the scholar thinks believers should act in the world. If believers follow the laws in these books, good for them and their future; if they do not, then there is no immediate consequence in most cases. Besides, legal scholars have never had the hard power necessary to enforce the rules contained in their books, but more on that in the next chapter.

The third major reason why looking at books of fiqh will not help us understand Muslim belief and practice is that no single book can claim to represent the beliefs of all Muslims. Muslims have no single clerical hierarchy, and so there is no central authority to say which interpretations or laws are truly Islamic and which are not. Moreover, Muslims are notoriously diverse in their legal opinions; they do not agree with Consensus except on a handful of laws, such as that there is only one God, one must give charity, murder is forbidden, and the like. That means that most laws are up for grabs.

This might have led to complete anarchy, but over time Muslims developed quasi-authority structures that believers may choose to follow. Fiqh-minded Twelver Shi'as, for instance, often identify authority figures, known as *marja' taqlid*s, from whom they can take guidance on Islamic law. This person will have published a treatise on Islamic law, often at the behest of peers, and will have demonstrated mastery over multiple religious sciences. Shi'as do not all agree on who these individuals are, or even how many there are at one time. Some will say that there are about fifty or sixty at any one time, whereas others will insist that there are only one or two. One can choose to follow a *marjaʿ taqlid*, trusting that they will take a principled approach to deriving law, or get trained to derive Islamic law for oneself and no longer need to follow the legal opinions of a *marjaʿ taqlid*.

Sunnis also developed quasi-authority structures, which take the form of what are now called schools of Islamic law. These are four large groups, each of which has a long, illustrious history of legal thinkers and texts. Most Sunni Muslims adhere to one of these four schools and often use them to describe their brand of Sunnism. Sunni Muslims regularly designate themselves as belonging to one of these four schools, known as the Hanafis, Shafiʿis, Malikis, and Hanbalis. A minority of Muslims state that they do not follow any school and instead follow only the Qurʾan and the practice of Muhammad. This is a very interesting group known as *salafi*s, about whom much has been written, but they remain a statistical minority among Sunni Muslims, the vast majority of whom identify with one of the four legal schools.

Each school claims to have official positions on legal issues. There is, for example, a distinctly Hanafi way to hold one's hands while standing in prayer (clasped at the wrist just below the navel), and there is a Maliki way to price cloth (by length as opposed to weight). There is a Shafiʿi way to read Qurʾan 22:77 (with a prostration immediately after its recitation) and a Hanbali way to begin ritual ablution (by making an intention and saying, "In the name of God, Most Merciful, Most Compassionate"). Each school follows different rules for deriving and interpreting laws, which results in each having distinct practices. Decoding why, for instance, members of one school hold their hands by their sides in prayer while members of another hold their hands clasped at the chest often involves complex legal reasoning. Instead of figuring out each school's reasoning on each issue and then deciding which one to follow, most Muslims just follow the school of their parents, friends, or neighbors. Following a school, much like following a *marjaʿ taqlid*, simplifies things a great deal: on any given issue, people can simply ask a scholar about their school's "official" position and not worry themselves with the methodology behind the law.

Sunni legal scholars have long held that following any one of these four schools will lead to salvation. Although one might think that one's own school is better than the others, each is considered acceptable. A recent document signed by over five hundred leading Muslim legal scholars, titled "The Amman Message," declares that following any major Sunni legal school—as well as the popular Shi'a legal school called the Ja'fari school—will lead to salvation. "The Amman Message" may have other exclusionary doctrines, but on this point it accurately reflects the belief of most Muslims that they are both safe and saved when they follow the opinions of any major school of law.

Through these schools, Sunni Muslims are linked to an ancient tradition of law and to "official" positions that are deemed acceptable by most Muslims. Since most Sunnis agree on the practice of following a legal school, it must be okay to follow one because of the hadith that says, "My community will never agree upon error." The logic is that since following a school is an agreed-upon practice by most Muslims, and Muslims cannot agree on error, following a school's official position can thus never be erroneous. Obviously, when two schools have different opinions, one might be more right and the other might be more wrong, but the person following the "wrong" opinion can tell God on the Day of Judgment that they were simply following their school's official position and then be absolved of all sin. As we learned in the previous chapter, following a "correct" legal opinion results in two rewards on the Day of Judgment, while following an "incorrect" opinion results in only one reward. One reward is not as good as two, but it is still not bad.

Despite the emphasis on following a school's "official" opinions, a trained eye can tell that schools do not actually have official, unchanging opinions. Schools change their opinions all the time, sometimes advocating the exact opposite of a position they had previously held. For example, in the ninth century, Hanafis officially believed that one could recite a translation of the Qur'an during prayer. Hanafis were unequivocal that if, for example, a Persian translation were highly accurate, it could be used in worship. Today, the official Hanafi position is that the Qur'an must be recited in Arabic during prayer and that any other language is completely unacceptable. Until the seventeenth century, the official Shafi'i opinion was that the mandatory alms tax (*zakat*) could be given only to the Caliph. Today, the official opinion is that it can be given to any bona fide charity organization or needy person. There are a number of examples, some of which we will see in chapter 6, of schools changing their official opinions, and Islamic Studies scholars have done a wonderful job identifying and describing many of them.

Schools change their dominant opinions all the time, but for the casual observer it's hard to tell exactly when and how they do so. Scholars do not come out and say, "Our school used to hold such-and-such opinion, but now we're going to go another way." Recall that although laws must change according to time and circumstance in order to be relevant, they must also be ancient in order to have authority. That means that Islamic laws must be both ancient and contemporary at the same time. And so Muslim scholars, when they come up with new and changed laws, describe how those new laws are completely in line with historical legal opinions, which themselves are presumed to follow the principles-of-Islamic-law methodology.

A relatively recent example of this comes from the Muslim Personal Law reforms made in India in the 1930s. As mentioned in chapter 1, the colonial codification project forced Muslim legal scholars to quickly throw together Islamic laws that would be applied on the state level, and in their scramble to do so, they often imported laws wholesale from historical fiqh books. Those fiqh books were written in a time in which judges could apply laws with some discretion, and it was assumed that the laws found in legal texts would be interpreted and applied only as appropriate. But the new codified law made judicial discretion very difficult, since judges were now forced to rule as much as possible according to the codified law. This put Indian Muslim scholars in a bind. To ensure that justice was served, scholars needed to change certain laws to make up for the lack of judicial discretion. But those changed laws also had to be ancient if they were to have any authority in the community.

One instance in which Indian Islamic legal scholars, who mostly identified with the Hanafi school of law, found that they needed to change an "official" Hanafi law was the case of a woman whose husband went missing. The central legal question that they grappled with was this: if a woman's husband goes missing, how long does she have to wait before she can remarry? This is a serious issue because in all classical fiqh books, a woman cannot be married to more than one man at the same time, and she cannot have sex with anyone else while married to her husband. If she were to have sex outside of her marriage, that would be adultery, for which many fiqh books prescribe corporal punishment. And so, if a woman's husband were to go missing, she would have to be absolutely sure that he was either dead or never coming back before remarrying. But how long should she have to wait before being reasonably sure that her husband was gone forever? It would be cruel to make her wait indefinitely, but it would also be unreasonable to annul a marriage just because a husband went missing for a few days. There had to be some reasonable, "Islamic" time between forever and a few days in which a woman could presume that her husband was not coming back and have the marriage annulled so that she could remarry.

In the early centuries of Islam, scholars from different legal schools considered this question and set about determining an appropriate waiting period for a woman with a missing husband. Hanafi scholars, for their part, held that the only way for a wife to really know that her husband was never coming back would be to wait until he was missing for such a long time that he would surely be dead. That effectively meant that she should wait about one lifetime; then there would be no danger of her being married to two men at the same time, and she could rest easy in her new marriage knowing that her missing husband would never return. The Hanafi opinion is based on a hadith that was graded a weak transmission by hadith collectors, meaning that it was likely an inauthentic narration. The hadith in question says, "The wife of a missing person will remain his wife until it is known that he died." Hanafi scholars figured that no one lives longer than 120 years, and so they set that as the baseline: the wife of a missing husband should wait before remarrying until such time has passed that her missing husband would have celebrated his 120th birthday. If she wasn't sure how old he was, she should wait about ninety years before remarrying, just to be safe.

Of course, prescribing a ninety-year waiting period is the same as saying that a wife with a missing husband can never remarry. But recall from the previous chapter that these texts were written in a time when it was assumed that judges would use their discretion when pronouncing judgments; therefore, scholars could afford to be purely theoretical and unconstrained by practicality. That is, scholars knew that even though their text might prescribe a ninety-year waiting period, a judge would look at the situation and come to his own decision. A woman might come to court after her husband was missing for, say, five years to plead her case, and a Hanafi judge, while recognizing the theoretical waiting period in legal texts, might nevertheless grant her a divorce from her absentee husband, leaving her free to remarry. The judge had the discretion to make such decisions despite laws written in legal texts, and there is ample evidence that judges in the precolonial period regularly did so.

That was the context of the precolonial period, but in colonial India, judges no longer had such wide discretion, because the state imposed a uniform law for all Muslims. In their frenzy to codify the law, Muslim scholars in South Asia simply lifted laws from precolonial Hanafi texts to rule that women whose husbands go missing must wait a minimum of ninety years before remarrying. Thereafter, that was the law, and judges were bound by it. Muslim scholars in colonial India recognized that it was an unjust law that would eventually need to be patched or hacked, and over the years its injustice became clearer and clearer as Muslim women with missing husbands were repeatedly denied the right to remarry.

In the 1930s, Muslim legal scholars came together in a bid to hack this and other unjust laws, but they faced a major problem regarding hacking and public opinion. Remember that fiqh-minded Muslims believe that Islamic laws stem directly from the foundational sources of Islam and ideally should not change. You cannot simply discard laws and replace them with new ones whenever you want; rather, a fiqh-minded believer must submit to laws whether or not they are convenient. For the fiqh-minded, that submission is at the heart of Islam, and it is what separates true believers from mere pretenders. If legal scholars simply said that they were changing the laws to be more just, they would lose all authority in the eyes of the fiqh-minded. That is why scholars could not offer a new law based in the Qur'an or refute the "weak" hadith on which the law was based. They had to demonstrate that their reform was a continuation of the legal tradition rather than a break from it. And it was necessary that they do so; if they failed to hack the law, Muslim women would continue to suffer, and the law would reflect a vision of sharia in which widows were stigmatized rather than supported.

So, the predominantly Hanafi Indian legal scholars came up with a way to change the law that did not appear to be a radical break from the precolonial tradition. They turned to ancient fiqh texts from the rival Maliki legal school, which hold that a woman can get a divorce and remarry if her husband goes missing for only four years. It was tempting to adopt the Maliki opinion in this case, but the Indian Hanafi scholars could not simply import it wholesale. That would seem as though they were simply picking and choosing convenient rulings from rival legal schools. What was the point of being Hanafi if you abandon the school whenever it is inconvenient? Moreover, this kind of marriage dissolution, known as a *faskh*, was historically a point of bitter contention between Hanafis and Malikis. The Indian Hanafi legal scholars, who were nonetheless desperate to adopt the Maliki law, solved their problem by resurrecting a statement from a respected nineteenth-century Hanafi scholar, Ibn ʿAbidin (d. 1836), who himself quoted a sixteenth-century Hanafi ruling about a different topic that said, "In times of need, there is no harm in adopting a legal opinion [*fatwa*] from the Maliki school." The Indian Hanafi scholars could thereby say that they were justified in adopting the Maliki ruling as their own.

It's important to note here that Hanafi scholars neither simply changed the law on their own nor simply imported the Maliki law. Instead, they looked into their own legal texts and followed a saying of a historical Hanafi scholar to justify their actions. They could then say that their choice to adopt the Maliki waiting period actually flowed from the Hanafi tradition. The new law was shown to have an ancient Hanafi pedigree, even as it broke from Hanafi precedent.

If you were to ask an Indian scholar today about the Islamic legal position on the length of time that a woman must wait before remarrying after her husband goes missing, the answer would be four years. There would be no need to get into the technicalities and history of the law, and doubtless, most scholars do not know or care about how the law was changed or even that it was changed at all. All that matters is that today in South Asia, Islamic law says that a wife with a missing husband must wait four years before remarrying.

In the following chapters, I will provide many more examples of how Islamic law was patched and hacked in the past, but here I want to focus on how patches and hacks are discussed among fiqh-minded Muslims. They are neither seen as new laws nor justified by appeals to justice. Rather, they are ancient laws promoted by legal scholars from previous centuries; they stem from the past and, as far as we know, will continue to be applied in the future. In the example above, it does not matter that the four-years rule had no precedent in Hanafi law, and there is no guarantee that the law will be the same ten years from now. What matters is that the law has some root in the Hanafi legal tradition, and one can therefore trust that it accords with the "principles of jurisprudence." When laws are historically rooted in this way, they gain authority among fiqh-minded Muslims.

This, again, is a feature of any legal system that relies on an origin story. Almost every community tells stories of early heroes who developed systems of law that the community follows today. Even when laws change so much that they would be unrecognizable to those early heroes, contemporary laws are thought to represent their original spirit and intention. Laws themselves help provide order and meaning, but the stories behind the laws compel people to buy into that order, to believe in it, and to trust that following the law is a good thing. Islamic law follows that same dynamic. Almost any Islamic law can be patched or hacked, and almost any new law can be proposed, as long as it is shown to have an ancient and principled pedigree.

This might seem distasteful to those both inside and outside the Muslim community. If a law is thought to be unjust, why not simply replace it with another that is more just? After all, the Qur'an repeatedly commands Muslims to stand up for justice, even when it's against their own interests. And the Prophet would change laws when he found that they caused unnecessary hardship. The Qur'an states that "God wishes ease for you, not hardship," and the Prophet reportedly said, "Make things easy, do not make them hard." In fact, numerous hadith suggest that Muhammad thought the five daily prayers to be too onerous, and he reportedly pleaded with God to reduce their number to save Muslims from undue hardship. If the Prophet had that attitude regarding something as central as daily

prayer, why not bring that same attitude to bear on the rest of Islamic law and change it when necessary to promote justice and ease?
Why bother with this game of looking for historical legal opinions
or of demonstrating that new laws are actually old? The whole process looks like outright hypocrisy: we can hack the law any way we
wish as long as we don't say that we're hacking the law.

However justified, such outrage misses the point of Islamic law
as a religious law. For fiqh-minded Muslims, following the law
connects one to a larger tradition, to glorious scholars, to an illustrious past, and to God. The law is part of a bigger historical and
cosmic order, and so aligning yourself with the law means aligning with history and the cosmos. Success comes from finding one's
place within that order, not in subverting it. So fiqh-minded Muslims must demonstrate, at least rhetorically, that they are always op-
erating within the tradition, even when in practice they are breaking from it. The contents of the law are almost secondary; what is
most important is demonstrating that the laws, whatever they might
be, are part of something bigger, older, and wiser than you.

Islamic Law as Ethics

There's an old saying in seminaries around the world that's based on
a statement attributed to Muhammad's cousin, 'Ali ibn Abi Talib.
The saying goes like this: "If Islamic law were supposed to make
sense, we would wipe the bottom of our socks." The saying refers
to the ritual ablution made before prayer, the last stage of which
involves washing feet. Washing your feet can be cumbersome at
times; it involves taking off shoes and then socks, washing your feet,
and then drying them so that you can put your socks back on. Fortunately for many fiqh-minded Muslims, there are hadiths that state
that when Muhammad was traveling, he simply wiped the top of
his socks during ritual ablution rather than removing them entirely
to wash his feet. Muslim scholars concluded that, under certain circumstances, believers are allowed to follow Muhammad's example

and wipe the top of their socks rather than wash their feet. This is a huge relief for people who need to do ritual ablution while on a plane, at work, at school, or in any number of situations in which it would be awkward to remove your socks and wash your feet.

But wiping the top of your socks doesn't make much sense; socks are dirty on the bottom, not the top, so wouldn't it make more sense to wipe the bottoms of socks? In Islamic law, this logic is irrelevant; Muhammad reportedly wiped the top of his socks, and so must believers if they don't want to wash their feet. For many scholars, this proves that Islamic law doesn't have to make sense in order to be followed. Thus the saying goes, "If Islamic law were supposed to make sense, we would wipe the bottom of our socks."

Practicality—like what part of the sock is dirty and needs washing—does not determine or even explain law for the fiqh-minded; it is supposedly a disinterested observer. Why, for example, does a woman have to wait four years for her husband to be missing before remarrying? Why not three years, or five years, or two weeks? The short answer is: because the law says so. Illustrious scholars of the past said, "Four years," and we trust that they derived laws according to principles. That is reason enough: the law is the law because legal scholars in the past said it's the law. This kind of circular reasoning shows that when it comes to Islamic law, content is not as important as process. When trying to change the law regarding how long a wife has to wait before remarrying, the Indian Hanafi legal scholars did not discuss whether four years was a good or just time period. They asked instead, "Is there a precedent or some methodology by which we can justify less than ninety years?" Once they found that precedent and methodology, the law shifted, and the new law became virtuous and good.

The content of the law can and does change all the time, but the general story of how we get to the law must stay the same. I find it helpful to think of Islamic law as a ritual, like prayer or fasting. Rituals are based on an internal logic that does not require external validation. There is no rational answer, for instance, to a question like, "Why do Muslims pray four cycles in the noon prayer?" Muhammad was reported to have prayed four cycles for the noon prayer, and that is reason enough. While on a journey, Muhammad was reported to have prayed two cycles for the noon prayer, and so Muslims are allowed to do the same when traveling. There is no rational explanation behind praying two cycles while on a journey as opposed to one or three; all that matters is that there is a methodology that justifies praying two cycles. When you pray four cycles while at home and two cycles while traveling, you are connected to God, Muhammad, and a long line of illustrious Muslims. Understanding why you are praying four cycles or two is unnecessary.

This might all sound a bit scary, as though fiqh-minded Muslims blindly follow laws that make no sense, regardless of their impact on people and society. But it is important to note that just because fiqh-minded Muslims believe they should follow certain laws whether or not they make sense does not mean they enact those laws in their lives. Recall from the previous chapter that in the era before codified laws, Islamic legal manuals were about how the world *should* work, not about how the world *does* work. Similarly, for most fiqh-minded Muslims, obedience is not so much about following the law but about believing that one *should* follow the law. Fiqh-minded scholars put it this way: praying is good and not praying is a sin, but believing that you don't have to pray is blasphemy. If you don't pray, you are committing a sin and will have to ask God for forgiveness. So, if you miss a prayer, you should feel bad and ask forgiveness, but if you think that you don't have to pray at all, that is denying God's command altogether. Similarly, if you do not enact the law in your daily life, that is sinful, and you should ask God for forgiveness. But if you think that you don't have to enact the law at all, that is blasphemy, and you risk putting yourself outside of the community altogether. So, a fiqh-minded Muslim might believe with all her heart that she must pray the noon prayer in four cycles, but that does not mean that she actually prays the noon prayer at all.

There is a key difference here between believing in the law and acting on it. Fiqh-minded Muslims say that in order to gain entry into paradise, one needs to believe that the law should be enacted but does not actually have to live according to the law. The laws themselves are an impossible ideal; no one can follow all the laws contained in a fiqh book. That is okay, because God is merciful and will forgive you when you fall short. But rejecting the need to follow laws altogether is seen as a rejection of God, and that is to be avoided at all costs. Fiqh-minded Muslims therefore pay regular lip service to the importance of the law, even when they do not follow it themselves.

This is the *religious* nature of the law; it is why precolonial Muslim scholars could promote horribly unjust laws, such as the one about the wife whose husband went missing, without concern for practical ramifications. They knew that those laws would not be enforced and that judges would acknowledge the law but deviate from it. They also knew that if they did not strictly enforce the law that would be okay because God is forgiving and merciful. We have numerous examples of precolonial judges saying things such as, "We find you guilty of sexual immorality, and according to Islamic law, you should receive corporal punishment. But we're not going to do that; pay a fine instead, and please don't do it again." That is why Islamic law did not need to make sense and needed only to accord to some methodology: if the methodology yielded an unjust law, then people and judges did not have to follow it.

That was all well and good in the precolonial period, but it poses a major problem now, when countries have sharia source laws and codified sharia. Now, judges must rule according to these laws, and they have to work within the rhetoric of Islamic law, in which appeals to justice and personal judgment have little place. Laws that might not have been applied in the precolonial period—such as those that systematically disempower women, demonize converts out of Islam, and restrict social freedoms—are now the law of the land. This is a very difficult context in which to discuss Islamic legal hacking, but if we keep in mind that Islamic law is more concerned with method than it is with content, we can see a path forward.

As long as a methodology is followed and new laws are demonstrated to have an ancient pedigree, laws can change and still be considered Islamic. Yesterday, the waiting period for the wife of a missing husband might have been ninety years, but today it is four years, and tomorrow it might be one year. The exact law is not what is important; rather, the way we get to the law and the story we tell about it is what is important. That means that for the Islamic legal-hacking conversation to progress, hackers must move, perhaps counterintuitively, away from conversations about justice and toward conversations about method.

Indeed, internal legal debates among fiqh-minded Muslims are obsessed with method. Concerns about justice are certainly at play, but they are expressed in sterile, methodological language. To understand how this plays out, let's make a simple distinction between morality and ethics. People have proposed many different definitions for morality and ethics, but for our purposes let's make a naive one: morality is about whether something is good or bad, whereas ethics is about how to do something properly. So, for example, we might debate the ethics of the death penalty. To do so, we would talk about humane ways of killing someone, whether by electrocution or lethal injection or firing squad. We might agree that skinning someone alive is an unethical way to enact the death penalty, but hanging might be more ethical. All these issues sidestep the question of morality: is the death penalty itself good or bad? Morals concern the bigger issues of right and wrong, whereas ethics are about the proper way to do something, not so much about whether that thing is right or wrong.

The Islamic legal conversations are, in this context, about ethics. How do you pray, eat, pay taxes, declare war, make love, and divide your inheritance? Legal scholars did not spend a lot of time discussing whether any of these actions were good or bad in and of themselves but instead described how to do them. They would debate about the ethics of these different topics and would come up with ethical arguments for how best to enact them. It was assumed that if a law was ethical, then it would be moral to follow it.

And so, fiqh-minded Muslims rarely ask, Is it moral? Instead, they ask, Is it ethical? To see this in action, let's take the example of slavery. Up until about a century ago, Muslim jurists were very comfortable with the idea of slavery. They wrote treatises about the ethical ways to beat a slave (no more than eighty lashes), how to sell a slave (mothers and their children should not be separated), and how slaves could earn manumission (through a *mukataba* contract). Jurists did not dwell on the morality or immorality of slavery as an institution in their legal works—although many did in their nonlegal works—but instead talked about the ethics of slavery.

In the modern period, however, legal scholars united in their abhorrence of slavery as an institution. But rather than dwell on the immorality of slavery, legal scholars focused their efforts on arguing that there is no circumstance in which owning a slave could be ethically justified. In particular, they imposed conditions on slavery that made it practically impossible to draw up a contract that would allow buying, selling, or owning persons. Thus, they used contract law to argue that there is no ethical way to engage in any part of the slave trade. Since there is no ethical law for slavery, it would be immoral for a Muslim to own a slave, not because slavery is immoral but because the contract law that slavery is based on is unethical. They added that since Muslim-majority countries had all passed antislavery legislation, there is Consensus that slavery cannot be practiced.

It seems cold to have religious conversations, especially about laws related to institutions as immoral as slavery, in the language of ethics rather than morality. Besides, isn't religion supposed to be about morality? Shouldn't slavery be illegal because it is evil rather than because of contract law or Consensus? We normally assume that religion and morality go hand in hand, or that at least that they should. But that assumption is a big reason why modern calls for reform fall on deaf fiqh-minded ears. Islamic law is certainly concerned with morality, but it expresses that concern in the calculated language of ethics. The move to ban slavery did not come out of a vacuum; rather, there were huge movements across the Muslim world demanding its abolition. Likewise, the move from a ninety-year waiting period to a four-year period was spurred by the obvious immorality of the prevailing law. But when fiqh-minded scholars turned to patch and hack those laws, they expressed their moral concerns in the language of ethics.

Just to drive the point home, let's return to the example of prayer. When determining whether to pray three or four cycles for the noon prayer, it makes no sense to ask whether one is more moral or just than the other. It does, however, make sense to ask whether one is ethical or unethical: is this what Muslims are supposed to do or not? Once it has been determined that it is ethical to pray four cycles for the noon prayer (there are numerous hadith that attest to this as well as scholarly Consensus) and unethical to pray three cycles (there are no hadith that attest to this, and there is scholarly Consensus against it), it then becomes a moral duty to pray four cycles, and it is immoral to pray three cycles. It is moral to follow ethical arguments and immoral to follow unethical arguments. Morality does not exist in fiqh-minded legal discussions apart from ethics.

To take this back to our larger discussion of sharia as a moral vision for a just society, Islamic law is a scientific language that describes the ethics of that moral vision. So someone might believe that the sharia supports gender equality as a moral good, but in debates on Islamic law, that person would need to translate her ideas about that moral good into the language of ethics. Thus, if someone wanted to argue with fiqh-minded Muslims about the virtues of gender equality, she would have to do so in the cold, calculated language of Islamic law, not in the impassioned language of sharia. She would have to demonstrate that gender equality is ethical and stems directly from historical legal opinions, not that it is a moral good that should be adopted out of a concern for justice.

As strange as that may sound, it is not unlike how we engage with modern state laws. We do not ask, for example, whether the capital gains tax is moral or immoral. And even if someone were to argue that the tax is, for some reason, immoral, it doesn't really matter. She would still have to pay the tax, and if she did not pay it, she would have to justify her actions. A judge or legal official would decide her case based on whether she followed the law, not whether she thought the law was moral or immoral. Conscientious objectors pay fines or go to jail; defense arguments like "I didn't think the law was moral" do not fly in the courtroom.

To take the analogy further, arguments about morality do not in and of themselves change modern state laws. For example, abortion activists believe that it is immoral to deny women access to a full range of family-planning services. When making a legal argument, however, they do not have to prove that denying such services is *immoral* but that it is *illegal*, regardless of its morality. The same is true for Islamic law, in which the ethics of certain practices are subject to debate, but their morality is not. Someone can have a moral position that animates her argument, such as, say, "Slavery is immoral." But until she can prove that slavery is unethical according to Islamic law, her argument will have no weight among fiqh-minded Muslims. That is not because they disagree with the sentiment but because they are speaking different languages.

Hacking Islamic law means speaking an ethical language from within the rhetorical story of Islamic law. A good hack will change a law in its entirety using only the ethical language of Islamic law.

If you were to ask the average fiqh-minded Muslim today whether Islam allows slavery, you would get an unequivocal *no*. More than that, people will say that the Prophet himself wanted to outlaw slavery, that this was always the intention of the law, and that slavery will be abolished in perpetuity. This complete attitudinal shift suggests that the hack was a good one, that it effectively spoke from within the tradition, and that it will have a lasting impact.

A bad or incomplete hack will only partially change a law, and only for a limited time. In the case of the woman with a missing husband, the law was patched to reduce the waiting period to four years, but that left many other problems. For example, a husband whose wife goes missing can remarry without any waiting period at all. Also, a wife cannot end a marriage on her own, whether her husband is missing or not. She must go to a judge to request a divorce. A more comprehensive hack would have changed the waiting period, made marriage rules equal for men and women, and given women equal rights in divorce, all while demonstrating that those changes actually stem from the historical Hanafi tradition. Creating that hack would also have been more challenging, taking time and energy, but it would have more fully captured the moral belief that the sharia treats men and women equally, which was animating the effort in the first place.

Many more difficult hacks than this have been made in Muslim history, and Muslim scholars have been hacking the law using ethical language for over a thousand years. Slavery used to be legal, but now it is illegal. It used to be illegal to give the *zakat* tax to anyone other than a governmental authority; now it is legal. Coffee was once forbidden in Mecca, and now there is a Starbucks just opposite the King Abdulaziz Gate of the Kaʻba. Whenever a law is hacked to accommodate new beliefs and circumstances, it is done using internal, ethical language. Almost any law can be changed through this internal method, whereas external attempts to change the law are dismissed out of hand. Once a law is hacked, it becomes moral to follow the new law and immoral to follow the old one. This is not a unique feature of Islamic law; rather, it seems to be characteristic of most legal systems.

The added religious dimension of Islamic legal hacking is that it is also virtuous. Going through all the trouble of hacking the law reflects deep religious devotion, not the lack of it. If someone did not care about the law, there would be no need to hack at all. One could simply choose to abandon Islamic law or to come up with one's own personal version of it. Delving into the language of Islamic law to propose hacks that are in line with the legal tradition is a sign that one will only engage in an action if it is proved to be ethical. That is what it means to submit to the law—not a slavish obedience to its contents but a commitment to its methods for determining ethical behavior.

This commitment to method is at the core of the hacking project. It is what allows the law to be contemporary and ancient at the same time. Even when the laws are new, the method for deriving them is old, and so, in a sense, they are not really new at all. As we will see in the coming chapters, it is not always easy to strike that balance between new and old, and proper hacking requires time, study, and energy. Yet hacking has always been a mandate for the Muslim community. If it is true that "my community will never agree upon error," then Islamic law must always reflect the community's evolving beliefs about the sharia. Whenever Muslim beliefs about the sharia shift—whether with respect to governance, human rights, environmentalism, or any other innumerable concerns—legal scholars are tasked with capturing those beliefs in the language of Islamic law while staying true to the historical legal tradition. Hacking makes this possible, just as the communal ethos makes hacking necessary.

The need to hack Islamic law has taken on newfound significance in the age of sharia source laws and codified sharia. Many states now claim the exclusive right to determine what is and is not Islamic law, and they have appointed state-sponsored scholars who speak in the name of the state. These state-sponsored scholars, as several studies have shown, are often woefully out of touch with the majority of Muslims and do not represent popular Muslim interests. Fortunately, as mentioned in the previous chapter, putting sharia into state constitutions inadvertently gave all Muslim citizens the right to weigh in on what they think Islamic laws should look like, a development that works perfectly with the idea that the community as a whole is a source of authority. In order for citizens to engage in meaningful debate and respond to these state-sponsored scholars, they need to be able to express their beliefs in the internal, ethical language of Islamic law and to hack the law with precision and authority.

We will learn how to do that in this book, but before we do, we'll need to know what, exactly, makes someone qualified to hack the law. Hacking is not easy, so what are the qualifications needed to hack? What makes someone a "legal scholar" who can hack the law, and who gets to be one? Since there is no official hierarchy in Islam, who decides which scholars are legitimate and which are not? These are highly contentious questions, fraught with political and religious implications. We will see that there is a concerted effort to restrict hacking to a small coterie of individuals but that many more people are qualified to hack Islamic law than we have been led to believe. Understanding the identity politics that accompany Islamic legal hacking will bring us one step closer to fully entering the hacking conversation and to determining where you, the reader, fit into it.

CHAPTER 3

Who Hacks Islamic Law?

IN THE PREVIOUS CHAPTER, we saw why hacking is an integral part of the Islamic legal tradition. Hacking is how Muslim scholars keep Islamic law ancient and contemporary at the same time, rooted in a historical legal tradition yet relevant to Muslims in different times and places. Hacking is itself a religious virtue: it demonstrates fidelity to God and a desire to translate deeply held beliefs about sharia into the language of Islamic law. I said earlier that Muslim scholars have been hacking the law since the earliest times and continue to do so today, but I didn't describe who these hackers were. To fully understand the social context of hacking, we need to know what makes someone a "legal scholar," what the qualifications are for hacking, and where we find these hackers.

Today, hackers are found all around us, although many are hesitant to recognize them as real legal scholars. That hesitation is largely a reaction to the sweeping legal changes brought about by the colonial experience. In chapter 1, we saw that the conversation about sharia and Islamic law changed dramatically with the onset of colonialism. One of the most significant of these changes was that, with law codified, states no longer needed Muslim legal scholars to come up with new laws. What was the point of legal scholars if the law was already set? Certainly, they were needed every now and again to officiate proceedings and interpret vague laws, but the new legal codes effectively sidelined legal scholars, and they no longer received plum government posts. Citizens started to see the institution of Muslim legal scholarship as a quaint holdover from older times, relevant perhaps to fiqh-minded individuals but not to most. Consequently, centers of Islamic legal learning, *madrassas*, lost much of their funding and prestige, graduates were no longer guaranteed a livelihood, and legal scholars were forced to square precolonial Islamic laws with modern constitutional codes in order to stay relevant. Muslim legal scholars struggled to find their place in a world in which they were increasingly marginalized, and, in general, the study of Islamic law stagnated as the best and brightest in Muslim-majority countries opted to pursue more lucrative, exciting, and relevant fields.

A truism has emerged that "real" legal scholars are now extinct and that Islamic scholarship basically disappeared when colonial powers entered Muslim lands. Madrassas, lacking qualified scholars to teach the art of deriving law, are now thought to teach only by rote, such that students simply memorize precolonial legal texts and then regurgitate them with no understanding of how Islamic laws are meant to be applied differently in different circumstances. Modern scholars are seen as inferior to premodern scholars because the former are presumed to know only about laws contained in precolonial texts but not about the wisdom behind those laws or their proper application. Many Muslims now believe that the rise of nation-states with codified laws, combined with the dismantling of the madrassa system, has all but ensured that real legal scholars will never return.

The changes brought about by colonialism will no doubt be lasting; there is no returning to precolonial times, despite the wishes of some modern Muslim movements. The madrassa system has indeed changed drastically, and legal scholars no longer enjoy the patronage that they once did. But the difference between precolonial Islamic scholars and modern Islamic scholars is not as stark as it might first appear. Yes, there are now codified laws, and yes, there are now nation-states, whereas in the precolonial period there were none. Still, the sophistication with which modern Muslim scholars discuss Islamic law mirrors the way it was discussed before colonists ever came on the scene. It is easy to have an overly romanticized notion of precolonial Islamic society and to valorize precolonial scholars, but that can lead us to miss similarities and exaggerate differences. Precolonial society was certainly different than ours, but it was still inhabited by people like you and me who lived their religion in ways that were surprisingly similar.

The tendency to romanticize precolonial Islamic scholars—and Islamic law's role in precolonial societies—is perfectly understandable. Many Muslims yearn for a time when Muslims led world powers and high-quality Islamic scholarship was the norm. Modern fiqh-minded Muslims often presume that the worldly power that Muslims enjoyed in the precolonial period was somehow linked to excellent Islamic scholarship; specifically, they think that Muslims had power in the precolonial period because Islamic scholars were excellent and that both leaders and the laity valued that excellence. One reason that modern Muslims might have this presumption is because precolonial scholars often said so themselves.

Precolonial Islamic scholars regularly presented themselves as highly knowledgeable, widely respected, and politically powerful. They placed themselves at the center of Muslim society; they said that sultans relied on them for legitimacy and that the people relied on them for guidance. Precolonial Islamic scholars, in their own telling, kept society humming, and to ignore their wisdom was to put society at risk. This is in contrast to today's scholars, who are seen as being of a lesser caliber, if only because they are so disempowered.

It is important to note, however, that just because precolonial Islamic scholars claimed to be powerful and indispensable does not mean that they actually were. Besides, we should not rely on scholars to give us an accurate account of their own role in society; that would be a bit like assessing a politician's importance based only on her memoir. Of course we might want to believe that Islamic legal scholars are more truthful than politicians since Islamic scholars are supposed to be pious, but even the most pious people can have trouble recognizing their place and power in society.

In fact, precolonial Islamic legal scholars regularly aggrandized themselves and their role in society, although not purely out of self-interest. On the contrary, scholars had religious reasons for exaggerating their own importance. Islamic legal scholars believed that they held the keys to a prosperous society and that, through law, they could connect society to God. If they underplayed their own value, people might not feel the need to follow scholarly opinions. But if scholars presented themselves as central to good governance and essential for prosperity, then people might be more inclined to listen to their decrees and follow Islamic law.

And so legal scholars described themselves as "heirs to the Prophet" and "custodians of the tradition," without whom society would devolve into lawlessness and godlessness. They were stand-ins for Muhammad, and they were thus owed obedience and respect. Scholars explicitly wrote that if the scholarly community became angry, then God would be angry, and God's favor would be lifted from the people. They said that if society flourished, it was because legal scholars were being respected and obeyed, and if society failed, it was because leaders and the populace failed to heed scholarly admonitions.

Consider the following two stories about Ottoman sultans. These stories are not historically accurate, but Islamic legal scholars regularly cited them to illustrate the link between scholars, Islamic law, government, and societal success. The first story involves Sultan Mehmed II, known as al-Fatih, the Conqueror. He captured Constantinople—later renamed Istanbul—from the Byzantines, conquered much of Anatolia and Crimea, and pushed the boundaries of the Ottoman Empire into southeastern Europe. His political gains were undeniable, as he transformed the Ottoman Empire into a world power, but his personal piety was somewhat in doubt. Despite building many Islamic institutions and championing religious freedom, he famously clashed with legal scholars and rejected many of their edicts. Muslim scholars nevertheless told stories praising his religiosity and respect for Islamic law, like this one:

> Around the year 1471, Sultan Mehmed al-Fatih wished to build a mosque in his own honor to rival the famous Hagia Sofia church in Istanbul, which had 20 years earlier been converted into a mosque. He hired a renowned architect, an Armenian Christian by the name Sinan, to design the entire structure. When the building was complete, the mosque proved smaller in height than the Hagia Sophia. Outraged, Sultan Mehmed amputated the architect's hand. Sinan, having lived for some years now in Islamic lands, and thus being well aware of the power of legal scholars, complained to a Muslim legal scholar that he had been treated with injustice. The scholar agreed, and ruled that, according to Islamic law, Sinan was entitled to retribution (*qisas*) for the wrong committed. Sultan Mehmed had no choice but to concede to the scholar's ruling, and agreed to have his own hand amputated in retribution. Sinan, amazed at the beauty of a system in which even the sultan was subject to the law, pardoned the sultan, and converted to Islam.

There is no evidence that this ever happened, and it is not mentioned in any of the major histories of the Ottoman Empire. Given Sultan Mehmed II's regular flaunting of Islamic law and scholarly dictates, there is no reason to believe that it is true. But it was told and retold by Ottoman legal scholars, and it tells us about how they saw themselves: they were the ultimate authorities, and when rulers submitted to their authority—as the sultan did in agreeing to have his hand amputated in accordance with Islamic law—society would flourish, as it did during Sultan Mehmed II's rule.

Similarly, legal scholars said that when political leaders did not obey Islamic law, the state would founder. Consider this second story about the far less effectual Ottoman sultan Mehmed IV, who is often a villain in Islamic religious texts. Known as "the hunter" for the time he spent hunting instead of governing, Mehmed IV handed over many of his responsibilities to his grand vizier to free up more leisure time. He seemed uninterested in governance, and as his reign progressed, the Ottoman army faced a series of disastrous defeats. In one story, which has certainly been embellished, Sultan Mehmed IV intervened in a case involving the application of Islamic law:

An Ottoman Muslim woman was accused of adultery, and was brought before a judge. If convicted, the Muslim woman faced either lashing or death by stoning. According to Islamic law, the prosecution would need to produce four reliable witnesses in order to convict, each of whom had to have witnessed the act of adultery first-hand. The prosecution failed to produce the necessary four witnesses, but the presiding judge was overzealous, and managed to, on his own, secure some dubious witnesses who provided circumstantial evidence. Their testimony was accepted, despite their not having personally witnessed the act of adultery, and the judge sentenced the woman to death. This produced an outcry amongst the Ottomans, both citizens and scholars; besides the obvious failure to follow judicial procedure, no one had ever been sentenced to death for adultery in the Ottoman Empire. Demonstrations were held, and several prominent legal scholars urged Sultan Mehmed IV to intervene and nullify the ruling. Instead, the Sultan supported the judge over the scholars' protestations, and upheld the ruling. Ottoman society was scandalized, and upon seeing the convicted woman stoned, the Sultan reportedly felt great shame and outlawed stoning as a punishment for adultery, saying, "From now on, I do not want such disgrace in the Ottoman lands."

Here, Mehmed IV doubly spurned the scholars. First, he failed to listen to them when they demanded he nullify the judge's ruling. Then, in response to a miscarriage of justice, the sultan outlawed stoning for adultery altogether, regardless of whether the necessary four witnesses were produced. The sultan's arbitrary, tyrannical ruling style was seen as an affront to the institution of Islamic law; under his rule, the law was determined by the sultan's whims rather than through careful scholarly research. The sultan was described as regularly flouting Islamic law, whether he was ignoring the scholars or pursuing all manner of debauchery. It is no wonder, the scholars explained, that the Ottoman Empire suffered under his rule.

Muslim scholars around the world regularly linked society's relative success with the respect that political elites gave to Islamic law and to scholars themselves. Yet, even when scholars recounted stories like these, they revealed an important dynamic between themselves and the ruling elite; namely, that scholars had power only when the sultan wished them to have it. In the case of Mehmed II, he himself agreed to have his hand cut off. Presumably he could have refused and the scholars would have been powerless to stop him. Mehmed IV changed Islamic law when he saw fit, and he did not have to answer to anyone. The underlying message in both stories is that if a sultan wants to rule by Islamic law, then good for him and for society, but if a sultan chooses to ignore Islamic law and legal scholars, he is free to do so and ruin society. In either case, ultimate power rests with the sultan, not with the scholars.

In fact, this was the case not only with sultans but also with every political functionary on state and local levels: political elites always had more power than Islamic legal scholars and could accept or reject scholarly opinions at will. We know this for several reasons, the most obvious of which is that whenever an Islamic legal scholar stood up to challenge political authorities, the scholar *always* lost. It did not matter whether they were famous or not, scholars could neither compel political elites to obedience nor ever win in a conflict. Muslim history is bursting with examples of scholars facing persecution from political authorities; in fact, it became a badge of honor to have spent time in prison because of one's beliefs.

Anyone familiar with historical Muslim personalities will recognize names like Sufyan al-Thawri, Abu Hanifa, Malik ibn Anas, Ahmad ibn Hanbal, al-Bukhari, al-Tabari, al-Juwayni, Ayn al-Qudat, Ibn Rushd, Ibn Taymiyya, and Ibn al-Qayyim. All of these people, and many hundreds more, were persecuted by political elites, and some were executed for their insubordination. Their slights might have been real or imagined, treasonous or trifling; all that mattered was that they offended those in power. Muhammad ibn Ahmad al-Sarakhsi (d. 1090), perhaps the most celebrated scholar of the largest Islamic legal school, once criticized his local governor for having contracted a marriage improperly. He reportedly urged the governor to redo his marriage contract in accordance with Islamic law. The governor took umbrage at al-Sarakhsi's suggestion and imprisoned the great scholar in an underground dungeon for ten years.

There is no question that precolonial Islamic scholars had less power than political elites. That did not mean that they were powerless, though, just less powerful than they would have us believe in their own writings. The scholars had what is known as "soft power," that is, power through persuasion rather than through coercion. They were well respected for their religious knowledge, and people often turned to them for answers to personal questions about everyday problems. These questions could have been about anything under the sun, from rules of prayer to raising a child, conducting business, achieving spiritual ecstasy, giving charity, understanding zoning restrictions, or dividing inheritance. If one wanted to know how to do any of these things ethically, one would ask the scholars. The scholars did not have the power to enforce their opinions, but they were still authorities on how to do things right in the eyes of God.

That is the true power of the scholars: they were authorities of more than just law; they were authorities of *religious* law. They determined which actions would lead to salvation and which would lead to damnation. Very few people—especially in the legal profession—can honestly say that their job leads people to heaven and saves them from hell. So, even though scholars had limited hard power, they had a great deal of soft power among religious Muslims. It is true that Islamic legal scholars sometimes had power in courtrooms, but courtrooms represent only a small slice of Islamic law in daily life, especially since most people never go to court. The most influential arena for legal scholars was that of daily life; if a Muslim wanted to live a pious life in accordance with God's will, she would naturally turn to the scholars for guidance. And, more cynically, if members of the political or social elite wanted to publicly demonstrate their piety, they would give money or positions of honor to Muslim scholars. It was therefore a virtue to defer to the scholars and a social disgrace to ignore them.

Defining the Scholars

So, who were these precolonial, soft-power-wielding, socially influential Islamic scholars? The Arabic term for "scholars" is *ulama*, which literally means "learned people." It is easy to talk about the ulama as an abstract whole, as though they formed a unified and coherent group, but the fact is that they were many and varied. Some ulama believed that Islam is best expressed through law and that following Islamic law is the most important thing a Muslim can do to please God. This is a fiqh-minded group among the ulama. An example of this kind of scholar is the aforementioned al-Sarakhsi, who wrote,

Indeed the greatest deed, and most honorable in the sight of our community, is—once having learned the basic principles of this religion—to exert all of one's efforts to learn the law, following the model of our sages. For laws help one differentiate the licit from the illicit, and, as God Most High has clearly stated in revelation, that is the greatest good.

Other ulama were less fiqh-minded and argued that although law is important and good, the goal of life is to achieve communion with God. Laws might help one achieve communion with God, but once that communion is reached, laws are no longer necessary. For example, the poet and mystic Jalal al-Din al-Rumi (d. 1273), himself a distinguished legal scholar, said,

Religious Law is like a candle showing the way. Unless you gain possession of the candle, there is no wayfaring . . . and when you have reached your journey's end; that is the Truth. Hence it has been said, "If truths were manifest, the religious laws would be nothing." As, when copper becomes gold, or was gold originally, it does not need the alchemy which is the Law, no need it rub itself upon the philosophers' stone, which is the Path; as it has been said, it is unseemly to demand a guide after arrival at the goal, and blameworthy to discard the guide before arrival at the goal.

Ulama could be found all along the spectrum—some of them touted Islamic law as the most important manifestation of Islam, and others described it as important but not central or even necessary. All of them, however, believed that Islamic scholars must be consulted and respected for individuals and society to flourish.

Since this is a book about how visions of sharia are expressed in the language of Islamic law, we will be focusing on the more fiqh-minded ulama. These are scholars for whom law is absolutely essential, for whom law is the best way to reach God, and for whom salvation is impossible without following the law. These fiqh-minded ulama are referred to in Arabic as *fuqaha* (singular *faqih*), which is derived from the word used for "Islamic law" (*fiqh*), and it refers to those who have legal training. Depending on who is doing the naming, the fuqaha might be further subdivided. Some fuqaha are referred to as *mufti*s, meaning that they are qualified to issue personal legal opinions (*fatwa*s). Others are known as *mujtahid*s, meaning that they are skilled in the practice of *ijtihad*, in which independent reasoning is used to interpret, derive, and hack Islamic law.

This book is concerned with deriving and hacking Islamic law, so when we speak of ulama, we are speaking mainly about mujtahids. Again, many today claim that "real" mujtahids no longer exist and that there is no one with the necessary training and intellectual capacity to truly derive new laws and hack Islamic law from within. But as we will see later, there are many, many mujtahids today, even if they do not call themselves by that name. Most of these mujtahids simply call themselves ulama, and so we will do the same here. From here on out, I will use the term *ulama* to refer to fiqh-minded mujtahids, meaning those skilled in the science of using independent reasoning to derive and hack laws. This is done for pragmatic reasons; if you were to have a conversation about Islamic law and mention mujtahids, few people would know what you're talking about. Use the term *ulama*, though, and people will get your meaning. Just know that there are, in reality, many types of ulama, some of whom are fiqh-minded and some less so.

Mujtahids, hereafter called ulama, are mainly concerned with the following question: what are the rules and regulations that, if sincerely followed, will lead to salvation? They agreed on the big issues: pray five times a day, fast during the month of Ramadan, give charity, don't eat pork, and so on. But the ulama disagreed about the details of those actions. How, exactly, does one pray? When does the fasting day end—is it when the sun dips below the horizon or when the sky goes completely dark? How much charity must one give? If one should not eat pork, can one eat vegetables from a dish that was used to cook pork? The answers to these questions matter because getting the law right means having a better shot at getting into heaven and building a flourishing society.

So ulama set about enumerating as many Islamic rules and regulations as possible in order to ensure that every action is done correctly. For example, Muslims are commanded to purify themselves for prayer by performing a ritual ablution. The ulama agreed on some minimal requirements for purification and on basic steps for ritual ablution, but they disagreed on questions like:

1. Once pure, do you have to perform ritual ablution again before the next prayer, or only if you get impure in between prayers?

2. What does it mean to get impure?

3. What substances can be used for purification? Does it have to be water, or can it be any liquid, or does it even need to be liquid at all? Does a sponge bath count? How about a dust bath?

4. Can dirty water be used for purification? If so, how dirty can the water be before it becomes impure?

5. What if a pig drank from water that might be used for purification? Does that make the water impure? What if a pig only walked through the water? What if a pig spent several days wallowing in the water, and then left—how would you know when the water is pure again? What if you're pretty sure that an animal was in the water for a good amount of time but weren't 100 percent sure that it was a pig? What if you weren't sure how long the pig or other animal spent in the water? What if a pig fell in a well and died—is all of the well water impure? What if a cow, whose meat is licit for eating, fell in a well and died—can the well water still be used for purification? What if a donkey, whose meat might

or might not be licit for eating, depending on whom you ask, fell in a well and died—can the well water still be used for purification?

6. If water becomes impure, whether because of pigs or for some other reason, is there a way to purify it so that it can be used for ritual ablution again?

7. If you store water in a pot that was used to cook pork, can that water be used for purification? What if you're not sure whether the pot had pork in it? What if you're sure a pot was used to cook pork, but then that pot got mixed in with other pots that normally hold water, and now you're not sure which pots were used to cook pork and which were used to hold water—can any of those pots now be used to hold water for ritual ablution? What if the pots were not used to cook pork, but a pig licked the inside of the pots? What if a pig licked only some pots? What if the pig licked only one pot, but then that pot got mixed in with other pots?

And so on and so forth—the ulama tried to deal with every possible scenario that might come up. These questions might seem trivial—what are the chances that a pig will get into your pot supply? But the answers matter to fiqh-minded Muslims. Since Muslims are commanded to purify themselves before prayer, their prayers would be invalid if they were not pure. That would mean that one of the most central commands in Islamic law—the command to pray five times a day—would go unfulfilled.

One could reasonably argue that indulging these questions is unnecessary, that God knows one's intention, and that you should just do your best and move on. So what if a pig did happen to get into your pots? Just clean the pots and get on with your life. That might make some sense to most of us, but it ignores the central feature of religious law, and especially Islamic law, that was discussed in

the previous chapter. Namely, that for fiqh-minded Muslims, finding the answers to these questions is good in and of itself. It doesn't
matter so much whether these laws address scenarios that ever come
up, or even if you follow the laws when they do; what matters most
is believing that you *should* follow the law.

Remember that these laws are not like modern state laws; they
are aspirational, and their ultimate goal is to describe how individuals and societies *should* work if they want to achieve success in this
world and the next. Writing and teaching about Islamic law is a religious ritual that is meritorious in its own right. Asking scholars
their opinions is a virtuous act, whether or not their opinions are
acted on. That is why precolonial ulama were comfortable portray-
ing themselves as highly virtuous people who should be respected
and obeyed, even if in practice they were not. The ulama knew that
their laws would not be applied in the way we apply laws today, but
that reality did not make their laws any less real or important.

Joining the Scholarly Ranks

In the precolonial period, there was great prestige in being a member of the ulama and in being a scholar of law. Ulama would get
great government jobs, and they would work as secretaries, actu-
aries, judges, market inspectors, and more. But even if one didn't
work for the government, one would still be seen as virtuous. People would pay the ulama respect, if not money, for their wisdom
and salvific role. So how would someone join this prestigious class?
Certainly, some kind of rigorous training and the ability to interact
with Islamic legal ideas and texts were required, but the road to becoming a member of the ulama might take one of many paths.

Much of our knowledge about the ulama and their training is
biased and taken mostly from their own works and biographical
dictionaries. In their writings, ulama described themselves as highly
learned and very important. But it's hard to get a read on a scholar's
skill and prominence by reading his own works; scholars tended to

have overblown ideas about their own importance, which is as true today as it was in the precolonial period.

Biographical dictionaries, too, were full of personal agendas and biases. An author of a biographical dictionary might include and highlight more of his allies and might exclude or denigrate those with whom he disagreed. For instance, some of the most famous and authoritative biographical dictionaries in Muslim history do not even mention the towering figure Abu Mansur al-Maturidi (d. 933), who founded the largest Muslim theological school, as measured by number of adherents. By not mentioning his name, authors of biographical dictionaries effectively erased him from history, at least for their readers. A scholar might be praised in one book for his expertise in Islamic legal reasoning but lampooned in another book as completely inept. We can't, therefore, take at face value what scholars said about themselves and what they said about one another.

One thing we know for certain about the ulama is that there were lots of them. Thousands upon thousands of legal scholars were engaged in the ritual of writing and teaching about Islamic law. Some of them we know about, but most of them we don't; in just about every village and hamlet in which Muslims lived, there were ulama who would teach their communities about Islamic law. Their teachings were highly personal, and Islamic law would look different from town to town based on the teachings of the local scholar. That local scholar might have had some formal schooling but was more likely to have been taught by a family member or community leader.

Although most people in the precolonial period lived in rural areas, we know much more about precolonial urban life than we do about precolonial rural life. Urban ulama were usually trained in madrassas, the most famous of which were located in big cities. These schools had set standards for their students, and although classes were often open to the public, "graduating" from a madrassa meant meeting some requirements, after which you would be "licensed" as a mujtahid and could derive legal opinions for yourself. These requirements varied from school to school. Some were vague and lenient; for example, the Hanafi patriarch Muhammad al-Shaybani (d. 804) said that people could issue legal opinions if they were "right more often than wrong." The Maliki scholar Ibn Juzayy (d. 1340), however, required prodigious memorization before deriving any new legal opinions.

Most ulama fell somewhere in between. They required some expertise and memorization, but these were usually not onerous. Precolonial legal theory manuals often cite the following four criteria as necessary and sufficient for becoming a mujtahid.

1. **Literacy in Arabic.** Literacy might seem like a given to us now, but it was a big deal in the precolonial period. Most towns had no formal schools, and those that did usually taught rote memorization and what has been termed *maktab literacy*, or, enough literacy to engage in the marketplace. Even in major cities with formal schools, like Cairo and Damascus, only one-third of all males attended elementary school. Even then, attending school did not guarantee literacy; there are ample stories of students who, despite attending school for years, could not read. Only successful, full-time students in excellent schools would learn to read and write Arabic or Persian or some other language. To get a sense of the literacy rates in the medieval period, consider that the Ottoman Empire in the nineteenth century had a literacy rate of 2–3 percent. We might then reasonably conclude, as many scholars have, that literacy rates in the precolonial period would not have exceeded 5 percent at any point.

Being literate automatically put one in the upper echelons of learned society. It gave one the ability to read texts from scholars around the world. Of course, not all literate people had access to these texts, the specialization required to understand them, or even the inclination to read them, but literacy opened the door. The language of scholarly discourse was most often Arabic, although Persian became increasingly popular in the medieval period. Persian Muslim scholars, however, wrote their most important tracts in Arabic, thereby lending their works a cosmopolitan, international flavor and proving the author's mastery over the language of the Qur'an. Writing in Arabic also ensured a wider audience; it meant that a Persian speaker writing in Uzbekistan might find readership in Morocco, even if that was highly unlikely. The aforementioned al-Maturidi, for instance, wrote a brilliant work of theology in Arabic even though his first language was Persian. Frankly, his Arabic prose was not very good, and the book is replete with odd word choices, awkward phrasing, and Persian technical terms. Even al-Maturidi's most ardent fans found the book frustrating to read. But the very fact that it was written in Arabic gave it an air of authenticity and authority and ensured a wide readership.

A level of fluency in Arabic was therefore a prerequisite for being a member of the ulama, and most madrassa curricula began with instruction in reading and writing Arabic.

2. **Awareness of laws contained in the Qur'an and** *sunna*. Scholars were expected to be aware (*'arifan*) of legal issues both in the Qur'an and in the well-known sayings of Muhammad. As mentioned in the last chapter, the Qur'an is mostly comprised of stories and exhortations for good living, and only about 10 percent of the Qur'an contains any legal content. Ulama were required to know of these verses, although they did not need to commit them to memory.

They similarly needed to have access to hadith collections, in which reported sayings of Muhammad were compiled. Again, students did not need to memorize hadiths; they just needed to have easy access to collections containing them (many of these collections are organized according to legal issues for ease of use). A minority of ulama nonetheless committed the Qur'an to memory, and a handful even memorized entire collections of hadith, but ulama were required only to be aware of those Qur'anic verses and hadiths that were relevant to points of law. Since the ulama were literate, they did not need to commit these sources to memory; they could always consult the Qur'anic text and hadith collections if a legal matter arose requiring their attention.

3. **Awareness of points of consensus.** Ulama were generally discouraged from coming up with new rulings when old rulings would suffice. They were especially warned against deviating from positions on which there was Consensus. If scholars were agreed on a law at some point in time, then it had God's implicit sanction. To ensure that they did not inadvertently come up with a ruling that violated Consensus, madrassa students had to be aware of the laws on which scholars within one's own legal school were agreed.

The ulama were divided about how to achieve this level of awareness. Some said that one should always consult prominent books of law within one's legal school before coming up with a new ruling. Others held that studying books of law and memorizing the rules of inheritance would be sufficient. Some believed that aspiring ulama should memorize some small text within their legal school that chronicled areas of general agreement. These books were between roughly thirty to eighty pages, like *Nur al-Idah* by al-Shurunbulali, *al-Zubad* by Ibn Raslan, or *Mukhtasar al-Akhdari*. These texts were designed for easy memorization, and some even follow a rhyme scheme. Take the following selection from the Shafiʿi text *al-Zubad* about wiping over socks. The relevant point of law here concerns whether a person can perform multiple purifications without removing her socks (see the previous chapter on wiping over socks). The immediate question is, How long can a person continue to wipe over her socks before being required to remove them to wash her feet? The author answers by stating that time periods differ for travelers and for residents:

> While in your hometown, you are given the right,
> To wipe over your socks, for one day and one night;

When on a short journey, travelers get a reprieve,
Of three days and three nights, starting after they leave.

The poet-jurist does not provide any justification for his claims about wiping over socks, nor does he need to. He is simply stating matters of Consensus for ulama within the Shafi'i school. Aspiring ulama need only know the rules contained in that poem and not contradict them. There are still many issues related to this topic that are not covered by the poem about which ulama can express their personal opinions. These are issues like: How far does one have to travel before no longer being "on a short journey"? What constitutes a sock? Does it have to be made of a thick material, or can it be any sheer covering? Can socks have holes and still be wiped over? If so, how big can each hole be, and how many holes are too many?

All of those issues are up for debate within the school, as there is no Consensus about them. That means that ulama have a good deal of latitude when determining Islamic laws. It also means that knowing all the points of Consensus is not too difficult, especially since these manuals are rather short (thirty to eighty pages). Whether consulting legal texts, memorizing a short fiqh manual, or studying legal texts and memorizing the rules of inheritance, being aware of points of Consensus is imminently achievable.

4. **Awareness of the principles of Islamic law (*usul al-fiqh*).** Principles of Islamic law texts, described briefly in the previous chapter, contain rules and regulations for deriving laws. Students were expected to know the most important of these before becoming ulama. To recap, the principles establish a legal hierarchy of sources, with the Qur'an as the most important source of law, followed by the *sunna* (practice of Muhammad, commonly understood to be contained in the hadith), Consensus, and then Analogy. Books on the subject include basic rules for reading these sources so that ulama would derive laws properly.

For example, these books teach ulama the difference between

general commands that are meant for all Muslims and specific commands that were meant only for Muhammad's time or for a subset of Muslims. They also teach the science of abrogation, in which one law contained in either the Qur'an or hadith supersedes another. For instance, there are hadith reports that Muhammad commanded his early followers to pray toward Jerusalem. That command, however, is considered abrogated by Qur'an 2:144, which commands believers to pray toward Mecca, and by several hadiths that affirm that Muhammad stopped praying toward Jerusalem and started praying toward Mecca. Ulama were expected to know when one law abrogated another so as to not apply an outdated law.

In madrassas, aspiring ulama were encouraged to memorize a short book on principles of Islamic law, such as the approximately thirty-page *al-Manar* of al-Nasafi or the roughly fifteen-page *al-Waraqat* of al-Juwayni, to fulfill this requirement.

Once students fulfilled those four requirements—literacy, awareness of laws in the Qur'an and hadith, awareness of areas of Consensus, and awareness of major principles of Islamic law—they were considered members of the ulama. Looking at those four requirements, it's hard to miss the fact that they are not all that stringent. One essentially needs to be literate and have access to a library containing the Qur'an and some hadith collections to fulfill the first two requirements. The third and fourth requirements require only minimal memorization work to prove that one is "aware" of the major issues in jurisprudence and *usul al-fiqh*. Even if one had not fulfilled all four requirements, one could still be considered a member of the ulama with respect to certain issues. As the legal scholar al-Ghazali (d. 1111) remarked,

> If someone is adept in forming analogies, he has the right to issue legal opinions based on analogy, even if he is not learned in hadith. For instance, someone who studies the issue of [inheri-

tance], it suffices for him to be a jurist in his own right with respect to the foundations of inheritance law and its meanings, even if he has not acquired knowledge of hadith reports concerning the prohibition of intoxicating substances, or the issue of marriage without a guardian. That is because [inheritance] has nothing to do with those hadith reports, and they are not relevant to this issue.

It would seem that almost anyone who can read and conduct research is allowed to issue legal opinions and participate in at least some of the activities of the ulama.

To institute some measure of quality control, ulama developed an internal system of checks and balances. The cornerstone of this system is a method of certification known as an *ijaza* (literally, "permission"). A teacher may confer an ijaza upon a student as proof of the student's mastery over a text or an area of study. To get an ijaza, a student approaches a well-known teacher or scholar to request certification. The teacher will then usually ask the student to recite parts of a text from memory. For example, if a student wants to prove that she has mastered the text *al-Zubad*, she would go to a prominent Shafiʻi scholar, who would then ask her to recite, say, the law of wiping over socks. If the student successfully recites verbatim the poem cited earlier in this chapter, she passes the test and is granted an ijaza. The student could then cite that ijaza as a testament to her scholarly ability.

Of course, this gives a lot of power to the teacher, who could offer or withhold certifications at will, based on personal, subjective standards. There are several examples of teachers having given ijazas to the newborn children of prominent personalities, and some scholars boast of having received thousands of ijazas, although they obviously could not have studied with thousands of teachers. The ijaza is a type of certification, it is true, but it is also a sign of mutual respect and an honorific. It is a way of saying, "I respect you, your knowledge, and/or your family, and I am willing to put that respect in writing." I once shared a taxi with an internationally renowned legal scholar, and during the twenty-minute ride we had an intense conversation about Qur'an interpretation. When we arrived at our destination, he offered me an ijaza in the science of Qur'an exegesis. I politely declined. In contrast, I studied Qur'an interpretation with a teacher I deeply respected, and it took years before he offered me an ijaza, despite my demonstrating mastery of several texts early on. Not unlike belts in martial arts, an ijaza might be granted with little or no effort or withheld despite years of effort, depending on the teacher and institution.

Ultimately, the requirements for becoming a member of the ulama were nebulous, and the process for certification was by no means systematized. To introduce a greater measure of quality—and political—control, social and political elites set up legal colleges in major cities. These were staffed by a few or, in rare cases, several legal scholars who would teach a set curriculum, conferring ijazas only after a rigorous course of study, usually when students were between the ages of eighteen and thirty. Students would graduate not only with an ijaza from a teacher but also with the blessing of the college. Not all legal colleges were equal; some were renowned and stringent, and others were lax and lesser known. Graduates from prestigious colleges had a certain cachet; they were in demand as religious leaders in local communities and as government functionaries, especially in the judiciary. Like today, students who attended the better-known schools were more likely to be offered positions of authority within communities, institutions, and government. Also like today, someone from a lesser-known school could still achieve fame and fortune.

Of course, not everyone could simply attend a legal college and become a scholar. There were institutional barriers to entry that made it challenging for many. Gender was the most obvious barrier; it was very difficult, if not impossible, for women to break into the ranks of the ulama. Even when women were literate and got permission from their families to study, they had a tough time finding male teachers who were willing to teach them. There are, indeed, examples of women's colleges and female scholars, but any reading of precolonial legal texts will demonstrate that legal scholarship was almost exclusively the domain of men.

Racism also played a prominent role in determining who could become a respectable scholar. Several studies have documented the overt racism and Arabism that characterized legal literature in the precolonial period, and racism influenced not only who could attend a legal college but also who would be granted a government job and who would be seen as an authority. Class could be a significant barrier to becoming a legal scholar as well. Anyone choosing to pursue a legal education needed to have the means to do so, the freedom from providing necessary labor for his household, and the connections to get into a good college.

These institutional barriers were reflected in the way that ulama articulated Islamic law. Arabs, for example, were given preferential treatment in the law, as were members of the nobility (*ashraf*). But the most pervasive result of these barriers is the ubiquitous patriarchy found in precolonial Islamic law. *Patriarchy* is a term that is used to describe a situation in which males exclusively hold the keys to power and in which male interests are privileged. In their legal works, precolonial ulama treated males as the law's normative subject, which means that the law was addressed primarily to men and only secondarily to women. Men were given the power to dispose of women's affairs, and many women's rights that were protected by the early Muslim community were systematically stripped away by generations of male ulama. Patriarchal ideals made their way into almost every aspect of the law, from prayer to pilgrimage, from marriage and divorce to financial contracts and political leadership. Institutional barriers ensured that those with power would remain in power and that those without power would be spoken about but would not do the speaking. They also effectively ensured that the ranks of the ulama were reserved for those who themselves had some amount of power.

For male, nonblack, moderately wealthy individuals, however, legal scholarship was a respectable path to religious enlightenment, gainful employment, social standing, and soft political power. Although there were thousands of these legal scholars, only a select group of ulama would serve in high posts in government or have serious soft political power. These elite ulama were learned well beyond the four requirements listed earlier; they studied for years in seminaries and read voluminous books on jurisprudence and legal theory. They were well versed in the rules of pots, pigs, prayers, and many other topics, from child custody to international relations. They appreciated the intricacies involved in legal matters, not just those on which there was Consensus but also on those about which there was disagreement. They lived in a world created by legal texts and worked to square that world with the reality outside the texts.

It is important to remember that these elite ulama, even when given government positions, did not have hard but only soft power. They had power within their communities and sometimes within the marketplace, but only when that power was conferred upon them by the ruling elite. They sometimes served as state-appointed judges, but judges were just as often political appointees, unstudied in Islamic law. Even when ulama did serve as judges, their rulings could always be reversed by state authorities. Nonelite ulama could disagree with elite ulama with few, if any, repercussions, and nonscholars were under no obligation to follow scholarly edicts.

In this world of soft power, the best way to wield influence was to promote fully coherent legal arguments that were relevant to societal concerns. In the following chapters, I will explain more about how scholars created coherent and relevant arguments, but suffice it to say here that argumentation was a scholar's prime method of increasing his authority and power. These arguments were sometimes explicit and sometimes implicit, and they were always made with an eye toward existing power dynamics. Elite ulama had these arguments inside and outside their own circles, using highly sophisticated language and technical terms. Ulama would write books and hold public debates in which they would use ethical legal language to describe the world that people should be working toward. In the public sphere, nonelite ulama could sometimes weave better narratives and command better audiences than elite ulama, but elite ulama had better access to the viziers and courts of the sultan. In each of these arenas, whoever could make a compelling argument about how Islamic law best captured the spirit of the sharia within the prevailing context would elicit more soft power.

This all sounds very dynamic and interesting, but if we recall that (1) most of the population was illiterate, (2) of those who were literate, few were taking part in these highly specialized debates, and (3) people were not compelled to follow the conclusions of these ulama, then it would seem that ulama were, for the most part, talking among themselves. That is a reasonable conclusion, and historical analysis reveals that, in most cases, that was true. Ulama might have had deep and detailed arguments about, let's say, tax law—when taxes should be collected, how much, what is taxable, what is exempt from tax, and so on. History shows, however, that rulers took whatever taxes they wished and that they decided to tax items based on state concerns, not on religious concerns. They might have imposed taxes in the name of sharia and, at the same time, deviated from Islamic tax laws in practice. That was not really a problem, because Islamic law is primarily a *religious* law, and so what is important is not so much whether the law is applied but whether the law, if applied correctly, leads to salvation.

The Ulama Today

Such was the situation of precolonial Islamic legal scholarship, and it is striking to see that not that much has changed. Today, anyone who is literate and has access to texts can call herself a member of the ulama, and indeed many do. There are now hundreds of thousands of people who refer to themselves as ulama, despite lacking any formal Islamic legal education. Among all the people who claim to be ulama, there are certain elite ulama who have attended madrassas, wherein they studied many and varied legal texts and distinguished themselves based on their knowledge of those texts and the ijazas they received. Nevertheless, their authority hinges on their ability to make cogent, coherent arguments that are relevant to their audiences. Regardless of whether someone is formally trained, they are authoritative only when audiences feel that they are accurately capturing the sharia in legal language.

To see this in action, visit YouTube and do a search for "Islamic law." Scroll past the videos that proclaim sharia to be the downfall of Western civilization, and you will find thousands of videos from as many individuals claiming to be members of the ulama, with titles like *shaykh, sidi, mufti*, and *ustadh*—all meant to convey a sense of being learned in the religion. These people are just as likely to have formal training as not, and some of the most famous personalities actually advertise that they have no formal training and are thus uncorrupted by the religious establishment. Their popularity lies in their ability to make sharia relevant to different audiences around the world in the language of Islamic law. Again, this is not law in the modern sense; rather, it is an aspirational law about how law should be applied in an ideal world.

One major and exciting difference from the precolonial period is that some of the institutional barriers that kept people from becoming ulama, such as gender, race, and class, have begun to weaken. They are still at play, but more voices have been added to the conversation than were possible before. Still, like their precolonial predecessors, today's ulama, regardless of gender, race, class, or formal training, all work in a theoretical world that does not necessarily correspond to lived reality. The ulama today have very limited hard power; instead, they wield soft power over those who are fiqh-minded.

This last part is key: the ulama have influence only over those Muslims who are themselves fiqh-minded, and this comprises only a minority of Muslims. That might be surprising; Muslims are often visually represented as praying at a mosque or attending huge rallies run by what seem like fiqh-minded Muslims. Internationally renowned legal scholars like Taqi Usmani and Hamza Yusuf regularly fill stadiums for their talks; and videos by scholars like Tariq Jameel and Habib Ali Jifri have millions of views on YouTube. Yusuf al-Qaradawi, who is known as the "global mufti," has a television program with a reported viewership of sixty million. Yet these numbers represent but a tiny fraction of the Muslim population, which is currently estimated at 1.6 billion. Polls suggest that legal scholars do not have much influence in day-to-day matters and that most Muslims neither attend a mosque on a regular basis nor listen to scholarly opinions. As mentioned in chapter 1, most Muslims do not attend even the mandatory Friday prayer, for which many Muslim-majority countries have a day off.

Opinion polls regularly indicate that Muslims are distrustful of ulama and that there is a general feeling that the ulama are undereducated and out of touch. Although many Muslims report that they find Islam to be important to their lives and believe that sharia is very important, they do not feel that the ulama represent their interests. As a result, although ulama are influential among fiqh-minded Muslims, most Muslims do not listen to ulama and, in both democracies and autocracies, ulama are not given much hard political power. This has been demonstrated in many Muslim countries in response to recent events:

- In 2001, reacting to the US invasion of Afghanistan, the major Islamic political parties in Pakistan came together to form a joint party, the Muttahida Majlis-e-Amal (MMA).

This party was stocked with ulama who declared the MMA to be the party of Islam and vowed to rule by Islamic principles and sharia if elected. Despite riding a wave of anti-US sentiment and new election laws that greatly helped their party, the MMA secured only 11 percent of the popular vote in the 2002 national elections. Their popularity steadily declined until they disbanded in 2008. In the 2013 Pakistan elections, no Islamic party received more than 3 percent of the vote.

- During the Arab Spring, the grand mufti of Egypt, Ali Gomaa, issued a fatwa supporting the sitting Egyptian head of state, Hosni Mubarak, and condemning those protesting in Tahrir Square. He commanded Muslims to stay home and urged parents to keep their children from joining the protests. Gomaa argued that protesting against a legitimate government violates Islamic law and that the protests were causing social chaos. Despite his edict, the protests continued unabated until Hosni Mubarak abdicated his rule.

- The aforementioned Yusuf al-Qaradawi issued a fatwa in June 2013 demanding that Egyptians support their then president, Mohammad Morsi, and that the Egyptian general Abdel Fattah al-Sisi stop putting pressure on Morsi to institute certain reforms. In the following weeks, far from obeying al-Qaradawi's fatwa, millions of Egyptians protested against the Morsi government, calling for his ouster. Within a month, Morsi was deposed, and Sisi is now the president of Egypt.

- In 2014, Saudi Arabia's biggest lender, the National Commercial Bank, decided to go public in an offering that some financial analysts called "the mother of all IPOs." The grand mufti of Saudi Arabia, Shaykh ʿAbd al-ʿAziz Aal al-Shaykh, decried the move and issued a fatwa saying that the IPO was a form of interest (*riba*) and thus violated the sharia. He said that the IPO was illicit (*haram*) and that it should be stopped by any means. The IPO nevertheless went forward without any delay, raising over six billion dollars.

In all of the above cases, we see that the ulama had little sway in the political arena and over the majority of Muslims. Ulama may issue fatwas and contest elections, but they neither exercise direct influence over political authorities nor command the obedience of the populace. But, just as in the case of precolonial scholars, that does not mean they have no power at all.

First, the ulama have influence over fiqh-minded Muslims. Even if their number is only somewhere between 15 and 20 percent of Muslims, that is still a sizeable group. Second, political authorities can lean on ulama to approve of their policies or to disapprove of the actions of political rivals. Although it may not alter the course of events, as we saw in the examples given earlier in this chapter, having the support of the ulama can nonetheless ensure support from a block of Muslims, even if it is a minority block. Third, with the support of the ulama, politicians can institute politically expedient laws and policies under the guise of sharia, thereby garnering support from a significant minority and securing a religious trump card against those who might question state policies. Charging someone with contravening the sharia is an especially potent criticism; it is akin to saying that someone is an apostate, which is a serious charge. It is perhaps no surprise, then, that many Muslim-majority countries employ official ulama and support institutions that educate ulama. These state-sponsored ulama are not mere puppets of the government, but they are certainly patronized and rewarded by the state when they comply with state policies and punished when they do not.

All of this helps explain why ulama, especially those that are state sponsored, have such a bad reputation with the majority of Muslims. They are seen as disconnected from society, reading and debating texts that have little relevance to the problems and social concerns of the day. Their methods of education are seen as outdated and impractical, and when scholars are not viewed as completely incompetent, they are considered to be cynical mouthpieces for the state, molding Islamic law to fit the desires and demands of political elites rather than the needs of the people. It is no wonder that Muslims regularly pine for the precolonial era, which boasted "real" scholars who derived and applied Islamic laws properly, even if the precolonial period they pine for never actually existed.

The animus toward today's state-sponsored ulama might seem a little drastic, especially since, as we have seen, the role of the ulama has not changed much since the precolonial period. Ulama still have no hard power, they still debate texts that have an internal coherence but no necessary correlation to lived reality, and they still primarily discuss how the world should be rather than how it is. So, what has changed? How did this same group, doing the same things, go from being highly respected to roundly reviled? The biggest reason is that Muslims have changed their expectations from ulama and ideas about law.

Muslims expect much more from their ulama than they used to, largely because the baseline for education has advanced tremendously over the past two centuries. Literacy is no longer an impressive scholarly achievement; literacy rates have skyrocketed, and many Muslims read and speak more than one language. Most people now have easy access to a library; many have personal copies of the Qur'an and of hadith collections in their homes and on their smartphones. Today, we can use searchable Qur'an and hadith databases, and we have access to thousands of digitized books via the internet. Anyone can now study legal texts directly, and memorization is largely unnecessary. Many fiqh books have been translated from their original Arabic or Persian, and those translations can provide answers to many legal questions that might come up. The

Islamic legal conversation has become richer than ever before, especially now that women are part of Islamic knowledge production, adding new and essential perspectives on Islamic law.

If anything, ulama today, whether formally trained or not, are better equipped than their precolonial counterparts, and their conversations are more sophisticated. Ulama with no formal madrassa education today would likely have been elite scholars in the precolonial period. And so, as Muslims become more and more educated, the once-extraordinary training regimen of the ulama looks less and less impressive. Today, Muslims expect their state-sponsored ulama to be better trained and more knowledgeable than an educated Muslim with an internet connection and are disappointed when they are not.

Along with these raised expectations, Muslims have changed their understanding of the term *law*, both what it is and what it does. Muslims, like almost everyone else, now believe that there should be one law in the land that should be applied at the state level without prejudice. This is a hallmark of the modern period in which nation-states stake their legitimacy on their ability to apply law equally. Judges are not supposed to use their discretion when adjudicating, even though they do in practice; rather, they are supposed to impartially apply laws found in legal codes. Thus, the virtuous argumentation and legal pluralism that characterized precolonial legal discussions are now seen as vices and fruitless distractions. When state-sponsored ulama argue about the law, it is now seen as a distasteful sign of dissension among their ranks. In any case, since ulama have no power to enforce or legislate laws, they are, for the purposes of state law, seen as somewhat useless.

All of this has led to widespread dissatisfaction with state-sponsored ulama, even among those who hold Islamic law to be a virtuous ideal. Mosque attendance is low, and it is common knowledge that state-sponsored ulama do not represent most Muslims.

There is a deep divide between these ulama and Muslim society, such that the two groups do not interact with and are mutually suspicious of one another.

Paradoxically, this appears to be just fine with state-sponsored ulama, who are no longer accountable to Muslim communities. Since these ulama are relegated to mosques—and mosques are the places where we usually look to find Muslim piety—state-sponsored ulama can claim that they represent all religious Muslims, even if they actually represent only a fraction of fiqh-minded Muslims. When the state wishes to enact "sharia law" to bolster its legitimacy, state-sponsored ulama are the ones who get to define what sharia is. Since reformist ulama and disaffected fiqh-minded Muslims are not part of their circles, state-sponsored ulama are free to discuss sharia on their own terms. If they consistently promote the most restrictive forms of Islamic law as the best representation of sharia, then that will be the official position, since there is no one to challenge them.

But these state-sponsored ulama comprise only one group of ulama today. Just as in the precolonial past, there are ulama at all levels of society who are promoting different, and sometimes competing, visions of sharia in legal language. These ulama are far more numerous than ever before and are found in disparate communities throughout the world; some have media platforms and educational institutes, and others have virtual followings online. We will take a closer look at some of these nonstate ulama in chapter 7, but for now I want to note two things.

First, these ulama have more than met the minimum requirements for being a mujtahid that were outlined in the precolonial period. They speak multiple languages and have access to a wider array of texts than did any precolonial scholar. Today's state-sponsored and elite ulama might question their status as ulama, but towering, precolonial legal scholars, like al-Ghazali, would not.

Second, when these ulama, whether state sponsored or not, express their visions of sharia in the language of Islamic law, they do so by working within the Islamic legal tradition, particularly through the methods of patching and hacking. By following these methods, they are able to ensure that their visions are grounded in an ancient historical pedigree while also being relevant to contemporary needs and concerns. When they are able to do this well, ulama gain followers who agree with their vision of sharia.

My aim in the next few chapters is to demonstrate how skilled ulama patch and hack Islamic law to express their moral convictions about sharia. My hope is that as more people learn how to do this and develop their skills, they will enter into fruitful, authoritative debates with the fiqh-minded elite and state-sponsored ulama. This will, ultimately, be in the interest of these latter ulama. It will help them enter into a meaningful conversation with the broader Muslim community, be relevant to the needs of changing times, and reclaim respect in the eyes of Muslims around the world.

CHAPTER 4

How Does Islamic Law Get Patched?

IN CHAPTER 2, we saw that hacking is a religious virtue. Hacking allows fiqh-minded Muslims to express evolving ideas about sharia in the language of Islamic law so that they can abide by Islamic law and please God without sacrificing their full participation in contemporary society. In chapter 3, we saw that an untold number of hackers today meet or exceed the precolonial requirements for being a member of the ulama and are hard at work hacking the law. And I have claimed throughout that Muslims have been hacking the law since the earliest times and will continue to do so as a matter of religious devotion. So, if that's the case, why don't we hear about hackers and their hacking?

A big part of the reason is that, as discussed earlier, while Islamic law has to adapt to context to be relevant, it must at the same time be ancient to have authority. Ulama are therefore simultaneously tasked with changing the law to adapt to changing times and with rooting those changes in the historical legal tradition. If they were to simply change laws without concern for historical pedigree, then those changes would lack authority, because they would be seen as breaking from a hallowed tradition that links believers to Muhammad and the earliest generations. Part of a good hack, then, is to show that the hack is not actually changing anything.

Demonstrating that new laws are actually ancient is doubly im-

portant in the postcolonial period, because, as we saw in the previous
chapter, modern ulama are viewed with suspicion and are thought
to be inferior to ulama in the past. Today, ulama need to root their
ideas and practices in a time in which "true" scholars roamed the
land. Modern ulama regularly say that they follow the principle of
istishab, which means sticking to historical laws unless there is some
pressing need to come up with a new one. It is commonly understood that, especially in the modern day, one should come up with a
new law only in dire circumstances and with extreme care. There is
a saying among the fiqh-minded that the best thing to do is to imi-
tate laws derived by ulama in the past and that the worst thing to do
is to innovate. It is for these reasons that modern hackers, although
they are plentiful and competent, are not vocal about their hacking. If their hacks were thought to be anything less than direct extensions of the precolonial legal tradition, they would be dismissed
as modern innovations promoted by inferior ulama. We do not hear
about hacking precisely because talking about it threatens to undermine its claims to historical authenticity.

The closest thing to hacking that ulama are willing to openly talk
about is a method that I call patching. Patches are stopgap measures
that don't really change laws in an abiding way. Patches are temporary by nature, and they tend to suspend or extend laws rather than
change them completely. Patches are, quite frankly, kind of lame.
They are easy to deploy, easy to rescind, and easily dismissed. They
confirm historical laws but argue that circumstances sometimes allow fiqh-minded Muslims to deviate from them a bit. Patching may
not be an effective tool for fundamentally changing Islamic laws, but
it is exactly for that reason that it can be discussed openly. Ulama
have used patching to great effect, and it is a proven method for enacting sorely needed legal reforms.

In this chapter, we will look at three patching methods that
ulama discuss freely and openly and that they consistently use. These
are known as *istihsan*, *talfiq*, and *istislah*. I will refer to them using

their original Arabic names since they are technical terms that we should get comfortable using. We will go through each to understand how ulama used patching as a socially acceptable way to extend or restrict Islamic laws. These patches present us with an interesting conundrum. Ultimately, they are unsatisfying because they do not permanently change laws. Yet they allow fiqh-minded Muslims to participate more fully in the modern world and to move in the direction of more fundamental change. We can see these patches as important bridges that, although temporary, might end up encouraging abiding hacks that better reflect the hopes, desires, and beliefs of Muslim communities.

Istihsan

Istihsan literally means "seeking what is best," and it is a little hard to define as a legal term of art. That is because it has meant different things to different scholars throughout history. Also, the way people talk about istihsan in public forums is different from how it's actually used among the ulama. Many people say that istihsan means something like "equity," meaning it is a principle that allows Islamic law to be derived based on equity. So, if a law results in inequity, ulama should replace it with a law that they think is more equitable. As we've seen, however, Islamic law does not work like that in the fiqh-minded world, and ulama are not supposed to use reason to come up with new laws or reinterpret old ones. If they were supposed to use reason, we would wipe the bottom of our socks.

Another common but mistaken explanation given for istihsan involves using context to abandon a strong Analogy in favor of a more appropriate law based in the Qur'an, hadith, or Consensus. A famous example of this concerns an Analogy about making up missed or broken fasts. Let's assume the following premises:

1. Muslims are commanded to fast during the day in the month of Ramadan.

2. Eating or drinking during the day invalidates the fast.

3. If Muslims miss or break a fast during Ramadan, they must make it up later.

Based on these premises, we can make an Analogy that if a person eats or drinks during the day in the month of Ramadan, she has broken her fast and will have to make it up later. But we can abandon that Analogy when someone absentmindedly eats or drinks during the day in Ramadan, because there is a hadith that says, "My nation will not be held liable for [actions resulting from any one of these] three things: forgetfulness, mistakes, and duress." Through istihsan, some argue, we can use the hadith to abandon our Analogy in the case of absentminded eaters in Ramadan, and we can conclude that absentminded eaters do not have to make up their fast later.

Istihsan may have functioned in one of those two ways early in Muslim history, but not today. Due to the societal constraints mentioned earlier, we cannot simply dismiss Analogies and existing laws just because we have new readings of the Qur'an and hadith. New readings are inherently suspicious, and so istihsan has come to be used in only three rather limited ways. These are known as necessity, custom, and free choice. Each of these patching methods assumes that one should always adhere to historical opinions whenever possible and ensure that any changes to laws are rooted in historical scholarly opinions.

THE FIRST FORM OF ISTIHSAN: NECESSITY (*DARURA*)
The most common form of the istihsan patch is known as *necessity*. The basic idea here is that historical laws can be suspended when there is a clear and demonstrated need to do so and that laws should only apply in ideal circumstances. For example, Qur'an 5:38 says that thieves should have their hands amputated. The necessity patch can be applied here to say that when thieves steal out of necessity,

the law of amputation should be suspended. So, when someone steals because they are starving, they are not stealing out of greed but out of necessity and so should not be subject to the law. We can then expand that patch to say that in times of famine or drought, the law of amputation ought to be suspended altogether, because people will regularly steal out of necessity, not out of greed. Similarly, Qur'an 2:173 forbids eating pork, but one could apply the necessity patch to say that the law against eating pork is suspended for those who are starving.

Necessity has been and continues to be an important method for patching Islamic law. Every school of law recognizes its validity, and necessity plays a role in most patches. It is also vague; one's person's necessity might be another person's luxury, depending on how one defines *necessity*. Take the example of going to the doctor if you are severely ill. Going to the doctor is certainly a necessity, but it could get complicated if the doctor is of the opposite sex. Fiqh-minded Muslims frown on fraternizing with unrelated members of the opposite sex, and touching is usually off-limits. But if you are severely ill and the only—or, according to some, best—doctor in town is of the opposite sex, fiqh-minded Muslims would say that it is permissible for that doctor to touch you out of necessity. But what constitutes being severely ill? What if you just have a cold? What about preventive medicine? Here, things start to get a little blurry, with some fiqh-minded Muslims arguing for an expansive definition of necessity, and others arguing for a more restrictive definition.

Necessity has been particularly popular for patching Islamic finance, especially when paired with *istislah*, as we will see later. The necessity patch in this case applies to precolonial interpretations of Qur'an 2:275–280, which forbids a type of financial transaction known as *riba*. Precolonial ulama described riba transactions in exquisite detail, but for our purposes, we just need to know that they defined riba as (1) any loan that increases a borrower's debt over time or (2) any transaction in which money is exchanged for money. This tends to describe most interest-bearing loans, and some ulama believe that interest-bearing loans are therefore prohibited. Using the necessity patch, however, many modern ulama say that the prohibition on riba should be suspended for, say, buying a home or purchasing a car. Some argue that car ownership is sometimes necessary for earning a livelihood. Therefore, those who cannot afford to purchase a car outright can take out an interest-bearing car loan, because that is a necessity. Other modern ulama object that this is an overly broad interpretation of necessity, but they have proven to be minority voices.

Necessity plays a key role in all the patches we will see later. But, as in the earlier examples, using necessity to suspend the law betrays a serious limitation that is characteristic of all patches; namely, that necessity suspends the law because of context but doesn't change the law. The law might still be that touching a member of the opposite sex is forbidden, as is taking out an interest-bearing car loan, except when context demands suspension of the law. That means that if there is another doctor of the same sex in town, or you can afford to buy a car outright, then the context disappears and there is no need to suspend the law. But what if you truly believed, on religious grounds, that there is nothing wrong with touching a member of the opposite sex or taking out an interest-bearing car loan? In that case, the law would need to be hacked altogether—not merely suspended—for it to reflect your religious beliefs. There is no need to suspend a law when the action in question is not forbidden in the first place.

Despite this serious limitation, necessity has been quite effective in patching laws, and it is effective precisely because it does not actually change the law. People can use the principle of necessity to engage in actions that are normally forbidden, all the while acknowledging that ancient Islamic laws are ideal but that context sometimes makes them impossible to apply. That is why necessity is so pervasive in Islamic legal conversations and why ulama can discuss it openly. We should bear in mind, however, that necessity and the patches that flow from it are always limited in their ability to fundamentally change laws.

THE SECOND FORM OF ISTIHSAN: CUSTOM

The Qur'an regularly commands Muslims to do good works and to act according to what is customary (*maʿruf*) in society. Customs vary depending on time and place, so there is always the possibility that, in new lands and with changing social values, some customs might conflict with historical Islamic legal opinions. Since fiqh-minded Muslims wish to follow both local customs and historical Islamic legal opinions, they have to figure out which to choose when the two conflict. It would be unreasonable to make Islamic law fully conform to all local customs, or what would be the point of having Islamic law at all? But it is also unreasonable to impose historical Islamic laws regardless of context, since that would be ignoring custom. Therefore, ulama must balance the two and decide when historical Islamic laws should be suspended in favor of custom and when custom must be ignored in favor of historical Islamic laws.

Ulama regularly negotiate between Islamic law and custom, sometimes saying that law trumps custom and sometimes concluding the opposite. Often, scholars disagree about when and whether one trumps the other. For instance, in certain cultures it is customary to bow when greeting someone, but bowing to anyone other than God is categorically forbidden in precolonial books of fiqh. This is an issue on which most precolonial ulama were in Consensus. Some modern ulama have argued that the law prohibiting bowing should be suspended in cultures in which bowing is customary, but other ulama have said that custom should be disregarded when historical scholars are in Consensus and that customary bowing is always prohibited.

There is a surprising amount of debate on the permissibility of customary bowing, which might seem odd. What are the chances that someone will be in a situation in which they must customarily bow to someone else? But the issue touches a nerve because it potentially infringes on a right reserved only for God. That is, bowing is a ritual act of worship, and acts of worship must be directed only toward God. The Qur'an mentions many times that people should not bow or prostrate to anything or anyone other than God. The question therefore arises, If one bows out of custom, is that the same thing as bowing in worship? Will you be insulting God by bowing to a person out of custom?

Many laws like this one, which we might not think much of at first glance, turn out to be very important to the ulama because they are about much more than the legality of the action itself. With the subject of customary bowing, the legal question touches on a deeper issue of theology. We see a similar dynamic in the debate over whether Muslim men are allowed to shave their beards. Recently, the Egyptian Dar al-Ifta ruled that, in places in which it is customary to be clean-shaven, Muslim men are allowed to shave their beards, despite many hadith and historical Consensus that Muslim men must maintain beards at all times. The Egyptian ulama explicitly referenced istihsan and argued that when custom demands a certain appearance, Muslims should conform and Islamic law should be suspended. This set off an international debate in which passions flared. That is because the underlying question was not one of law but of legal theory. The question was, To what extent are Muslims supposed to emulate the practice of Muhammad? Muhammad had a beard and encouraged Muslim men to have them as well. If the law is suspended because of custom, does that mean that people should not follow the Prophet's practice whenever it conflicts with custom? Where is the line between following the Prophet and following custom? Many tracts were written insisting that istihsan must not be used when it means that one can no longer emulate the Prophet and that severe restrictions should be put on the use of istihsan. Others have argued that *emulating* the Prophet does not mean *imitating* the Prophet and that, in any case, it is his personality that should be emulated, not his exact actions.

Appeals to custom, although popular among the majority of religious Muslims, have had very limited appeal among the fiqh-minded. Whenever an exception to Islamic law is made through an appeal to custom, it is seen as a dodge, a way to justify abandoning Islamic law out of personal weakness or capitulation. Further, the theological and theoretical problems that accompany appeals to custom immediately come to the fore. The vociferous fiqh-minded resistance to using custom as a method for patching Islamic law stems from the same underlying concern that we have encountered several times thus far: Islamic law should be ancient, even as it adapts to new times and places. Appeals to custom make it seem as though Islamic law changes with time and place, which is distasteful to the fiqh-minded.

THE THIRD FORM OF ISTIHSAN: FREE CHOICE (*TAKHAYYUR*)

There is another form of patching, known as *takhayyur*, or "free choice," that is a far more authoritative patch, although it is also far more limited. One of the reasons it is so effective is that it upholds the notion that Islamic law is ancient and that precolonial laws can still be followed today. Rather than suspending the law or subordinating it to custom, takhayyur allows contemporary ulama to look back into history for redemptive and helpful laws that may have thus far been overlooked. This allows one to trust that precolonial ulama had already laid down the answers to everything and that we can find those answers if we just look hard enough.

All legal schools use the free-choice patch, and it is the preferred patching method of the Hanafi school. To understand how it works, recall that in chapter 2, we saw that most Sunni Muslims belong to one of four legal schools (*madhhabs*). These schools each have a

millennium-long history of legal scholars who agree on core principles of the legal school but who disagree on many points of law.
Whenever major historical figures from one's legal school are in disagreement, one is free to follow any of their opinions. In the Hanafi
school, for instance, there are five foundational patriarchs: Abu
Hanifa, Muhammad al-Shaybani, Abu Yusuf, al-Hasan al-Lu'lu'i,
and Zufar. Any time these five figures do not all agree on a law,
Hanafis are free to choose from any of their opinions.

For example, all five patriarchs in the Hanafi school agree that
one has to purify oneself before prayer, and they all agree that one of
the steps in that purification involves washing both forearms. Four
of the patriarchs believed that forearms include the elbows, but one
patriarch, a student of Abu Hanifa named Zufar, was of the opinion that washing the elbows is unnecessary. Since there is no hierarchy in Sunni Islam or within a legal school, there is no way to determine whether Abu Hanifa or Zufar is "right." Neither the Qur'an
nor the "highly authentic" hadith explicitly mentions whether elbows are included as part of the forearms. In practice, most Hanafis
believe that elbows should be washed during ritual purification; if
someone wanted to patch the Hanafi law of washing elbows during
ritual purification, however, they had free choice to follow the opinion of Zufar and be fully justified.

When scholars wish to patch a law, whether out of personal preference or because the law is not working out so well as it is, the sim-
plest thing to do is to look back at all the historical opinions within
one's school and just pick a different one. This kind of patching happened and continues to happen all the time. And whereas the example of washing one's elbows seems pretty minor, free choice has
been used to make some rather sweeping reforms.

A prime example is found in the Ottoman Empire regarding institutions known as *waqfs*. A waqf is a charitable endowment in
which someone sets aside land or resources for exclusively charitable
purposes. One could, for instance, gift farmland to a local orphan-

age. Once gifted, that land and anything produced on it could be used only for the benefit of orphans. Orphans could use it to grow food to eat, or they could sell the produce for the benefit of the orphanage. No one could ever purchase the land or repurpose it, and the land, along with all its produce, is tax-exempt. People could endow schools, homeless shelters, or any number of charitable institutions by creating a waqf, and they could be sure that the land or resources would never be used for any other purpose.

To guarantee the abiding success of an orphanage, school, or shelter, the endowing patron could specify that a certain amount of money made from the waqf—whether from selling produce farmed on the land, or from tuition charged to students at a school, or from something else—be used to pay groundskeepers, administrators, teachers, and trustees who would ensure that the endowment is being used to its full potential. Patrons might create a waqf because it would give them a charitable legacy after their death. This is known as *sadaqa jariyya*, or a form of charity that perpetually sends blessings on a person, even after they have passed away.

As with any institution, a waqf has the potential for abuse. The patron might appoint family members to the board of trustees and pay them exorbitant fees for their services. The one measure that keeps waqfs from rampant abuse, however, is that the waqf must provide some public service that justifies its tax-exempt status, such as education or care for orphans. If the waqf is not being used for its original purpose, the government can seize it. But since orphanages do not generate huge returns on investment, it is unlikely that charlatans and tax cheats would use a waqf to make money in that way.

Some ulama, however, considered the tantalizing possibility that a waqf would be endowed not with land or a building but with cash. In that case, a wealthy patron would endow a large cash reserve to be lent out by a board of trustees. The money would be lent out free of interest to needy individuals, and the borrowers would be expected to pay the capital back over several years, plus administrative fees related to the loan. The administrative fees would be charged for things like keeping up financial records, following up on loan repayment, and, most importantly, the time and attention of the trustees who dole out the loans. In essence, this would make the waqf a tax-exempt bank that would enrich the board of trustees, who themselves would likely be friends and relatives of the wealthy patron who endowed the waqf in the first place.

The cash waqf, in that case, would be a kind of trust fund. For several hundred years, ulama frowned upon this practice and insisted that a waqf could never be endowed with cash, as that would subvert the whole idea of a waqf as a charitable institution. But despite the disapproval of the ulama, endowing cash waqfs was a widespread practice among Muslims living in Ottoman lands. They generated huge returns, and certain families got enormously wealthy. Those families put increasing pressure on the authorities and the ulama to legalize the practice so that they could expand their operations.

This is not such an odd request. Ulama are regularly asked to legalize forbidden practices and to criminalize legal practices. Sometimes they comply and sometimes they don't, as we will see in chapter 6. When there is a lot of pressure to change the law, ulama tend to find a way to comply. But the Ottoman ulama in this case faced two major, seemingly insurmountable problems: (1) Ottomans were mostly Hanafi, and historically, Hanafi scholars almost unanimously forbade endowing a waqf with cash; and (2) the whole setup looked suspiciously like banks giving out interest-bearing loans, even though the banks in this case were being called waqfs, and the interest was being called administrative fees. Lending out money on interest is considered riba by almost all Muslim legal scholars and is therefore forbidden almost by Consensus.

In order to get around the first problem, that of endowing a waqf with cash, the mostly Hanafi Ottoman ulama used free choice to identify a historical Hanafi opinion that seemed supportive. The aforementioned Zufar was reported to have said something that, maybe, if read in a certain light, might be interpreted as endorsing waqfs endowed with cash. It's a really weak argument, one that links Zufar's opinion on garden tools to cash waqfs, but it kind of works. However weak the link, many Ottoman ulama pounced on it and said that Zufar approved of cash waqfs. Using free choice, they could then choose to follow Zufar's opinion over those of all other Hanafis.

The Ottoman scholars then focused on getting around the second problem, that of cash waqfs lending out money on interest. They argued that whenever a waqf lends money, it is taking on some risk, because there is no guarantee that the loan will be repaid. Since a waqf shares risk with the borrower in case of failure, it stands to reason that the waqf should also share in the borrower's success. If the loan is used for a commercial venture, for instance, then there is nothing wrong with the waqf sharing in its profits, since the waqf's loan made the commercial venture possible in the first place. Profit sharing is not the same as charging interest, they reasoned; it's just business. Waqfs are allowed to engage in business, as long as the money all goes back into the waqf. When the capital and the profit is repaid to the waqf, the waqf can then pay the trustees an administrative fee for their time and diligence in devising the terms of and approving the loan. Those fees would be tax-free since they are basically reimbursements for time spent in service of the waqf.

That seemed to be a good enough argument, and thereafter cash waqfs proliferated throughout the Ottoman empire. By all accounts they were wildly successful, with some studies suggesting that they had a rate of return between 9 and 12 percent, making some families fantastically wealthy. Although cash waqfs were in vogue before the Ottoman ulama made them licit, the ulama gave the practice an official stamp of approval. Using the free choice patch, they legitimized cash waqfs as an institution fully in line with Islamic law.

Free choice can be used rather liberally to patch a great num-

ber of laws, and indeed it has been. Although Hanafis dispropor-
tionately use free choice to patch their laws, it is also a tried-and-
true method for patching laws within other schools. Of course, the
problem is that it can be used only when the foundational figures of
one's school are in disagreement. If there was unequivocal Consensus, for instance, that cash waqfs were categorically forbidden, then
there would be no favorable historical opinion to choose from. The
link to the past is what gives free choice its authority in Islamic legal
discussions, but it is also what hamstrings its potential for patching.

The limits of free choice were on display in recent debates about
female-led prayer. Many feminist ulama have been arguing that
females should be permitted to lead both men and women in all
prayers, whereas most state-sponsored ulama insist that only males
may lead mixed-gender prayers. Feminist ulama point out that the
Qur'an does not prohibit female-led prayer, and in fact there is evidence in the hadith that Muhammad appointed a female prayer
leader over a mixed-gender gathering. Feminist ulama have further pointed to several historical and prominent ulama who permitted women to lead prayer. The problem, though, is that the historical ulama that they cite did not belong to any of the four major
legal schools. Some ulama who permitted female-led prayer, such
as the famous Sufyan al-Thawri and Abu Ja'far al-Tabari, founded
schools of law that went defunct over time. The legal scholar Ibn
Hazm, who also permitted certain types of female-led prayer, was
a member of the Zahiri school, which is tiny in terms of adherents.
And no one would claim to follow yet another school that permitted female-led prayer, the much-reviled Khawarij, who never had
any measure of success after the tenth century, and whose name still
raises the ire of Muslims today.

The Hanafis, Malikis, Shafi'is, and Hanbalis do not have a history of permitting female-led mixed-gender prayers. That does not
mean that there is no room in Islamic law for this practice, just that
it was not permitted in the past, for a variety of reasons. The point

of bringing this up is to demonstrate that although feminist ulama have many strong arguments for permitting female-led mixed-gender prayers today, free choice is not one of them, at least not for convincing most fiqh-minded Muslims. Though free choice is a quick and easy move to make, it comes with serious limitations. For starters, there are only a finite number of historical opinions to choose from, and these historical opinions were all articulated by elite men who were privileged by and had a vested interest in promoting patriarchy.

More importantly, regular use of free choice breeds a kind of circular thinking: if the law can be patched simply by citing a historical opinion, perhaps the law cannot or should not be hacked when no historical opinion can be found. As we will see in the next couple of chapters, a lack of historical opinions does not keep ulama from making hacks, but it does make the process more difficult, because patching relies on and perpetuates the idea of necessity: that the law should change only when it absolutely has to.

These limitations aside, istihsan patches are quick, simple, and authoritative. They are seductive in their ease, but there is a trade-off between ease and effectiveness. When istihsan proves too limiting a patch to solve a thorny problem, ulama turn to other patching tools. These are slightly more expansive but also more controversial. The next patch that we will examine, *talfiq*, is a little broader in scope than istihsan and encompasses more possibilities, but it also generates greater unease among fiqh-minded Muslims.

Talfiq

Talfiq literally means "combining," but "borrowing" would be a more accurate description, because talfiq involves one legal school borrowing a ruling from a different legal school out of necessity. All legal schools engage in talfiq in some form or another, though they don't always admit to doing so. Talfiq is called on when there are no historical opinions within one's own legal school that address a contemporary problem. Free choice, then, would be unhelpful, since there would be no historical opinions to choose from. In such cases, ulama are forced to go beyond their own legal school and to borrow a ruling from a different school.

One example of this borrowing was seen in chapter 2, when Indian ulama were trying to reform the law about women remarrying after their husbands had gone missing. Hanafi law held that women could only get remarried after their husbands were missing for ninety years, and there were no major historical Hanafi ulama who offered a different opinion. When Muslim women with missing husbands started leaving Islam in droves to get remarried, Indian ulama looked beyond the Hanafi school for help. They found a solution in the Maliki school, in which women could get remarried four years after their husbands went missing. This is a textbook example of talfiq, a kind of last resort to subvert the dominant opinion of one's legal school in times of crisis or need.

For another example we can turn to the Shafiʿi school and its ritual purity law. Shafiʿi ulama believe that a person becomes ritually impure after touching a member of the opposite sex. That rule results from their interpretation of Qurʾan 5:6, which instructs believing men to ritually purify themselves if they have "touched women." Some schools interpret the phrase "if you have touched women" as a euphemism for sexual intercourse, but Shafiʿis believe in reading texts literally unless there is convincing evidence to do otherwise. As a result, Shafiʿi law requires believers who have literally touched a member of the opposite sex to redo their ritual purification—washing the hands, face, arms, and so on—before praying. That shouldn't be a big deal, since we normally don't touch people, whether of the opposite sex or not, all that often. But the law is untenable for Shafiʿis observing the hajj pilgrimage. During hajj, men and women pray and walk side by side, regularly touching as a matter of course. The Shafiʿi position on ritual purity would require constant ritual ablutions throughout hajj. Praying would be a near impossibility; if one needs to be ritually pure to pray, and touching a member of the opposite sex breaks ritual purity, then one cannot pray among the mass of two million unsegregated men and women.

To make it possible for followers of the Shafiʿi school to pray during hajj, Shafiʿi ulama borrow a ruling from the Hanafi school. Hanafis are more comfortable reading the Qur'an allegorically, and so they interpret the word *touched* in the phrase "if you have touched women" to mean sexual intercourse. Based on that reading, Hanafis hold that merely touching a member of the opposite sex does not break one's ritual purity. So, for the duration of hajj, Shafiʿis borrow this Hanafi law out of necessity, but once the pilgrimage is over, Shafiʿis go back to their original law.

Another example comes from the 1990s when Morocco was reforming its Personal Status Code (*Mudawwana*) at the behest of the king. One of the mandates of the reform was to allow Muslim women to marry without the consent of their male guardians. This was challenging, however, because most Moroccan ulama are Maliki, and precolonial Maliki law is agreed that a woman cannot marry without the consent of her male guardian. To remedy this problem, the Moroccan Maliki ulama borrowed from the Hanafi school, the latter of which believes that an adult female does not need permission from anyone, male or female, to contract her own marriage.

Although effective, fiqh-minded Muslims generally frown upon talfiq except in cases of necessity, and even then it should only be temporary. Their concern is not about mixing up laws from different schools but about mixing up methodologies. The Shafiʿi ruling on ritual purification, for instance, is not the result of random guesswork; rather, it reflects a methodological commitment to reading the Qur'an literally whenever possible. If Shafiʿis were to give up that commitment in the case of ritual purity, why not give it up in other areas? If you pick and choose rulings as a result of using different methodologies, then what is the point of following one methodology or legal school? Preserving methodological integrity has led ulama to use talfiq sparingly and only when dictated by necessity.

Istislah

The aforementioned patches of istihsan and talfiq are not so much about coming up with new laws as they are about either suspending laws or choosing from among laws that already exist. That gives some flexibility to the law, but it doesn't help when historical laws don't address a current problem in any meaningful way. What if, for example, Malikis also believed that a woman whose husband went missing must wait ninety years before remarrying? Or if Hanafis also believed that a woman needed the consent of her male guardian to marry? In those cases, talfiq would be useless. When historical laws inside and outside a legal school are of no help for dealing with a new situation, something more is needed. One would have to move beyond historical opinions and actually come up with new laws.

But new laws are inherently suspect, and there is a prevalent belief that laws must be ancient. To navigate this paradox and keep Islamic law relevant, a group of ulama came up with a compromise. Laws, they argued, sometimes change in response to changing circumstances, but the fundamental values that underpin those laws are universal and unchanging. By shifting the focus from individual laws to universal values, certain ulama, especially those from the Maliki, Shafi'i, and Hanbali schools of law, introduced a new method for changing laws to serve the needs of the community. They called this method *istislah*, which loosely means "seeking the common good," and which looks at Islamic law in light of what these ulama claim are its universal values.

By identifying universal values on which Islamic law should be based, they hoped to create a litmus test for all Islamic laws, both old and new. It might be that a historical law worked well in the past but when applied in a new context it ends up violating universal values and harming the common good. In that case, the old law should be replaced with a new one that better serves the common good. The universal values would be ancient and unchanging, while the laws themselves would change to meet new circumstances. All Islamic laws are, in this conception, subject to reassessment based on the context in which they are applied.

Over the centuries, ulama who championed this approach tried to identify those universal values, which they called the *maqasid al-shari'a*, or "the objectives of the sharia." These ulama argued that Islamic law, if it is to truly reflect the sharia, must protect the following five values: intellect, life, lineage, property, and religion. These five values were not decided upon arbitrarily; rather, they each correspond to what are known as the five *hudud* punishments in Islamic law. A literal reading of the Qur'an and certain hadiths suggests that corporal punishment should apply to those convicted of drunkenness, murder, adultery, theft, and apostasy. Corporal punishments are a big deal, and so some ulama reasoned that they must have been instituted to protect the most important, universal Islamic values. Working backward, they argued that if we figure out the reason behind each hudud punishment, we would understand the universal values that those punishments are meant to safeguard.

Let's take the hudud punishment related to adultery as an example. Adultery is a violation of the marriage contract, but not every contract violation results in corporal punishment. Ulama who championed the maqasid al-shari'a thought that there must be something especially bad about adultery to warrant such a response. They figured that the real problem was that adultery robs parent and child from being certain about paternity. Especially in tribal societies, knowing one's lineage is of paramount importance; it figures into status, inheritance, succession, and much more. Preserving lineage must be so important, they reasoned, that anything that threatens it must be punished corporally. They therefore concluded that lineage must be a universal value that the sharia is meant to preserve in all times and places. Similarly, drunkenness robs one of unrestricted use of the intellect, and so intellect must be a universal value. Murder robs one of life, theft robs one of property, and apostasy robs one of religion; thus, these ulama argued that each must correspond to a universal value that the sharia must always uphold.

Ulama who promote istislah argue that Islamic laws must always be checked to ensure that they do not violate any of those universal values. If and when they do, these ulama say, laws should not be applied, because universal values are always more important than particular laws. The Hanbali scholar Ibn Taymiyya was reported to have passed by a group of Tatars who were immersed in drunken revelry. One of Ibn Taymiyya's students wanted to report them to the authorities and have them corporally punished. Ibn Taymiyya stopped him, saying, "God prohibited wine because it distracts from prayer and rituals, but in the case of the Tatars, wine distracts them from murder, loot, and rape." In his own bigoted way, Ibn Taymiyya was trying to make the point that laws are intended to uphold larger values, and when they no longer achieve that goal, laws should be abandoned or reconsidered.

Istislah and the maqasid al-shari'a have received a lot of attention of late, but they weren't very popular in the precolonial period, when judges could apply the law with a good deal of discretion. As states began to codify law, however, patches were the easiest way to get around legal codes while maintaining authority, and the istislah patch had the potential to institute more sweeping changes than possible through either istihsan or talfiq. By identifying universal values, ulama could theoretically patch any and all Islamic laws to accord with higher ideals. Since the early twentieth century, reformers have been calling for a wholesale review of the Islamic legal tradition to see which laws no longer uphold universal values and so should be replaced with better ones. Today, there are many centers around the world dedicated to the study of the maqasid al-shari'a, and scholarship on the subject is plentiful.

Despite the popularity of this approach among reform-minded Muslims, it has neither gained traction among the fiqh-minded nor resulted in significant changes at the state level. Instead, what has happened is a kind of retrenching. Ulama now insist that state laws *already do* accord with universal values and therefore are in no need of patching or hacking. State laws that punish apostasy, for instance, claim to protect the value of religion; state laws punishing extramarital sex claim to protect the value of lineage, and so on.

There are, however, two fields in which istislah has been effective in patching. The first is in the realm of Islamic finance. Ulama regularly cite istislah and the maqasid al-shari'a when coming up with new financial contracts that seem to contradict precolonial Islamic laws. These are usually complex, and we will learn more about them in chapter 6, but for now we can examine a less complicated example: housing.

We saw earlier that some ulama say it is permissible to take out an interest-bearing loan to buy a car out of necessity. They argue that it is often hard to go to work and provide a life for one's family without a car, and long-term car rentals are prohibitively expensive and impractical. But whereas it is easy to make the case for taking out a car loan due to necessity, it is a little harder to make the same case for buying a house through an interest-bearing mortgage. One could, after all, rent a place, and never have to worry about taking out a loan. Buying a home is an investment and a privilege, not a necessity. But home ownership can also be seen to align with some of the universal values of the sharia. One could argue that it protects the intellect, because homes in affluent neighborhoods often have good local schools and libraries. Owning a home can protect life, especially when it is located in a safe neighborhood. Owning a home definitely upholds the value of property; in fact, some ulama have argued that renting is a waste of money, and wasting money is prohibited in Islam, so one should purchase a home when possible, even if that requires taking out an interest-bearing loan.

This logic has made it possible for numerous fiqh-minded Muslims to take out a traditional mortgage and still feel that they are following the sharia. Many banks hire ulama to explain why traditional mortgages are actually acceptable according to the istislah patch, and they have generally had a warm reception.

The second way that istislah has been effective is known as "blocking the means" (*sadd al-dhara'i'*). This is the flip side of making sure that laws accord to the universal values of Islamic law; namely, it prohibits anything that might undermine those universal values. Many states have instituted restrictive laws that forbid whatever might conceivably lead to violating a universal value. In Malaysia, where istislah is very popular, many government-affiliated ulama are worried that their pluralistic society might undermine the universal value of religion. They are now arguing that to maintain the sanctity of the Islamic religion, non-Muslims must be barred from using the Arabic word *Allah* for God.

Saudi Arabian ulama regularly cite blocking the means as their reason for outlawing any action that could possibly undermine a universal value of the sharia. Blocking the means was an especially good way to keep unrelated men and women from intermingling (*ikhtilat*). The concern with intermingling is that it will lead to extramarital sex, which undermines the universal value of lineage. In their crusade to minimize intermingling between genders, Saudi ulama until recently barred women from driving cars and currently restrict them from taking certain jobs, and they famously outlawed the sale of red roses on Valentine's Day. Aside from potentially undermining the value of religion—since Valentine's Day has Christian origins—the buyer of red roses would presumably give them to a member of the opposite sex, which would result in intermingling.

Blocking the means has turned intermingling into a sin that must be avoided at all costs and has made its potential to wreak havoc on society the stuff of legend. Intermingling has become an evil unto itself, much like the stereotype of dancing as the worst of all sins in the Southern Baptist tradition. There's an old joke that Southern Baptists prohibit extramarital sex because it might lead to dancing. The ulama's approach to intermingling is not much different. Here is the scholar Ibn al-Qayyim, whom we read about earlier, talking about the need to block the means of intermingling:

> Without a doubt, allowing women to intermingle with men is the root of all calamities and evils. It is one of the primary reasons why [God] sends down collective punishment, since it causes corruption in both public and private affairs, and because intermingling between men and women leads to the spread of immorality, adultery, mass extinction, and pandemic plagues.

Like I said, the stuff of legend.

It is interesting to note when and how istislah is used—whether in the sense of upholding the common good or in the sense of blocking the means—especially given fiqh-minded Muslims' anxiety about changing the law. Most often, istislah is deployed to give more power to the powerful. In the examples mentioned earlier in this chapter, istislah was used by banks to support modern Islamic finance, by the Muslim majority in Malaysia to restrict options for non-Muslims, and by men in Saudi Arabia to restrict women's freedom of movement and association. When istislah is used on the state level to enact laws, it is used in almost every case "with the goal of restricting citizens' rights and legitimizing executive dominance."

Many reformists have tried to turn the tables on governments' cynical use of istislah by using it instead to promote human rights. The thinking is that if state-sponsored ulama can restrictively patch the law in the interests of the powerful, why can't reformists patch the law expansively for the disempowered? Some reformists have argued, for instance, that corporal punishments should be altogether suspended because they no longer uphold the universal values of the law. The punishment for adultery, for example, is supposed to uphold the value of lineage, but now lineage can be determined through a simple DNA test. Furthermore, some reformists have argued that corporal punishments for things such as adultery and apostasy work only to uphold universal values in a just society, with a just ruler, and with a truly impartial judiciary. In the absence of these, the universal values will not be upheld, and thus corporal punishments will only facilitate injustice and vigilantism. Therefore, they argue, there should be a moratorium on all corporal punishments until and unless they properly uphold the universal values of the sharia.

Apart from the fact that these reformist arguments have had little impact on fiqh-minded Muslims and even less on autocratic governments, the proposed patches are severely limited. Each patch essentially tries to suspend laws when they no longer uphold universal values. There are two problems here. The first is, What happens if the ideal conditions of a "just" society suddenly returned? Would it then be okay to enact corporal punishment? We saw this scenario play out recently when Daʿesh declared a caliphate. They claimed to have established a just society and thus felt justified in carrying out corporal punishments.

The second problem with the patching method has to do with the fact that Islamic law is supposed to reflect people's deeply held religious beliefs about the sharia. What if someone's vision of sharia, based on a sincere reading of the Qurʾan and hadith, goes against something commonly accepted in the precolonial legal tradition, like, say, hudud crimes? For instance, what if someone truly believed not only that corporal punishment for apostasy should be suspended but that there is nothing wrong with apostasy? What if someone believed that corporal punishment is wrong altogether? What if someone believed not only that thieves should have their hands spared in times of famine but also that it is wrong to muti-late someone for having committed a crime? In these cases, argu-ments from necessity and istislah are of little help. What is needed is a hack that not only suspends the law but changes it entirely.

There are many instances in Muslim history when ulama did just that. But they did not come right out and say, "This histori-cal law is unjust according to my vision of sharia, and so we should change it." Instead, they enacted hacks that demonstrated that their visions of sharia were deeply rooted in the Islamic legal tradition. They worked within existing frameworks of law, doctrine, and hab-its of scholarship to create laws that work with the tradition rather than against it. These hacks were subtle and made within dense texts through sophisticated argumentation so that they were proven to be seamless continuations of the tradition. It was less patching the law from the outside and more recoding the law from the inside. This recoding was not meant to subvert or to flaunt the law; rather, it was a religious act that works through the legal tradition to dem-onstrate obedience to God.

It is important to remember that both patching and hacking are deeply religious acts. They are ritual offerings that seek to reflect be-liefs about God and the sharia in legal language. If someone simply wanted to get around the law, they would not have to go through this intricate and somewhat arduous internal process. Engaging in the process is itself a mark of religious piety and devotion.

With that in mind, we will now examine how ulama hack Is-lamic law. Hacking is far more authoritative for the fiqh-minded than is patching, and hacks have resulted in laws that have changed Muslim legal practice in abiding ways. Hacking requires ulama to work within the larger system of Islamic law, to speak its language, and to balance numerous legal, theological, and rhetorical issues at the same time. This may seem daunting, but keep in mind that any-one who meets the requirements outlined in chapter 3 for being a member of the ulama may hack the law and contribute to the Islamic legal conversation. Indeed, many more hackers will be required to get authoritative expressions of Islamic law to reflect contemporary Muslims' beliefs about the sharia. And as we will see in chapter 7, these hackers are present, ready, and willing.

CHAPTER 5

How Does Islamic Law Get Hacked?

AS WE SAW in the previous chapter, ulama can easily patch Islamic law by extending, limiting, or selecting from historical legal opinions. But we also saw that the patching method is necessarily limited. It can only suspend or extend the law out of necessity; it cannot create new laws that reflect changing ideas about the sharia. For example, we could use patches to argue for suspending apostasy laws because, under current conditions, apostates cannot be guaranteed a fair trial. But what if we sincerely believed that God did not want apostates punished at all? What if we believed instead that the sharia promotes freedom of religion? How could we create new Islamic laws that reflect that conception of the sharia? We would need laws that not only suspend punishments for apostasy but also uphold the right to religious freedom.

In coming up with such a new law, however, we would run up against the same problem we have seen time and again: Islamic law is supposed to be ancient, even as it addresses new times and circumstances. When we look back at precolonial opinions on apostasy, we find that ulama mostly balked at the idea of absolute religious freedom. They were okay with people practicing their own religions but less excited about people changing religions at will. It would seem that with no legal precedent, there would be no way to patch the law to unambiguously uphold religious freedom. Some ulama today conclude, on that basis, that absolute religious freedom will never be accepted in Islamic law, since it was not part of the legal tradition, and laws are not supposed to change.

But just because ulama claim that the law doesn't change does not make it so. In fact, ulama themselves change the law all the time, but they cannot say so outright. The ulama's claim of upholding an ancient tradition is key to their soft power. Ulama argue that people should listen to them precisely because they uphold traditional laws in the face of modern corruptions; they claim to be untouched by the seductions of the modern world, and therein lies their strength. If they openly admitted to changing the laws, they would be seen as poor custodians of the tradition and would lose authority in the eyes of the fiqh-minded.

We find that ulama regularly move beyond simple patching to hack Islamic law, often changing it significantly to reflect changing conceptions of sharia. We'll see just how regularly they do this in the next chapter, but for now we need to understand how they make hacks to fundamentally alter laws while escaping detection from anyone not paying close attention. The most effective way for ulama to present their hacks is to embed them within a commentary on an older, authoritative book. Commentaries claim to only clarify existing texts, with little or no input from commentators. In reality, however, commentators bring their personal beliefs to the texts on which they are commenting, and they change the way texts are read.

We see this most starkly in Qur'an commentaries. Qur'an commentators claim that they are simply explaining the plain-sense meaning of Qur'anic terms and phrases. They say that they are not interpreting the text as much as they are removing any ambiguity from it. But commentators regularly make the text fit into larger narratives that they bring to the text, even if that requires some fancy interpretive moves. They do this in a holistic way so that when you read the Qur'an through their eyes, it seems to lend itself to their narrative, even if you might have read it differently before.

Commenting on the Qur'an

Take, for example, the Qur'anic story of the prophet Jonah. The basic storyline, found in snippets throughout the Qur'an, is that God ordered Jonah to tell his people to shape up. They refused, so Jonah stormed off and boarded a ship to somewhere else. The ship encountered problems that, for some reason, required the passengers to throw one person overboard. The passengers drew lots to see who that would be, and Jonah drew the losing lot. He was thrown overboard and then swallowed whole by a fish. Jonah called out to God from the belly of the fish and was saved.

In the Qur'anic version of this story, Jonah does not come off very well. In fact, it seems as though God doesn't like him at all, as evidenced in the following verses:

> "And [Jonah], when he left in anger and thought that [God] had no power over him" (Qur'an 21:87).

> "And indeed Jonah was a messenger who fled in a ship, and then lost a drawing of lots, was swallowed by a fish and he was blameworthy" (Qur'an 37:139–42).

> "And don't be like the companion of the fish, who cried out in distress. If God's favor had not reached him, then he would have been left alone in his plight, for he was reprehensible" (Qur'an 68:47–48).

These verses, when taken together, present Jonah as someone who defied God and with whom God was angry. Maybe the problem was that he abandoned his mission when he "left in anger," or maybe he was overly confident, since he "thought that [God] had no power over him." Either way, God seems to have had a serious problem with Jonah. This goes against a doctrine held by most Muslims; namely, that God protects prophets from committing sins. Prophets are seen as blameless souls who wish only to do God's bidding. The story of Jonah seems to challenge that assumption, so ulama went to work producing Qur'an commentaries that explain how, in fact, the story is fully in line with popular beliefs about prophets and their infallibility.

Ulama started with Qur'an 21:87 and said that, although Jonah left in anger, his anger was directed not at God but at the people who rejected him. Further, it's not that he thought God had no power over him but that he didn't realize what God had in store for him. Ulama pointed out that the word for "power" (*qadar*) is the same word that is used for "destiny." So basically, Jonah left his people deeply frustrated and was unaware that his destiny included being swallowed by a fish. That reading saves Jonah of any sin and suggests that he trusted in God while doing his job.

Qur'an 37:142, however, says that Jonah was "blameworthy." That makes it seem as though he did something really wrong, eliciting the wrath of God. Ulama countered that the text is not clear about who, exactly, found Jonah blameworthy. We could just as easily read the verse as saying that he was considered blameworthy by his own people, not by God. Ulama point out that Jonah's people heaped undeserved blame upon him, and thus the verse is simply describing Jonah's relationship to his people.

That still leaves us with Qur'an 68:47–48, which says both that Jonah is not a role model ("and don't be like the companion of the fish") and that he was "reprehensible." As for the first part, ulama said that Jonah lived in a different time and had a different mandate than other prophets. God allowed Jonah to leave his people in frustration, but other prophets, including Muhammad, were commanded to persist in inviting their people to the way of God. Thus, Muhammad was commanded not to be like Jonah because the two prophets had different missions. In that light, Jonah did nothing wrong; he just had a different task. So, perhaps the whole being-swallowed-by-a-fish incident should be read not as a punishment but as God showing Jonah that he was still loved and protected despite being rejected by his people and being thrown out of a boat. Or perhaps the fish incident was meant to symbolize rebirth, and God was showing Jonah that he was as blameless as a newborn baby despite failing to convince his people of God's message. As for Jonah's being "reprehensible" in Qur'an 68:38, ulama said that the term should be understood as akin to "blameworthy" in Qur'an 37:142; that is, it was not that Jonah had done anything reprehensible but that his people unfairly thought him to be reprehensible.

With this interpretation, ulama gave readers a way to read the text that's in accordance with the belief that prophets are blameless. In order to support this new reading, they had to address each and every verse related to Jonah. If they commented only on one verse to imagine Jonah as blameless, then the other verses would challenge their views on prophethood. But by commenting on all the verses related to Jonah, ulama were able to create a reading of the Qur'an that fully supports the notion that prophets are all blameless in the sight of God, even one who might otherwise be thought to be blameworthy.

Commenting on the Law

Commentaries on Islamic law work in a similar way. Much like the story of Jonah, which is found in different chapters of the Qur'an, Islamic laws do not live in isolation. Rather, they exist within a network of laws and ideas that work together to create a religious legal system. Laws of prayer, for example, might pop up in a chapter on hajj or on apostasy. Similarly, laws on apostasy show up in chapters on prayer, inheritance, and trade. Islamic laws are interconnected, and when viewed from afar, they tell us a story. They tell us about which freedoms are valued, which restrictions are acceptable, which rights are given to different subjects, how lawbreakers are dealt with, and much more. When taken as a whole, a book of fiqh provides us with a grand narrative that describes a vision of sharia using legal language. Hacking any one law in a book of fiqh affects that overall vision, and so when you reinterpret one law, you have to also reinterpret all the laws related to it so that the vision still makes sense.

The challenge in hacking, then, is not in coming up with a new law and justifying it through the foundational sources; that would be easy. Rather, the challenge is in seamlessly fitting a new law into the larger network of related laws within a legal text so that the old laws and the new one continue to work together to produce a coherent legal narrative. Once that is done, it is relatively simple to demonstrate that the hack is part of the ancient legal tradition rather than a foreign imposition. Fitting a new law into a network of old laws, however, is tough, and this is where the commentary tradition comes in.

To prove that they are upholding the legal tradition when hacking laws, ulama compose commentaries on famous historical books. Rather than proposing new laws, these commentaries—sometimes called a *sharh* (explanation), *hashiya* (gloss), *mukhtasar* (abridgement), or *tahqiq* (recension)—claim to simply inform readers about what the authors of old books *really* meant to say in their texts. When writing a commentary, ulama say that they are not as much providing new interpretations of these old books as they are removing ambiguity from them. But in much the same way that Qur'an commentators claim that they are only explaining the Qur'an's *real* meaning even when they are clearly providing their own interpretations, ulama write legal commentaries that affirm the validity of historical legal texts even while changing many laws within them and creating new narratives.

Commentaries are plentiful, and composing a commentary is the preferred method for presenting new laws. For instance, when the renowned Shafi'i scholar al-Ghazali wished to write a book of fiqh, he did not simply come up with his own laws. Rather, he paraphrased what he said were al-Shafi'i's own legal opinions in a book titled *al-Wajiz*. About one hundred years later, the Shafi'i scholar al-

Rafiʿi (d. 1226) wrote a commentary of *al-Wajiz* to explain what al-Ghazali *really* meant to convey. About fifty years later, al-Nawawi (d. 1277) wrote an abridgement of al-Rafiʿi's book that he said captured the essence of what al-Rafiʿi was *really* trying to say. Then, Ibn al-Muqri (d. 1433) abridged al-Nawawi's book, and then Zakariyya al-Ansari (d. 1520) wrote a commentary on Ibn al-Muqri's book, and so on and so forth.

In each of these abridgements and commentaries, authors tailored the law to speak to their own time and place, but they did so by working within historical texts from their legal school. By the time we get to Zakariyya al-Ansari's commentary, many laws were different from those contained in al-Ghazali's original text written four hundred years earlier. The new laws were not presented as new; instead, commentators hacked existing laws so that they worked toward a new narrative. That means that the new laws had to meld seamlessly with all related laws in the original text to support a narrative that the commentator was trying to promote. Recall the earlier Jonah example: to make Jonah blameless, it is not enough to reinterpret one Qurʾanic verse, because the other verses will challenge your interpretation. Similarly, if a commentator is trying to hack one law, she would have to address every related law in the book being commented on or else the hack would look suspicious and out of place.

We see this play out in modern conversations on warfare. Many modern Muslim ulama have interpreted the Qurʾan and hadith to forbid any kind of aggressive warfare in which Muslims attack first. They believe that God wishes peace for all of humanity and that the Qurʾan and hadith allow warfare only in self-defense. That is a perfectly valid reading of the foundational texts, and the Qurʾan and hadith readily lend themselves to such a reading. So, these ulama explain how verses of the Qurʾan and hadith related to warfare should be read only in the context of self-defense, and their explanations are quite persuasive.

When it comes to laws of warfare found in precolonial legal texts, however, things get a bit more complicated. That is because although there are many laws that directly address the issue of defensive and aggressive warfare, there are also many other laws that tangentially relate to warfare in some way or another, and those would need to be hacked too. It would be easy to hack only the laws that directly deal with aggressive warfare; one could say, for instance, that what precolonial authors *really* meant when they discussed "aggressive" warfare was a preemptive strike when lives are at stake. So, any time one comes across a law that seems to allow aggressive warfare, one should understand that what is allowed is only a preemptive strike to save lives. But then one would still be left with all the other tangential laws that do not directly deal with aggressive warfare but that seem to assume that sometimes it's okay to attack first.

These are laws that deal with diplomacy, rules of engagement, fair warning, formal declarations of war, and taxing the produce of land captured in an aggressive war as opposed to in a defensive war. There is, for example, a debate about the status of contracts made with foreign nationals whose country of origin has declared war, as opposed to those whose country of origin has had war declared upon it. In light of these laws, a rereading of "aggressive warfare" as a "preemptive strike" looks, well, weird. If there is no such thing as an aggressive war, then what is, for instance, the law of fair warning about? Such laws pose a challenge to any reinterpretation, and one cannot simply reject them out of hand without losing authority. If the related laws are left as they are, then the new law looks very strange: Muslims are not allowed to engage in aggressive warfare, but when they do, all existing contracts with the opposing party will be deemed invalid. The story doesn't make sense, and the new law sticks out like a sore thumb.

But if each law in a precolonial book of fiqh were explained in a way that works with a law forbidding aggressive warfare, then the narrative might make more sense. One could perhaps say that the law of fair warning is meant only to signal a willingness to defend oneself if attacked. Or that "captured land" is actually land that is ceded in the course of a defensive battle. Or that "contracts" in this case refers only to government contracts, which become invalid only because a Muslim-led government that declares an aggressive war is in violation of Islamic law and thus demonstrates that it is itself illegitimate. Whatever new interpretation is given, it must apply to all related laws so that they all work together to form a coherent narrative. By following this method, ulama can demonstrate that they are not actually changing historical laws so much as explaining how they should be understood within a larger Islamic legal framework.

Ulama have openly stated that this is the only way to truly hack the law. They say that any new law must demonstrate that it works with all other related laws, a doctrine known as concomitance (*ittirad*). Every new law should, therefore, be judged based on its effect (*ta'thir*) on similar laws; if the narrative still works, then the new law should be accepted. Otherwise, the new law is suspect and should be rejected. Any new law, theoretically, can be proposed, and any old law can be removed; the key is to ensure that all the other laws still work within the new narrative. After all, Islamic law is supposed to reflect the sharia, and the sharia is supposed to be perfect and coherent. If the laws themselves are incoherent and in conflict with one another, then that is a spiritual as well as legal problem. When all the laws work together to form a narrative of good living, then one can be confident that following the law will lead to salvation.

The best way to ensure both an ancient pedigree and a coherent narrative is to produce a commentary on an ancient legal text so that the laws therein are made to work together in a new, internally consistent way. You can think of Islamic legal texts like a sound-mixing console, one of the big ones with seventy-two channels. If you want to, say, make something sound deeper, you can't only adjust one lever, or it will sound terrible. Instead, you will need to adjust a series of levers to balance out the sound. So, if you want something to sound weighty or serious, you might want to turn up the bass. But depending on the speaker setup, that might result in feedback or distortion. To make sure it sounds right, you might also have to turn down the treble, adjust the reverb to make sure there isn't an echo, and adjust the microphone volume, filter, pan control, amplifier gain, fader, and a whole host of other controls to make the perfect sound. You might have thought, *I just want this to sound deeper*, but in order to make that happen, you have to balance all of the related controls.

In the same way, if you change one law, then you must balance out all related laws so that they work together to form a coherent narrative. Once you've done that, it is possible and relatively easy to reinterpret the foundational sources in a way that justifies your new law.

To hack a law, then, you would take a historical—preferably precolonial—book of Islamic law, and take the following steps:

1. Propose your new law.

2. Identify all related laws in the text.

3. Reinterpret those laws so that they create a new, coherent legal narrative that accommodates your proposed law.

4. Reinterpret the foundational sources according to your proposed law.

It's a simple enough process, but it can be daunting. If someone is not an expert in the law, she might not know where to look to find all of the related laws and might not know how to address each one. Many state-sponsored ulama have played on this fear, insisting that they alone can hack the law and that nonexperts are doomed to fail. But we should not be intimidated by the effort required to hack Islamic law. Literacy is now widespread, and more people than ever have access to Islamic legal texts in multiple languages. Many precolonial books of law are digitized, and one can easily search for laws related to one's area of interest. This puts many more people in an excellent position to hack, and, as the saying goes, many hands make light work. We are starting to see teams of hackers working on difficult laws, together identifying related laws and systematically hacking them. Again, this is an act of religious devotion. Hackers feel that certain precolonial Islamic laws do not reflect the true intention of the sharia, and they are doing something about it.

Once a law is fully hacked, reinterpreting the foundational sources—the Qur'an and the hadith—to accommodate the new law is simple and straightforward. For the fiqh-minded, the law determines the way the foundational sources are read, not the other way around. Just as beliefs about prophetic infallibility drive the way the story of Jonah is read, beliefs about Islamic law color the way fiqh-minded Muslims read the foundational sources.

To get a concrete sense of how the entire hacking process works, I have provided a couple of examples. The first is a relatively uncomplicated hack that will give you a sense of how hacking works in theory, and it involves a law that we saw in the previous chapter, customary bowing. The second is far more difficult, for reasons that will be seen, and it has to do with women's rights.

PROPOSED LAW:

"CUSTOMARY BOWING IS PERMITTED"

Let's say that we believe that the sharia allows for any form of customary greeting, whether shaking hands, saluting, bowing, or something else. There are several contexts in which it is customary to bow, like in Japan and martial arts dojos, and in which it is considered rude not to bow. If we believed that such customs should be accepted and respected, then we would expect Islamic law to permit customary bowing. When we look back at precolonial legal texts, ulama didn't talk much about customary bowing since it didn't come up all that often, although when it did, it was in unflattering terms.

Almost all ulama in the precolonial period who discussed customary bowing forbade it categorically. The actual legal texts on the topic read something like this: "Bowing to any person or thing is categorically forbidden because bowing is a right reserved only for God." Bowing to anything other than God might even be seen as an act of polytheism, which is to be avoided at all costs. It would seem, then, that the road to permitting customary bowing is closed.

The lack of historical opinions certainly means that we can't patch the law. But if we look closely at legal texts, we can find ways to hack the law. Having proposed our new law—customary bowing is permitted—we would need to identify all the laws related to bowing in an authoritative precolonial legal text. We would likely find the issue of bowing discussed in two places. The first is in a chapter on apostasy—that is, actions that lead one out of Islam. At the top of the list of those actions is usually bowing or prostrating to anything other than God, which is strictly forbidden. The second place in which bowing would be discussed is a chapter on ritual prayer, of which bowing is a requisite part. This is a perfect entry point for a hack. If bowing is permitted only to God, and bowing occurs in prayer, then studying the rules of prayer will help us determine what, exactly, counts as bowing and what does not. Does nodding the head count as bowing in ritual prayer? If not, then nodding the head as a customary greeting would not count as bowing to something other than God and thus would not be strictly forbidden. By defining a bow within a prayer, we can define the limits of bowing outside of it. Put another way, hacking the law of bowing outside of prayer requires first defining the law of bowing inside prayer.

Defining what counts as a bow in prayer is a bit difficult, because ulama were vague about it. They generally identified two requirements: (1) that the hands should reach the knees and (2) that the bow should not be a continuous up-and-down motion; rather, the worshipper should find at least a moment's stillness in the bow. The first requirement is the most promising in terms of defining a bow. We know from that requirement that small bows of fifteen or twenty degrees don't count. One would have to go deeper and touch one's knees to have one's bow count in prayer. But how much deeper?

People have different limb lengths, and whereas someone with short arms and long legs might have to bow down seventy-five degrees, someone with long arms and short legs might have to bend down only forty-five degrees. Also, we know that touching the knees is a requirement for a bow, but is it also wholly sufficient? That is, does merely touching the knees make something a bow, or is that just one part of the bow? Obviously, if someone were to squat down and then touch their knees, that would not count as a bow. So then, what, exactly, is needed aside from touching the knees?

This was not a question that ulama dwelled on, as it likely didn't come up very often. But we need to ask it here in order to answer our question about customary bowing, so we will look for the answer in another Islamic law related to bowing in prayer. This law is about the person who comes late to congregational prayer. To fully understand it, we will need a little background about how congregational prayer works. Muslims have the option of praying the five daily prayers either alone or, when possible, in a group. Each prayer has a certain number of cycles, and each cycle involves five actions:

1. standing,
2. reciting from the Qur'an,
3. bowing,
4. standing again, and
5. prostrating.

Once these five actions are complete, they are repeated for a certain number of cycles. The morning prayer is composed of two cycles, the noon prayer four, the afternoon prayer four, the sunset prayer three, and the night prayer four. When praying in a group,

the congregation appoints a prayer leader, known as an imam, who
initiates all the motions for the group to follow. When the imam
stands, the congregation stands; when the imam bows, the congregation bows. If someone comes late to the congregational prayer
and misses a cycle, she has to redo that cycle on her own immediately after the group prayer is finished.

The question is, How does she know if she has missed the cycle or not? What if she comes in the middle of step one, or what if
she just catches step five? The ulama reasoned that in order to make
the cycle, one would have had to engage in some portion of each
of the five steps. But notice that standing occurs in two places in
the cycle: steps one and four. So technically, if someone joined the
prayer late and missed step one, they could still fulfill their need to
stand in step four. With respect to step two, ulama recalled a hadith from the Prophet that states, "The recitation [from the Qur'an]
by the imam suffices those being led in prayer." In congregational
prayer, congregants do not need to do step two, because the imam
recites the Qur'an on their behalf. That means that a congregant
who comes late also does not need to worry about step two, because
the imam's recitation counts for her. That leaves steps three, four,
and five; if a congregant comes late to prayer and misses any one of
those, her cycle is incomplete, and she will need to redo it later.

In essence, that means that if you join the congregational prayer
after step three, the step in which the imam bows, you missed that
cycle and need to make it up later. But now we need to ask what it
means to miss the bow. Does the congregant miss the bow if she
comes just after the imam starts bowing? Does she miss the bow
if the imam is just coming out of the bow? What if she joins the
prayer well after the imam comes out of the bow but before the
imam stands perfectly upright?

To answer this question, ulama turned to a saying from Muhammad's companion Ibn 'Umar, who reportedly said that a con-

gregant has bowed if she joins the prayer before the imam starts to move into the standing position. So, if the congregant comes late to prayer while the imam is going into the bow or is still bowing, then she gets credit for the entire cycle and does not need to make it up later. But if she sees the imam's head begin to come up from the bow before joining the prayer, she will have missed that essential part of the cycle and will have to make it up later. Basically, seeing the imam's head is the difference between making and missing the bow. That means that if the imam's head is visible, then the imam is no longer bowing.

We could reasonably conclude, then, that, outside of some physical disability, one is only considered to be bowing if one's head is invisible to those behind. That sounds like a bow of about ninety degrees—even a bow of eighty-five degrees would make the imam's head visible—and anything less than that is not considered a bow. If we interpret the law in the apostasy section of a fiqh book in that light, then only a bow of ninety degrees or more is strictly forbidden. We could then argue that according to precolonial Islamic law, customary bowing is permitted so long as it is at less than a ninety-degree angle, since a bow of ninety degrees or more is reserved only for God. That law works within the narrative of bowing created by all the other laws—hands on knees, rules for making the prayer cycle, forbiddance of a bow to anything other than God—and flows directly out of the Islamic legal tradition.

We can then take this law and use it to explain the foundational sources of Islam. For instance, the Qur'an repeatedly forbids prostrating to and worshipping anything other than God. We can wholeheartedly agree that pious Muslims should neither bow to anything other than God with the intention of worshipping it nor bow to anything or anyone for any reason at a ninety-degree angle or more.

Turning to the hadith literature, we find the following report that needs explanation:

> A man asked the Prophet, "One of us may run into his brother
> or friend, may he then bow to him?" The Prophet said, "No."
> The man said, "Should he then hold him and kiss him?" The
> Prophet said, "No." The man said, "May he then take his hand
> and shake it?" The Prophet said, "Yes."

We could explain that, to begin with, this hadith is not making a legal claim, since it is not illegal to hug or kiss one's brother or friend.
Rather, this is a suggestion about the best way to greet someone.
Besides, in light of our hack, we can say that the type of bowing
being asked about in the hadith is a ninety-degree bow, so the hadith was discouraging that, not a customary bow of less than ninety
degrees.

The point is that such interpretations of the Qur'an and hadith
are easy to make once the law is in hand. The Qur'an and hadith
will never change, and they can abide multiple interpretations. The
general rule among the fiqh-minded is that law comes first, and interpretation comes second. In seminaries across the Muslim world,
law is taught in every year, whereas Qur'an and hadith interpretation are taught only near the end of one's studies. The underlying idea is that knowing the law is a prerequisite for understanding the foundational sources, and without the law, the foundational
sources are not only unintelligible, they are dangerous precisely because they can be used to justify most anything.

Starting with law not only mirrors seminary education but also
results in stronger and more authoritative hacks than mere patching or reinterpreting the foundational sources could ever provide.
Rather than suspending the law or making an exception out of necessity, this hacked law makes customary bowing a fully Islamic
legal practice. In the above hack, all the precolonial laws of ritual
bowing themselves seem to validate a law permitting customary
bowing of less than ninety degrees. Further, if you were to look at
all the precolonial laws of bowing through this new interpretation,

those laws would still make perfect sense. The new law functions within the larger edifice of precolonial Islamic law, allowing believers to feel that they are following, not subverting, a historical legal tradition when they customarily bow.

Of course, someone could object to the hack and say that it is misleading. It could be argued that it is better to look at the laws of infirm congregants when defining the limits of bowing in prayer rather than at the laws of those coming late to congregational prayer. One of the laws of infirm congregants holds that those with back problems are allowed to bow only about thirty degrees, or, to use precolonial Islamic legal language, only as far as they would have to bend to touch with outstretched arms the congregants praying in the row directly ahead. Based on this law of infirm congregants, one could conclude that ritual bowing starts at about a thirty-degree angle and that Islamic law prohibits deeper bows to anyone or anything.

That would be a perfectly reasonable objection, but eliciting such a response is exactly the point: rather than being dismissed as a foreign intervention, the hack has sparked a legal debate. A hacker could counter that the law of infirm congregants is exceptional and that laws should be based on rules, not exceptions. The hacker could then buttress her argument with the hadith that says that when the Prophet bowed in prayer, his back was so straight that if someone poured water on it, the water would settle there, and therefore bows are meant to be at a ninety-degree angle. There would no doubt be an objection that the previous hadith refers to optimal bowing and not minimal bowing, and a back-and-forth would ensue. That back-and-forth would be proof that the hack is taken seriously. Neither argument is objectively right or wrong, but each can now vie for authority as an ideal aspirational law that accurately reflects the sharia.

Although this hack is strong and speaks from within the legal tradition, we should also point out its weaknesses. It is effective in the sense that it allows for most forms of customary bowing, but it only allows for bows of up to eighty-nine degrees. What if the custom in a certain place is to bow ninety degrees or more? In that case, this hack would be unhelpful, and a new one would be required. Perhaps hackers could do something with the law that requires bows in prayer to include a moment of stillness, or look to some other law somewhere else. That would require a new set of explanations to put all related laws in balance.

The trouble with coming up with good hacks is that it is painstaking and piecemeal, and hacks need to constantly adapt to new and changing contexts. The most sweeping hack for customary bowing would be to say, "It is permissible to bow to any depths in situations in which such bowing is done out of respect for custom and not for the purpose of worship." That would be a good hack, addressing multiple contexts and more accurately reflecting the underlying belief that is animating the hack in the first place; namely, that there is a fundamental difference between customary bowing and ritual bowing and that the two should not be equated at all. Such a hack, however, would require much more time and attention, because it encroaches on several other precolonial Islamic laws. That hack is not impossible, but it is very difficult. Again, it is a testament to the faith of fiqh-minded believers that they will not act contrary to the law until and unless an appropriate hack is found.

Short of making a comprehensive hack, one can patch the law or perhaps propose an incomplete hack that does not address all related laws. That can have severe consequences; changing only one law puts tremendous strain on the Islamic legal narrative, suggesting that the hack is foreign to the legal tradition and could end up creating a whole host of other problems. Bad hacks have the benefit of providing a quick fix to a single problem, but they can end up causing more problems than they solve, as we will see shortly. There is thus a constant struggle between good hacks and bad hacks. Bad hacks provide instant relief but result in other problems; good hacks can provide lasting solutions but take time and energy, luxuries not available to those suffering under unjust interpretations of the sharia. This tension between good hacks and bad hacks was recently on display in Saudi Arabia during a push to hack the laws of domestic violence.

PROPOSED LAW: "DOMESTIC VIOLENCE IS CATEGORICALLY PROHIBITED"

In 2013, the Saudi monarchy, under enormous national and international pressure and in the wake of several high-profile court cases in which domestic abusers were exonerated, decided to outlaw all forms of domestic violence. The resulting decree, implemented in May 2015, criminalized any kind of harm perpetrated by one spouse on another, whether by "exploitation, or physical, psychological, or sexual abuse, or the threat of it." The decree put Saudi ulama in a frenzy. State-sponsored ulama rushed to find Islamic justifications for the law, taking almost a full year to do so, while opponents lambasted it as an overreach of executive authority. Conferences were held, for and against, and passionate tracts were composed, for and against. One big reason for all the frenetic activity and controversy is this: in their books of fiqh, precolonial ulama unambiguously upheld the right of a husband to physically discipline his wife.

That is deeply depressing but not entirely surprising, given that precolonial ulama lived in a time in which men were thought to be superior to women. That was their narrative of how the world worked, and they argued for laws that reflected that narrative. Such laws spanned almost every subject: women were barred from leading prayer, traveling without a related male escort, leading a nation, serving as the guardian of their families, divorcing unilaterally, and much more. Men, on the other hand, were empowered to take leadership positions and were placed firmly at the head of the family. As heads, men were charged with the physical and moral well-being of their families. That meant that under some circumstances, they might be permitted to discipline family members, a right that precolonial ulama understood to include physical discipline.

As Ayesha S. Chaudhry has exhaustively demonstrated, precolonial ulama all agreed that a husband could hit his wife and disagreed only about how he should hit her. They all said that he should hit her in a "nonextreme" way, but they disagreed about what that meant. Some said that nonextreme hitting meant not breaking bones or causing open wounds, whereas others said that it meant not leaving a mark of any kind. Some were comfortable with husbands hitting their wives with a whip, whereas others said that it should be done only with something like a toothbrush and that it was preferable not to hit at all. Much like legal scholars around the world at that time, precolonial ulama might have differed on *how* a husband should hit his wife, but they did not question whether a husband *could* hit his wife. That seemed reasonable to ulama based on their narrative of sharia in which men were in authority over women and responsible for their moral well-being, and they proposed a host of laws that supported their narrative.

With these laws in hand, precolonial ulama argued that the foundational sources of Islam validated their laws. In particular, they cited the latter part of Qur'an 4:34, which they interpreted to say, "And as for those [wives] from who you fear recalcitrance, admonish them, abandon them in their beds, and hit them." They followed that interpretation up with a hadith in which Muhammad, near the end of his life, stated, "My last recommendation to you is that you treat women well. Indeed, they are your helpers, and you have no rights over them beyond that, except if they commit gross indecency. If they do that, then abandon them in their beds, and hit them in a nonextreme way." For precolonial ulama, these texts were clear and fully justified their Consensus that a husband ought to be allowed to hit his wife, even if in a restricted manner.

Today, the narrative has shifted. The majority of Muslims no longer believe that men are superior to women or that men are responsible for the moral well-being of their families. Instead, they tend to believe that each person has an independent, unmediated relationship to God and that each is responsible for her or his own moral well-being. Further, Muslims overwhelmingly believe that domestic violence is wrong. Yet, despite this huge shift in attitudes and beliefs, legal change has been slow in coming. One reason is that the narrative of precolonial ulama, which assumes male superiority, is found in innumerable laws in precolonial fiqh books. Hacking one law will strain that narrative and expose any single hack to suspicion. What is required is for the legal narrative itself to change, and to do that, all the laws that give men superiority over women need to be hacked.

That is a task of epic proportions and will take years of concerted effort. In the meantime, some ulama have proposed patches, whereas others have proposed rereading foundational texts. One of these rereadings centers on the Arabic verb in Qur'an 4:34 that is often translated as "hit" (*daraba*) but can be understood in many different ways. The Arabic verb *daraba* might also mean something like "walk away" or "cite to an authority," depending on the context. Some modern ulama have said that the term "nonextreme" that Muhammad reportedly used to describe the manner of hitting actually means "metaphorically." For them, the command to "hit" in 4:34 is meant metaphorically as well, as in "hit the road" or "hit the right note." They believe that the Qur'an must be telling couples to separate, seek counseling, or something else, but definitely not to hit. They assume that God would not possibly sanction any kind of domestic hierarchy that leads to abuse, since men and women are supposed to be equal, and, in any case, people are forbidden from hitting one another, whether married or not. Ulama also point to the many hadiths that counter domestic abuse, such as the statement from Muhammad's wife 'A'isha, who said, "I never saw the Prophet hit anyone: not a woman, not an animal, not a slave." Or they point to the even more direct hadith containing Muhammad's command: "Do not hit the maidservants of God."

Yet these compelling readings of the Qur'an and hadith have

had little effect on laws in many Muslim countries that have sharia
source laws. That is because the law on domestic violence in precolonial legal texts is part of a much larger precolonial narrative in
which other laws are firmly lodged. Even if we were to reinterpret
Qur'an 4:34 or call on hadiths that forbid domestic violence, the patriarchal laws in legal texts would remain the same in their privileg-
ing of men over women and in their granting men dominion over
family affairs. A changed law on domestic violence would immediately look suspicious because it would be so out of place. That fact
was not lost on Saudi ulama. They had no choice, however, but to
support the monarchial decree forbidding all forms of domestic violence, so they went to work identifying all precolonial laws related
to domestic violence in order to make their hack.

They found that the right of husbands to hit their wives stems
from an underlying assumption about male dominance in the family. This is itself an extension of a broader idea that men are in charge
of women, as in the beginning part of Qur'an 4:34 that precolonial ulama interpreted to mean, "Men have authority over women."
Again, this verse could be read in many different ways, and, indeed,
it has been read in many different ways by modern ulama. One of
these ways is to see the verse as descriptive of seventh-century Arabia and not as prescriptive for all times and places. That is, the verse
merely relates that men were financially responsible for women in
the seventh century; it is a statement about how things were, not
how they ought to be. But the problem here is not with the verse
or its interpretation; rather, the problem is with the legal narrative
found in numerous laws that give men dominion over all family affairs. Remember that among fiqh-minded Muslims, Qur'an 4:34 is
interpreted based on the law, not the other way around.

According to the precolonial legal narrative, men had full authority (*qiwama*) over their families and their family members' affairs. They were owed obedience from wives and children, and they
controlled finances, restricted family members' movements and as-

sociations, and had the sole right to unilateral divorce. Among these and other rights given exclusively to husbands was the right to discipline family members who misbehave. Misbehavior was defined broadly; it could include failing to pray, leaving the house without a male guardian's permission, or wasting money. To deal with misbehavior, precolonial ulama gave husbands limited power to personally discipline their wives and children with what is known as discretionary (*ta'zir*) punishment. When wives were deemed to be recalcitrant or when children were thought to be in need of discipline, men were given the right to discipline using discretionary punishment. This could include admonishment, abandonment, and various levels of "nonextreme" hitting. Wives and children could both be subject to discretionary punishment based on the patriarch's assessment, and on this point, precolonial ulama were in Consensus. All of this was predicated on the idea that men have qiwama over their families.

If we were to map out the precolonial Islamic law on domestic violence in its larger narrative, we would see that it fits into a framework based on qiwama in family law. Discretionary punishment, for instance, makes sense only if a man has qiwama over a family. One slice of a concept map for the legal consequences of qiwama would look something like what is shown in the figure.

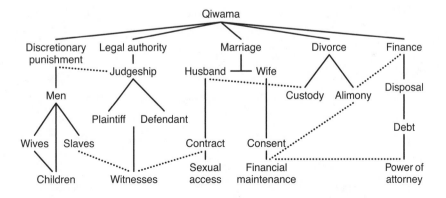

It's no wonder, then, that many reformists have tried to reinterpret qiwama in order to change all the laws associated with it. The thinking there is that if people change their conception of qiwama, it will have a beneficial effect on all the laws related to qiwama. But it is also no wonder that state-sponsored ulama are so averse to that approach: reforming qiwama would require a huge overhaul of Islamic law, affecting issues as diverse as who can serve as a judge and who can assume power of attorney. And all the laws shown in the figure, which represent only a subsection of qiwama, are further broken down into thousands of subsidiary laws—for example, whether a woman can travel without her husband's permission to visit her dying father, what happens when a husband fails to provide maintenance, who can serve as a child's custodian, and so on. All of those laws would need to be hacked as well. Further, different legal schools have different laws that would need to be hacked in different ways. Hanafis, for instance, make a sharp distinction between *wilaya* (legal authority) and qiwama, so *wilaya* would have to be hacked separately for them. Every law is counterbalanced within a larger system of laws, and all laws must work together toward a coherent narrative if they are to have any authority at all.

This is an anxiety that ulama face whenever they hack Islamic laws, and this is the situation that Saudi scholars found themselves in when an executive order was given to criminalize domestic violence. The government was clear that not only would physical violence no longer be permitted but neither would any harm perpetrated by one spouse against another, whether that be "exploitation, or physical, psychological, or sexual abuse, or the threat of it," including spousal neglect or abandonment. The state-sponsored ulama were charged with hacking Islamic law to accommodate the new decree, going against over 1,200 years of scholarly Consensus. Emergency conferences were held, and vigorous, international debate ensued.

Feminist ulama were not only excited about this turn of events, they were prepared. Feminist ulama had been reinterpreting Qur'an

4:34 for years, in ways that are both nonviolent and nonhierarchical, doing away with male dominance altogether. The Saudi ulama, for their part, made little use of feminists' arduous work. In their deliberations, one sees the fingerprints of feminist thought, and some key ideas are reproduced, but for the most part the Saudi ulama were having a different conversation. There are two reasons for that. First, the clerics were not trying to reinterpret Qur'an 4:34; instead, they were trying to come up with a new law that would achieve the seemingly impossible goal of both upholding and violating precolonial scholarly Consensus. If they were to reinterpret Qur'an 4:34, then that would exceed their mandate and impinge on other laws that are currently sanctioned in Saudi Arabia, such as females needing permission from their male guardians before traveling. Likewise, ulama would fall short of their mandate if they were to spend their time reinterpreting the Arabic verb *daraba* to mean something other than "to hit." Even if *daraba* were assigned a different meaning, the precolonial interpretation of Qur'an 4:34 still advises couples to separate beds, which could be construed as spousal abandonment, illegal under the new Saudi decree.

Second, state-sponsored Saudi ulama didn't take up feminist interpretations because they felt no need to dismantle the patriarchy. They could fulfill their mandate just by coming up with a new law that prohibits domestic violence. If they could prohibit domestic violence without changing laws that, say, deny women the right to unilateral divorce, then so much the easier for them. They wanted a law that would only minimally disturb the larger narrative of precolonial Islamic law, which in this case involved criminalizing domestic violence while maintaining patriarchy.

The ulama wanted to make a tightly focused hack that would disallow a husband from hitting for any reason without disrupting the other manifestations of qiwama. Thus, they turned their energies toward hacking the concept of discretionary punishment. This was a bit challenging; if they got rid of the right to implement discretionary punishment altogether, they would be making a pretty obvious change that would likely ripple through other laws, particularly those related to the judiciary. Discretionary punishment is a tool that judges rely on when adjudicating both civil and criminal cases, so doing away with it altogether was a nonstarter. The task was to develop a hack that would maintain a husband's right to dispense discretionary punishment but take away his ability to use it for harm. That would leave most things in their place, most notably the patriarchy, but change the law of domestic violence.

To hack the law, Saudi ulama chose to redefine discretionary punishment by focusing on the distinction between judicial discretion and civilian discretion. In a court of law, they said, judges had to use their discretion to determine how to punish someone based on the specifics of the crime, especially when the crime has no precedent. Let's say someone walked into a neighbor's house and shaved the neighbor's cat. There is no text in the Qur'an or hadith about that kind of crime, and there is no discussion of it in precolonial Islamic law. A judge must use discretion to determine whether to jail, fine, or otherwise punish the offending party. Judges have to come up with discretionary punishments as a matter of course, otherwise they wouldn't be able to make punishments fit crimes.

Civilians, the Saudi ulama claimed, do not have similar discretionary powers. They cannot sentence anyone to jail, extract a fine, or enact corporal punishment. The most that civilians can do is use their words; anything more than that is the purview of the state. Thus, they concluded, husbands do have the right to discretionary punishment but only to "scold, reprimand, and rebuke." A husband cannot discipline his recalcitrant wife any more than that; all other discretionary punishments are reserved for the courts. In the Saudi ulama's hack, husbands do still retain the right to use discretionary punishment, just in a more restricted way that does not include hitting or abandonment.

In making this hack, ulama affected other, related laws. If you look back at the figure of precolonial qiwama earlier in this chapter, you will note that husbands were given the right to impose discretionary punishment on their wives and children. Hacking the law at the high level of discretionary punishment has implications for all levels below. Specifically, if civilians do not have the right to impose any physical discipline at all, that means that fathers cannot physically discipline their children; otherwise the hack would lose coherence. The Saudi ulama accepted this consequence and went on to argue that it should be illegal for parents to hit their children. This was a self-conscious move—beyond their mandate—to maintain the coherence of the legal narrative. The Saudi ulama explained that, in fact, precolonial ulama always said that a husband could not hit his wife or children, that there was always a difference between judicial and civilian discretionary privileges, and that no civilian could discipline another beyond a stern lecture. Thus, this hack was presented not as new but as simply an explanation of what precolonial ulama had really been saying all along.

Interestingly, the Saudi ulama then went back to the foundational sources and reinterpreted them to according to their hack. Qur'an 4:34, they said, starts out talking to husbands, and it gives them the right to admonish their wives. It then shifts to address state functionaries, saying that if a couple comes to court with a domestic complaint, judges have the right to discipline a husband or wife by ordering a separation or a restraining order—which is their interpretation of the phrase "abandon them in their beds" in Qur'an 4:34—or with corporal punishment, depending on the severity of the complaint. They highlighted hadiths that feminist ulama had been touting for years, in which Muhammad castigated men who hit their wives, as proof for their position. Some ulama even cited the istislah patch as the reason for why their reform should be adopted. All these, however, are secondary justifications for the law that they already came up with. The justification flows from the law to the foundational texts, not the other way around.

This hack should be praised insofar as it gives religious sanction to a just policy, and it criminalizes a heinous practice. But it perfectly captures the incomplete nature of most fiqh-minded hacks and the tension between good hacks that address problems at their source and bad hacks that address only one symptom of a problem while leaving its root cause intact. In restricting the discretionary privileges accorded to men, Saudi ulama reinforced a mind-set that leads to domestic violence in the first place; namely, that men have exclusive rights over women. To truly combat domestic violence, men and women need to be seen as equals, and men should not have *any* exclusive rights over women. Domestic violence is a symptom of the much larger problem of male dominance and patriarchy; it is not simply the practice of a few sick individuals who can be dealt with through a single law. Domestic-violence rates around the world suggest that there is a pervasive belief among men that they are dominant over women, and every law that reinforces that belief ensures that domestic violence will continue to be a problem, whether or not it has religious sanction or there is a specific law criminalizing it.

The real problem for the ulama, then, is hacking all laws related to the institution of qiwama. The phrase in Qur'an 4:34 that states that "men have authority over women" is not itself the problem; Muslim scholars have been offering egalitarian and nonhierarchical interpretations of that phrase for decades. Rather, the problem is the many laws based on precolonial interpretations of qiwama that sanction patriarchy. These include laws that allow fathers to contract the marriages of their daughters, grant men sole custody of their adolescent children, give men the exclusive right to a unilateral divorce, restrict women's freedom of movement, and many more. The list of unjust laws that trace their origins back to precolonial readings of qiwama is huge. It is for this reason that Ziba Mir-Hosseini says that the precolonial narrative of qiwama is "the DNA of patriarchy in the Islamic legal tradition."

Good Hacks, Bad Hacks, and the Politics of Power

A good hack that ensures gender equality, then, will be very difficult. It will have to address thousands of related subsidiary laws and put them in balance. That should not be cause for pessimism, however. It simply outlines the extent of the problem. With enough minds and time, each law can be hacked in due course. Until then, every bad hack is still instructive. The Saudi law is incomplete, to be sure, and it allows the establishment to claim that they are promoting women's rights, even though they are promoting them in only one area while suppressing them in others. But it also points the way to a better hack that might still be in the making. The many bad hacks related to gender over the last century have not removed patriarchy from state interpretations of sharia, but they have given religious authorization for Muslim women in many countries to work, contract their own marriages, and serve as judges and heads of state, among other rights and responsibilities.

Fully hacking the laws related to qiwama will require concerted effort from thousands, if not millions, of committed Muslims. The Saudi hack, as bad as it was, took over a year to develop. With more minds at work, it might have taken less time and been more comprehensive. As we saw in chapter 3, there are now multitudes of qualified hackers who can interact with Islamic law and offer new interpretations of it. The task may be enormous but so is the pool of hackers. The only thing they lack is the kind of sponsorship given to state-sponsored ulama, like those in the Saudi hack discussed earlier, who are themselves connected to powerful interests.

Ulama are regularly funded to collectively hack Islamic law when it is in the interest of those in power. These cooperative, well-financed efforts resemble extended hack-a-thons. An Islamic legal hack-a-thon—often called an *ijtima* or *majlis al-shura*—involves intense debate among ulama who are trying to hack laws while maintaining a coherent legal narrative. The result is usually a book that looks like it is merely commenting on precolonial Islamic laws but that really contains many new laws. In the seventeenth century, for instance, about five hundred ulama gathered in India to create a book of fiqh known as *Fatawa al-Hindiyya* (or *Fatawa-e-Alamgiri* in Urdu), which looks just like a collection of historical laws but effectively inaugurated a new legal narrative, typified by unprecedented restrictions on judicial discretion. In the nineteenth century, an Ottoman commission of ulama spent eight years producing a civil law known as the *Majalla* (or *Mecelle-'i Ahkam-i 'Adliye* in Ottoman Turkish). The ulama claimed that this was merely a compilation of civil procedures according to historical Hanafi law, but it introduced sweeping reforms that, among other things, gave non-Muslims greater rights and effectively abolished many types of slavery.

A recent example of such a hack-a-thon comes from Indonesia. In the 1970s, Indonesian political and religious leaders recognized that precolonial Islamic legal texts needed updating to reflect widely held beliefs about gender justice. In the 1980s, leaders of the largest Muslim scholarly organization in Indonesia, the Nadhlatul Ulama (NU), began calling for reform, noting that precolonial Islamic laws clashed with ideas of gender equality that they found in the Qur'an and hadith. Several conferences were convened that, at first, sought to separate out a pristine, gender-equal sharia from its patriarchal manifestations in precolonial Islamic law, often by reinterpreting the Qur'an and hadith. Those early attempts were successful in spreading the message of gender equality as a social good but had little effect on how gender was taught in seminaries and discussed in sermons across Indonesia.

In the 1990s, the NU took another tack. They noted that, whatever the rhetoric about gender equality being promoted by the government, religious educators and preachers would instruct their congregations using precolonial Islamic texts and would end up promoting the laws found therein. So the NU embarked on a multiyear hack-a-thon in which ulama systematically reread a historical legal text, titled *'Uqud al-Lujjayn*, related to gender. Rather than come up with a new book of law, which might be viewed with suspicion for being modern and therefore corrupt, they composed a commentary on this older legal text that was already treated with reverence in Indonesia. The NU ulama dissected each law in that text, finding weak hadiths that promoted misogyny and replacing them with more authentic ones that promoted gender equality. They balanced each law in the book, and in 2001, produced a commentary that was just as coherent as the original *'Uqud al-Lujjayn*. They explained that the author actually championed gender-equality laws, including a woman's right to work, travel, and contract her own marriage.

The new commentary found a ready audience and is now taught in seminaries and mosques throughout Indonesia. The text is available online for free download. The commentary's allure is that it is built on a historical foundation so that the text is not really new. In fact, anyone promoting certain gender-equal laws can now cite the *'Uqud al-Lujjayn* without mentioning whether they are citing the original or the commentary. The new text is a major step in the right direction, even though it does not address all Islamic laws on gender. For that, there are NU-related groups that sponsor short-term hack-a-thons in which specific laws are targeted. These might have to do with reproductive rights, HIV/AIDS, transgender rights, or whatever happens to be needed at the time. In this systematic, measured way, precolonial Islamic laws are being hacked by Indonesian ulama so that they align with contemporary conceptions of the sharia and the larger ethos found in the Qur'an and hadith.

These types of systematic hacks change the law in a sustainable way. More than simply patching the law, they promote a coherent narrative that allows believers to adopt modern norms and still feel part of an ancient tradition. The catch is that good systematic hacks take time and resources. They require immense support, whether political, social, or economic. These kinds of hacks do not occur spontaneously. The Mughal *Fatawa al-Hindiyya*, the Ottoman *Majalla*, and the Indonesian *'Uqud al-Lujjayn* were all expensive and time-consuming endeavors. That means that they required support from powerful sectors of society who were keen on hacking the law and had in interest in accepting the hacks once they were made.

There is always some external pressure that leads to hacks being made, and societal interests determine whether a hack will be taken up. Even if a hack is really good and addresses all related laws in a systematic way, it will not gain currency unless there is some powerful sector of society supporting it. There isn't much demand for a law that allows for customary bowing, so that hack, despite being easy to make, is not likely to get hackers' attention. An executive decree in Saudi Arabia, however, ensured that the domestic-violence law would be hacked by a group of seasoned hackers, even though it was relatively more difficult. At the moment, a good hack on customary bowing is less likely to get publicized and adopted than a bad hack on domestic violence. If the Muslim population in Japan—currently at 0.08 percent—were to suddenly grow, then we would likely see a serious debate on hacking the law of customary bowing. That is because Islamic laws get hacked only in response to demand, and hacks are adopted only when they serve the interests of the powerful.

This is frustrating for many hackers, because popular demand, unfortunately, is not always enough to make a hack succeed. There is currently popular demand, for instance, for a hack of the laws of apostasy, and many ulama have proposed excellent hacks. But since those excellent hacks do not currently serve the interests of the powerful in many countries with sharia source laws, they have been ignored by the state. It is just as frustrating when bad hacks get adopted for no other reason than that they serve powerful interests. There are cases, however, when popular demand is enough, and hacks are accepted by the state even against its will. And there are times when the interests of the political and economic elite align with popular demand so that hacks serve a wide swath of society. Networks of power are always at play in hacking culture, and in the next chapter, we will see how societal forces determine how, when, and why hacks are either embraced, ignored, or suppressed.

CHAPTER 6

When Does Islamic Law Get Hacked?

COMING UP WITH a good hack is only the first step in changing Islamic laws. Good hacks are often ignored and left by the wayside, and bad hacks are often embraced even when they create more problems than they solve. Why is it that some hacks get adopted and others are ignored?

The answer is simple: power. A hack is adopted only when it advances the interests of the powerful. No matter how technically sound hacks might be and no matter how systematic or comprehensive they are, they will never be adopted if they fail to play into existing power networks. Likewise, bad hacks are sometimes elevated and adopted only because they somehow benefit the powerful.

And who, exactly, are the powerful? We normally think of state actors when we think of law and power, and that is for good reason. It is the job of state actors to legislate laws that serve multiple and varied interests. They might legislate on behalf of political leaders, economic elites, the military, the populace, or some mix of these interests. But state actors do not legislate purely for the greater good with no regard to power, even though we wish they did. Their job is to support the state, not to dismantle it, so it should come as no surprise that they are on the lookout for hacks that preserve the status quo and that they dismiss or ignore those that do not.

Although we normally think of the state when we think of law and power, state actors are not the only ones with power. The general population also has power, and they have their own demands of the law. They can threaten revolt if their interests are not served or if state actors ignore their needs. The general population is on the lookout for hacks that preserve their rights and increase their quality of life, and they might dismiss hacks that disempower them or make unjust demands on them.

The military has power, the press has power, the wealthy have power; each of these groups tries to identify and promote hacks that serve their own interests. In this power vortex, ulama have an exciting and interesting role. They have soft power to influence all sectors of society and have the ability to reflect multiple needs and desires in Islamic legal language. In that sense, they are power brokers. They can express the desires of the state to the populace just as they can express the demands of the populace to the state. They can throw their support behind one group or another and provide religious legitimacy to the cause of their choosing.

The ulama must be cautious, however, about how they exercise their soft power. Those employed by the state must ensure that they do not bite the hand that feeds them, yet they must not appear to be mere puppets of the regime. The ulama must champion the people's demands but only when they have the overwhelming support of the populace. Otherwise, they might end up in jail or worse. Many ulama have found a huge payday serving on the boards of Islamic banks, yet they must appear above serving at the pleasure of the wealthy or else they will be dismissed as paid spokespersons. Thus, whenever ulama promote certain hacks, they are always navigating networks of power and negotiating their role therein.

These complex power networks explain why Islamic laws get hacked and adopted only when they serve the interests of some sector of society. This is not a unique feature of Islamic law but is how law works in general. Legislators do not, on their own, get together to hack laws against their own interests. We should never expect the powerful to give up power of their own accord; rather, legal change always results from some overwhelming pressure that forces a shift in the balance of power. In representative democracies, these pressures tend to be things like mass movements, Supreme Court rulings, or existential threats. In more autocratic regimes, these tend to be executive orders, international pressure, or uprisings.

At the turn of the twenty-first century, for example, the now-deposed Egyptian dictator Hosni Mubarak decided to move Egyptian family laws toward gender justice. The regime ordered a slew of legal reforms, giving women greater rights in divorce and custody, among other things. Egyptian ulama struggled and grumbled as they tried to come up with new laws, but they did not have a choice. Hacking the law toward gender justice was not their idea, but they had to do so because they were being forced by the ruling regime. Most ulama complied, though only grudgingly, and derisively called the required reforms "Suzanne Mubarak laws," a reference to the dictator's wife. The prevailing theory was that Hosni Mubarak must have been pressured by his wife to order the family-law reforms, and ulama were now hacking the law just to appease her. But regardless of whether the impetus came from Suzanne Mubarak or Hosni Mubarak or foreign governments threatening to cut off aid, the hack was ultimately in the service of some driving, powerful interest, as hacks always are.

Whether in a democracy or autocracy, we do not find lawmakers coming together on their own to hack laws to make them more just. Rather, they hack laws in response to outside pressure, whether the laws concern universal suffrage, civil rights, immigration, or global trade. Every law can be linked back to some external pressure that led to its adoption, and the same is the case with Islamic laws. Even the Nadhlatul Ulama hack-a-thons that we saw in the previous chapter were encouraged and funded by the Indonesian government as part of a larger modernization effort.

That is just how law and society work: the powerful do not spontaneously band together to give up their power. We should not expect, therefore, that ulama, especially those who are state sponsored, will come together to collectively relinquish what meager power they presently have. Take the system of qiwama, which, as discussed earlier, grants men power over women. Since state-sponsored ulama are almost exclusively men, we should not expect that they will, of their own volition, overhaul the qiwama system and thereby lose the power that qiwama grants them. Instead, there will have to be some kind of external pressure that will force them to hack laws related to qiwama. The initial hacks will most likely be bad and incomplete, but when there is enough pressure, support, and time, good hacks can be made.

In this chapter, we will look at three major external pressures—political, social, and economic—that have forced ulama to hack the law. Sometimes their hacks are quick and minimal, other times they take a while and are far more extensive. Some hacks are better than others, and by recognizing how external pressures work on hacks, we will see why they are required from time to time and understand why bad hacks are sometimes taken up and good hacks are sometimes ignored. We will also learn how hacks should be framed if they are to be successful and how to keep hacks from running afoul of powerful interests, which would scuttle their chances of being adopted.

Political Pressures
Political elites are the most visible drivers of Islamic legal hacking. When new regimes come to power, or when an existing regime makes a policy shift, Islamic law must respond. The ulama do not always comply, and there is a long and illustrious history of ulama who resist the machinations of the political elite. When they push back too hard, however, they are persecuted, imprisoned, beaten, or killed. Most ulama fall into line with the ruling class, often outright supporting their policies, or at least not antagonizing them.

Whenever new regimes come to power, ulama roll with the

changes and adjust Islamic law to fit their new realities. Prominent ulama go to work for the ruling class and then hack Islamic laws to legitimate the practices of their rulers. One of the best examples of this is found in the court of the Ottoman sultan Suleyman the Magnificent. Suleyman was a beloved sultan who employed a coterie of scholars to come up with Islamic laws, basically on demand, to deal with his growing regime. These ulama claimed, of course, that they were only clarifying inherited Islamic law, but in practice they were charting new territory. Ottoman ulama who were not part of this elite coterie nevertheless embraced the new Islamic laws being proposed, and why would they not? Taking on Suleyman's court would have been foolish from a career and safety perspective, and since Suleyman was so popular, rogue ulama would have gotten little sympathy from the populace.

Even when the political class does not expressly demand specific hacks in its favor, some ulama go out of their way to come up with ruler-friendly hacks. Doing so might improve prospects for patronage, and schools of law vie with one another to prove that they best represent the ruling class's interests. An excellent example of this comes from Mamluk Egypt. Before the Mamluks came to power in the thirteenth century, Shafi'is represented the undisputed legal school of choice for Egyptian rulers. Shafi'is held prime government posts, and their seminaries were heavily patronized. The arrival of the Mamluks, however, threatened to undo all of that, and for good reason.

Shafi'is found themselves in an embarrassing position with the Mamluks because of Shafi'i slavery laws. The root of the problem is that according to Shafi'i law, the new Mamluk rulers were technically slaves. The name *Mamluk* literally means "one who is owned," and it denotes a certain kind of slave. Indeed, the Mamluks came to power as the result of a slave revolt. The Mamluks started out as slave-soldiers of Turkic and Circassian ancestry, often born Christian but captured in battle, enslaved, converted, educated, and groomed to serve in the military, either as soldiers or as statesmen. These slaves mounted a revolt against their masters in the thirteenth century and established a dynasty in Egypt that would last three hundred years.

Now, obviously these triumphant Mamluks were no longer slaves, in that they were not owned by anyone. They still referred to themselves as Mamluks, however, and they had not received any certificate of manumission from their masters. According to Islamic law, they were rebels who had run away from and, in some cases, killed their masters. By law, the rebellious Mamluks should have been prosecuted for their crimes, and they certainly should not have been ruling over their former masters.

But such was the reality of thirteenth-century Egypt; Mamluks were rulers, and the ulama had to adapt. Shafiʻi ulama were in a particularly difficult position because, according to Shafiʻi law, slaves cannot occupy government posts. Shafiʻis believed that since slaves live under the authority (*qiwama*) of their masters, they can never truly exercise independent and impartial judgment. Serving as a government authority requires one to be impartial, so under traditional Shafiʻi law, slaves, women, and children—all of whom live under someone else's qiwama according to precolonial conceptions of Islamic law and therefore could not be truly impartial—were banned from assuming positions of authority. Changing the law to allow Mamluks to be government officials would require Shafiʻis to overhaul their entire system of qiwama, which, as we saw in the previous chapter, is a herculean undertaking. But failing to do so would likely lead the Mamluks to patronize some other school that allowed slaves to be government officials, and the Shafiʻis would lose their dominance in Egypt.

Hanafi ulama, for their part, saw this as an opportunity to play up their relatively "better" slavery laws. Under Hanafi law, slaves and women could serve as government officials, because Hanafis linked government service not to qiwama but to the law of witness-

ing. The Hanafi thinking was that if someone's testimony was accepted in a court of law, then their judgment should be accepted in
all matters. Since slaves and women were allowed to testify, Hanafis
figured that they should therefore be allowed to serve as government officials. The Hanafi ulama therefore lobbied their new Mamluk rulers to privilege the Hanafi school as the most suitable school
of law for the new dynasty. This had the desired effect, as some
Mamluks were impressed with Hanafi laws on slavery. They were
less enthusiastic about Hanafi laws allowing women to serve as officials, but they nonetheless considered promoting the Hanafi school
over all others.

The Shafi'is were at risk of being surpassed, and they scrambled
to come up with a solution that would prove that they, too, celebrated their new rulers. Their first attempts were clumsy: the chief
judge of Cairo reportedly advocated auctioning off all the Mamluks
to sympathetic buyers who would then free them *en masse*. Needless
to say, that did not happen, but it was the only option that did not
require hacking the law.

Shafi'is certainly could have patched their law by engaging in
talfiq, borrowing Hanafi law out of necessity. But that would have
wreaked havoc on the rest of their legal system. If Shafi'is had suspended the law prohibiting slaves from serving as government officials in order to adopt the Hanafi law, that would have meant suspending all other laws related to qiwama, of which there are many.
They had to come up with some reason for why it was necessary to
adopt the Hanafi position on only one law related to qiwama and
not all others. Moreover, borrowing laws would have only proven
that the Hanafi school had more Mamluk-friendly laws, and it
would have proven that Shafi'i law accommodated the Mamluks
only out of necessity and did not actually embrace them as rulers.
Shafi'is needed a hack that would maintain their laws of qiwama
yet celebrate the Mamluks and allow them to serve as government
officials.

The hack that the Shafi'is devised was incredibly subtle; so subtle, in fact, that no one seems to have noticed it up until now. In pre-Mamluk Shafi'i texts, there are very clear stipulations that a government official must be

> a free, sane, mature, and righteous Muslim male, with full faculties of sight, sound, intellect, and the ability to engage in independent legal reasoning (*ijtihad*).

These requirements are repeated several times in prominent Shafi'i books of law; they are deemed necessary for being a judge, a market inspector, a governor, and any number of other government posts. The problematic requirement for the Mamluk-era Shafi'is was that the government official must be free, which suggests that a slave can never be a government official. But Shafi'i scholars noted that while we know what it means to be free, there is some ambiguity over what it means to be not free. Obviously, if you are not free you are enslaved, but they pointed out that in Islamic law, there are many different categories of enslaved persons. Turkic and Circassian slave-soldiers were referred to using the term *mamluk*, whereas enslaved blacks who were victims of the slave trade were called *raqiq*s. Domestic slaves were referred to as *khadim*s, and female slaves were referred to as *jariya*s. In legal texts, there were many different ways to refer to enslaved persons, and anyone else who was considered not free.

The Shafi'is focused their attention on this categorization of not-free people to make their hack. They wrote legal commentaries in which they explained that each requirement for being a government official—free, sane, mature, and so on—needed to be understood in terms of its opposite, that is, what it meant to be not sane or not mature. For example, the requirement to be sane meant that insane people could not be officials, the requirement to be male meant that females could not be officials, and so on. According to this line of reasoning, Shafi'is argued that the requirement that one be free meant that a *raqiq*—a black slave who is a victim of the slave trade—could not be an official.

It's easy to miss the move here: Shafi'i scholars said that the opposite of free is *raqiq*, and a *raqiq* is a different kind of slave than a *mamluk*. Technically, then, Mamluks—Turkic and Circassian slave-soldiers—were allowed to serve as government officials, not because they were free but because they weren't not free. Black slaves were still out of luck, and until and unless they mounted their own revolt, they would remain not free and unable to serve as government officials.

If you look carefully at Mamluk-era Shafi'i texts, you'll see that they regularly use the term *raqiq* to refer to slaves. Any time pre-Mamluk Shafi'i texts granted slaves lesser rights than they did free persons, later commentators would clarify that those lesser rights were meant only for *raqiq*s, not for *mamluk*s. Women still could not serve as judges, and black slaves were even more marginalized than they once were, but at least Mamluks were no longer vilified. The hack was technically sound, but it was also lame, in addition to being racist. They changed one little thing, a definition that nobody really noticed, and that made all the difference. It is a seductive hack, because it keeps the Shafi'i legal narrative intact, applying to all other parts of Shafi'i law without disturbing too much; it fulfills a political need while fully supporting the legal framework of qiwama.

The hack's technical soundness and political expedience encouraged Shafi'is to champion this otherwise unimpressive hack. It seems to have worked: Shafi'is retained their privileged status in Mamluk Egypt and celebrated their new rulers. The Mamluks, for their part, were happy to accept the hack. The Shafi'is were already popular in Egypt, and promoting them would give the Mamluks social legitimacy. Thus, there was a reciprocal interest in the hack: Shafi'is got patronage and power, and Mamluks got a huge support base. Both parties wanted this hack, and they both wanted it to work.

It is vitally important for both parties to want a hack to succeed. To see why, compare the Mamluk-era Shafi'i hack with the modern one responding to Hosni Mubarak's family-law reforms. One of Mubarak's proposed reforms was that women be admitted to the Egyptian judiciary. A decree to this effect was passed in 2003, and thirty women were appointed to the Court of First Instance. Egyptian ulama, including many employed by the state, were forced to come up with a hack to make that decree align with Islamic law. But they had no real incentive for making a good hack. They were not trying to impress women or to curry favor with them; women were not an empowered force that would reward the ulama for making a good hack. Mubarak, for his part, did not care whether the hack was good or not, as long as it accommodated the decree. And so, Egyptian ulama did the absolute minimum required to allow women to be judges. Rather than engage in an intricate study of the law or compose a commentary that allows for female judges, they simply patched the law using talfiq. Citing necessity, they borrowed the Hanafi permission for women to serve as judges, and with that, they were in line with the executive decree.

Necessity is not a very welcoming line of reasoning, which is why Shafi'is in the Mamluk era did not use it. Necessity in the modern Egyptian case basically says to women that they will be tolerated only because of an executive order but that in an ideal world they would not be judges. It suggests that the bench is an unnatural place for women and that Islamic law allows them to serve only as an exception rather than as a rule. This attitude has resulted in tangible impediments to women's participation in the Egyptian judiciary. Although women are technically allowed to serve as judges, it is, in practice, very difficult for them to do so. There are strong institutional barriers to success for female judges, and state-sponsored ulama do their part to ensure that women neither join the judiciary in large numbers nor rise through the judicial system to assume positions of power. Since 2003, women have joined the judiciary only by executive order, once in 2008 and again in 2015. When women have applied for appointment to the judiciary through the standard channels, their applications have been routinely rejected. Including the 2015 class, there are a total of seventy-two female judges in Egypt, a country of over eighty million, and they are not allowed to preside over criminal cases. The talfiq patch allowed Egyptian ulama to tolerate female judgeship in Egypt, but a genuine hack will be required for them to embrace it. Without some external pressure to make a good hack, one will not be forthcoming.

We see a similar dynamic playing out with respect to Morocco's 2004 Mudawwana reform. This was a sweeping attempt by King Mohammed VI to move Moroccan family law toward greater gender equality. As in Egypt, Moroccan ulama were forced to hack the law against their wishes, and, as in Egypt, they hacked the law only to meet the king's minimum requirements. Those minimum requirements, however, were far grander in scope than the family-law reforms instituted in Egypt. Rather than simply reforming a few outdated laws to allow for greater female participation in the state, the Moroccan ulama were tasked with doing away with male authority (*qiwama*) in Islamic law altogether. As mentioned in the previous chapter, qiwama animates almost all of precolonial Islamic family law, and doing away with it would require a complete legal overhaul. The Moroccan ulama, rather than going to all the trouble, settled for a statement that says qiwama is no longer an operative concept in Moroccan family law. They then affirmed certain laws decreed by the Moroccan Parliament, such as a minimum marriage age and restrictions on men's right to polygamy, but left the rest of the laws unchanged.

The results of this weak hack have been widely documented. Although Moroccan family laws no longer include the word *qiwama*, the precolonial Islamic laws that Moroccan ulama refer to when adjudicating cases remain the same. It should not be surprising, then, that when women go to family courts in Morocco, the male judge, often trained in precolonial Islamic law, adjudicates based on his training. Until laws are hacked to adequately reflect the complete abolition of qiwama in family law, qiwama will continue to influence how Islamic law is applied in Morocco, inside and outside of the courtroom.

In the modern Egyptian and Moroccan examples just discussed, ulama had no perceived incentive to hack the law. Obviously, women's full and equal participation in society has been demonstrated to be the most significant source of political and economic prosperity, but that is a long-term, somewhat abstract result. Women's membership in the judiciary will not immediately benefit the ulama, and, in fact, ulama have a short-term interest in keeping women out of the judiciary, if only to maintain the status quo. Many male ulama therefore do not feel compelled to make good hacks toward achieving gender equality, and they see benefit in making weak ones. Weak hacks don't change very much, which seems to suit the state-sponsored ulama in these countries just fine. By barely cracking the door open for women to attain a judgeship, they can say that they are being inclusive and gender equal without actually changing their rhetoric or practices.

The ulama would have more of an incentive, however, if there were sustained social or economic pressure to make their hacks more thorough. Although there are strong women's rights movements in Egypt and Morocco, polls also suggest that there is a strong faction that favors the status quo. In authoritarian regimes, ulama who support the status quo tend to be given outsized importance, since regimes are interested in staying in power, not in sweeping legal reforms. But even in authoritarian regimes, social pressures can be very powerful and have historically influenced Islamic legal hacking in often unexpected ways.

Social Pressures

As power brokers, ulama occupy an interesting space in society. Sometimes they seek state support and recognition, and sometimes they claim to uphold the desires of the people over the desires of the state. In a way, they are always playing both sides. This is a tricky game; erring on the side of the state might mean being branded a sellout by the people, and erring on the side of the people might mean being persecuted by the state. But when played just right, ulama can flex their soft power to push back against political elites, especially when the people are on their side. They can champion popular ideas despite the wishes of rulers, and when popular sentiment is overwhelmingly on the side of the ulama, rulers have to concede or risk revolt. The clearest examples of such situations have to do, perhaps unsurprisingly, with drugs.

In the late-Mamluk and early-Ottoman periods, political elites were worried about the rise of coffeehouses, which were becoming very popular and were out of the government's direct control. Who knows what was going on in there? People could be up to all manner of debauchery, or, even worse, they could be plotting against the state. Political elites in many major cities tried to work with the ulama to shut them down. Several political leaders expressly asked members of the ulama to forbid coffee under Islamic law and thus end the scourge of coffeehouses. Some even gave ulama a prefabricated legal rationale, which was that coffee is an intoxicating drug just like wine and so should be similarly forbidden. Political elites figured that would be an easy argument to make.

Although some ulama complied and tried to outlaw coffee, most rebuffed their leaders. Given the immense popularity of coffee, the idea that it would be suddenly forbidden was a nonstarter. Indeed, early attempts to shut down coffeehouses resulted in riots. Ulama, for the most part, left coffee alone, ignoring pleas from the political class. It's interesting to note that despite having the support of political leaders and a ready-made legal argument in the coffee-wine analogy, ulama nevertheless chose not to pursue a hack that would ban coffee. They figured that the argument was a loser, not because it was poorly reasoned but because the people wouldn't stand for it. It doesn't matter how strong a hack is; if people will not accept it, there is simply no point.

This is the case with modern-day Yemen, which, along with its heartbreaking political problems, has been struggling with a Class C narcotic called qat (also sometimes called khat or gat). Qat is a leaf that is chewed by more than three-quarters of the Yemeni population and on which Yemenis spend an estimated $4 billion annually. If chewed in large quantities and stored inside the cheeks for several hours, it produces a mild high, much like an amphetamine. Recently, it has proved to be an economic and agricultural menace, edging out coffee plants, cereals, and other vegetation and consuming about 30 percent of Yemeni GDP.

In 1972, the prime minister of Yemen sought to ban the drug and asked the ulama for help. He, like political elites before him, thought that it would be easy to make an analogy between qat and wine and that the ulama would be natural allies. He noted that ulama in countries in which qat is less in demand had already forbidden it for two reasons: (1) it is an intoxicant like wine, and (2) it keeps people from prayer, since you have to chew it and store it in your mouth for hours, and you cannot eat while praying. The Yemeni ulama, despite these arguments, refused to go along with the prime minister's plan to ban qat. The Yemeni populace was outraged when they found out about the initiative, and it failed utterly. Within three months, the prime minister was ousted, and analysts cite his stance on qat as the reason for his downfall.

No Yemeni politician thereafter dared to attempt to outlaw qat until 1999, when qat was proved to pose an existential crisis for the country. Land surveys showed that about one-third of the Sana'a Basin groundwater was being diverted to qat cultivation, and groundwater levels were dropping at a rate of three to six meters per year. In late 1999, then president Ali Abdullah Saleh announced that he would start phasing in a ban on qat use throughout Yemen. Almost immediately, the chief justice of the Yemeni Supreme Court issued a fatwa stating that qat is absolutely permitted in Islam. He did this by citing many historical ulama who did not outright condemn qat, and he confirmed that qat was not an intoxicant on the level of wine or opium, but rather that it was more like coffee.

Scores of Yemeni ulama agreed and added another line of defense. Remember that ulama from other countries forbade qat because it keeps people from prayer. In response, Yemeni ulama, along with ulama from other countries in which qat is heavily used, like Ethiopia and Somalia, initiated a campaign to argue that qat actually helps in prayer. They reasoned that since qat is a narcotic, it increases concentration, thus making for better worship. It appears that this campaign was highly successful; in a recent poll in an Ethiopian town in which qat is legal, 80 percent of chewers said that qat helped "gain a good level of concentration for prayer, facilitate contact with God and prevent them from crime."

The Yemeni ulama were nevertheless faced with one powerful criticism of qat and its relation to ritual prayer. That has to do with the fact that qat is chewed and stored in the mouth over several hours to get its full effect. This creates a problem for fiqh-minded Muslims who wish to pray five times a day because, according to Islamic law, one cannot eat or drink anything while praying. There is a general rule that "whatever invalidates a fast invalidates prayer," and since eating while fasting invalidates the fast, the same would hold true for prayer. Yemeni ulama would have to hack this law if they were to argue that qat does not, in fact, keep one from praying.

To do so, they examined specific laws around eating while fasting. When fasting, the conscious ingestion of any food or drink invalidates the fast. That includes opening one's mouth to eat anything of any size. But even if one doesn't open one's mouth, there is still a way to break the fast. Let's say a piece of food eaten during the predawn meal, before the fast begins, gets caught in your teeth. If you dislodge it and swallow it during the day, the fast will be considered broken. That might sound a little unreasonable; if there is a small bit of food caught in one's teeth, is it such a big deal if it is swallowed? It would be onerous to constantly spit out tiny pieces of food, especially while fasting, when saliva is in short demand. So precolonial Islamic legal scholars made this hadith-based rule: if the bit of food is smaller than the size of a chickpea, it is considered part of the saliva and can be swallowed, but if it is bigger, then it is considered food and must be spit out.

Here is where Yemeni legal scholars made their hack. First, they said that qat chewers could pray while chewing as long as they don't open their mouths or stick out their tongues during prayer. If their lips stayed sealed throughout prayer, there would be no chance of anything new being introduced. Second, they said that the juice from chewed qat should be considered part of the saliva, since it is not ingested anew but already found in the mouth when prayer begins. Third and finally, if for some reason a little bit of qat were ingested during prayer, it would probably be smaller than a chickpea and thus would not break the prayer. A minority of Yemeni scholars found this to be an unconvincing argument, but most thought it was genius. Walk into a Yemeni mosque today, especially those in western Yemen, and you will see in attendance males with bulges of qat in one side of their mouths, lips sealed, chewing away.

The qat crisis in Yemen continues, and even before the recent Saudi bombings, the World Health Organization described the health and agricultural situations in Yemen as dire. Many ulama around the world have denounced qat as forbidden in Islam, and it is shunned in almost every Muslim-majority country. But even as the current chief justice of the Yemeni Supreme Court recently conceded that qat might be harmful, he has not forbidden it, and neither have other prominent Yemeni scholars. Their resistance to government attempts to outlaw qat suggests that ulama believe civilians to hold the power in this fight. Yemenis were willing to bring down one prime minister because of qat, and they would surely do so again. If the Yemeni government were stronger, it might be able to counter the demands of the people. In that case, we would surely see many ulama siding with the government and declaring that qat is forbidden under Islamic law.

Of course, hacks are not always the result of one powerful group prevailing over another. Sometimes whole societies are agreed that hacks are needed and that certain hacks would benefit all sectors of society. This was the case with the next hack that we will examine, in which economic need resulted in hacks that overturned centuries of Islamic legal precedent.

Economic Pressures

Since there is no official clerical hierarchy in Islam, there is never an "official" hack that is accepted by everyone, and there will always be opposition, whether from the state, the ulama, or the general public, to any hack that is proposed. But every once in a while, there is a chance to hack Islamic law in a way that benefits almost everyone and on which most people will agree. We witnessed this recently with the rise of Islamic finance in the latter half of the twentieth century.

After World War II, several Muslim-majority countries fought for and won independence from colonial rule. They inherited economies ravaged by colonialism, and many struggled to find their financial footing. Some countries moved toward fascism, with ruling parties that treated national treasuries like personal piggy banks. Others moved toward communism and nationalized major economic engines. Some countries instituted forms of democratic capitalism, with varying levels of success. Regimes rose and fell as elites tried to balance political control, international pressure, and domestic governance.

During this turbulent time, it was easy to claim that one's economy was following Islamic law, regardless of whether it leaned capitalist, communist, or fascist. As long as central banks neither took nor lent money based on interest, countries could claim that their economies functioned according to Islamic law. Of course, most Muslim countries did take interest-bearing loans from international organizations such as the IMF and the World Bank, but that was chalked up to necessity. Once the country got on its feet, the thinking went, it would wean itself off those loans and institute a no-interest policy. Then, in the 1970s, the foundations of the world economy shifted.

Islamic economic theory was faced with an existential challenge when major world powers steadily moved away from the gold standard after World War II. To explain this briefly, before World War II, all major currencies were backed by gold. Since paper currency has no intrinsic value other than the paper it is printed on, countries would say that each unit of its paper currency could be exchanged at any time for a fixed amount of gold. This policy required countries to maintain vast gold reserves in case their citizens wished to make an exchange. Some countries experimented with alternatives to the gold standard after World War I, and after World War II, many countries began to back their currencies with US dollars instead of gold. This resulted in a gold-standard exchange, the details of which are interesting, but for our purposes, we just need to know that it ended up giving foreign powers influence over the US economy.

To counter this foreign influence, the United States decided in the early 1970s to let its currency temporarily float. That is, the US dollar was thereafter backed by nothing but faith in the US economy. One could not exchange a dollar for a fixed amount of gold or any other currency; today, one thousand dollars might buy one ounce of gold, whereas tomorrow it might buy ten, depending on a host of factors. While floating, the US dollar might rise or fall in value, but it would have no fixed worth. Since most foreign currencies were at that point linked to the US dollar, they would also fall whenever the US dollar lost its value. One by one, countries began to delink their currencies from the US dollar so that today, every major currency in the world floats, backed by nothing but faith in the economies of the countries that issue them.

In this new international monetary system, in which currency values fluctuate, governments must assert some control over their currency's value. Assume you are running a country; if your currency is valued highly, then you will be able to buy more foreign goods with less money, but it will be harder for foreign entities using their less valuable currency to afford the goods that your country makes. Your country will import cheaper goods but will not be able to export its more expensive goods. If your currency keeps getting stronger as time goes on, and goods become more and more affordable for your citizens, they might put off purchases for later, hoping that goods will be even cheaper when the currency gets even stronger. With people spending less and holding out for lower prices, the economy stalls, which is known as deflation.

On the flip side, if your currency has a low valuation, then foreign entities can afford to buy more of your goods with their stronger currency, and money will flow in. But all foreign goods will be more expensive for you with your weaker currency, and your currency risks inflation, meaning that it will buy fewer and fewer goods and services as time goes on. Ideally, you want some kind of sweet spot in which your currency loses value at a rate at which foreign trade is balanced with domestic spending, employment, and production.

Finding this sweet spot is incredibly challenging, especially when currency values are in constant flux. Governments and economists have devised a series of tools that aim to maintain some form of equilibrium. Of course, since currency has no intrinsic value, governments could always just devalue their money or print more money, but these moves have uncertain consequences. The most powerful and reliable tools with relatively stable results have to do with regulating the money supply and fixing the interest rate (we're getting to Islamic law, I promise).

To influence money supply, governments' central banks issue documents known as securities—in the forms of bonds, debentures, and similar instruments—and sell them to other nations, individuals, and institutions. Securities are essentially IOUs; if you buy one from a central bank, the bank promises to buy it back from you after a number of years with interest. When a security matures, you can trade it in to the central bank and collect your profit. This system works only if you trust that the currency will be worth something at the time you trade it in. If you don't, you'll be less likely to buy, so central banks have to set an interest rate that will entice buyers. When people buy lots of securities, there is less money in circulation, at least in the short term, and currency gains value. To decrease the value of currency, central banks buy back the securities that people own or set low interest rates that discourage people from buying securities. That puts more cash in circulation, thus devaluing the currency.

Another tool that central banks use is fixing an interest rate at which they lend money to private banks and at which banks lend money to one another. If a central bank sets the interest rate low, then private banks will borrow more money and lend it out to others more readily, putting more money into circulation. If a private bank ends up lending money to someone who doesn't pay it back, that's not so bad because the private bank borrowed its money at a very low interest rate, so at least they're not on the hook for a huge interest payment. If, however, the central bank sets the borrowing rate high, then private banks will be more cautious when lending money, and there will be less money in circulation, leading to a revaluation of the currency.

Central banks use these and a variety of other tools to try to maintain balance in international trade, currency valuation, employment, and more. Without them, economies with floating currencies would fluctuate wildly, with nothing to anchor or guide them. All of these tools require some way to set and manipulate an interest rate. Whether it's the rate of return on a government-issued security or the interest rate for lending money, interest is an integral part of the modern financial system. It is not a mere vanity or optional appendage that raises profits; rather, it is fundamental and necessary to economic survival.

This posed an enormous challenge for ulama in the early 1970s. As we learned in chapter 4, precolonial ulama held that any form of trade known as *riba* was categorically forbidden. To review, precolonial ulama defined riba as either (1) any loan that increases a borrower's debt over time or (2) any contract in which only money is exchanged. An example of the first definition is when I sell you a bike for $100 and allow you to pay for it over time, charging 10 percent interest every month until it is paid in full. An example of the second definition is when I lend you $100 for one month for you to spend however you wish, and I require you to pay me back $110 at the end of the month. Both of these definitions of riba, of course, describe how the modern-day financial system works at its most fundamental level. The system is based on loans that increase the debt of the borrower over time and in which only money is exchanged. Modern ulama thus had to find some way to square this new financial system with precolonial Islamic law to avoid throwing their economies into chaotic cycles of boom and bust and to keep their currencies from wild fluctuation and manipulation from both insiders and outsiders.

The easiest thing for ulama to do would be to say that central banks in Muslim-majority countries could set an interest rate and sell interest-bearing securities out of necessity. But economic success depends on everyone fully participating in the system. Surely the central bank of a Muslim-majority country could sell interest-bearing securities out of necessity, but why would Muslim institutions or individuals feel compelled to purchase them? A fiqh-minded Muslim would, in fact, want to avoid buying securities at all costs, choosing instead to invest her money in a profit-sharing business or something else.

This is a serious problem: banks have to set interest rates and give out interest-bearing loans for the health of the economy and for the valuation of currency. If no one is willing to either buy securities or take out loans, then the system breaks down. It would be hard to argue that someone "needs" to buy a government-issued security or take out an interest-bearing loan to build a new garage or expand a business. To ensure full participation in the new global economy, ulama needed to devise not just a patch that would help the economy bump along but rather a strong hack that would make the economy thrive. They needed a hack that allowed fiqh-minded Muslims to fully participate in the system without feeling that they were engaging in riba.

One way to do that would be to change the definition of riba, in much the same way that some feminist ulama tried to change the definition of qiwama. Indeed, some took this approach and argued that riba refers only to predatory loans that either target poor people or charge exorbitant interest rates. Such arguments are based on sophisticated studies of language and the context in which the Qur'an was revealed, but most fiqh-minded ulama find them unconvincing. The problem is that precolonial Islamic legal texts are so clear about the definition of riba: it is a loan that increases debt over time or a transaction in which only money is exchanged. Precolonial ulama insisted that any increase in debt was forbidden, even if that debt increase was only one dollar over a hundred years, and that financial transactions must involve an actual commodity, not just currency. The pervasiveness of that definition meant that modern ulama had to find some other hack.

The hack that they devised is instructive in its utter simplicity. One would think that an intricate and highly complex solution would be required for such a difficult problem as allowing for interest. Instead, ulama zeroed in on a little-known financial instrument that precolonial ulama condoned, known as a deferred-payment (*murabaha*) contract. "Deferred payment" means that a buyer agrees to pay a higher price for a good or service if the seller is willing to be paid at a later date. So, if a bicycle costs $100, but you don't have $100 right now, you can ask the seller to hold on to it for a month when you will have the money. In return, you agree to pay $110 for the bicycle. Precolonial ulama said that as long as the terms and the sale price are agreed upon up-front and the money is being used to buy something, then the contract is not riba, because the debt does not increase over time, and money is being exchanged for an actual commodity.

Modern ulama used this contract as the basis for their hack. They devised scenarios in which banks would lend money at an agreed-upon price, setting a future date for repayment. They could then incorporate a specific markup (*ribh*) in the contract that would otherwise be called interest. That helped ulama hack the first definition of riba: a debt that increases over time. To understand exactly how this works, let's say you wanted to buy a house that costs $100,000. Since you don't have the money right now, you could ask the bank to lend you the money and agree to pay it back over twenty years along with a fixed markup. Under a traditional mortgage, that markup would be some percentage of interest. But if you simply come up with a dollar amount—let's say $50,000—that you will pay instead of interest, then the debt does not increase over time. The total cost for the house will always be $150,000, regardless of whether you pay it back in one year or twenty years. In essence, the house costs $150,000 because of the $50,000 markup charge for deferred payment. This skirts the first definition of riba, since the debt stays constant.

But ulama still had to confront the second precolonial definition of riba—that is, a contract in which only money is exchanged. In the scenario above, you asked for a $100,000 loan and agreed to pay back $150,000 over twenty years. That is still riba, because you are giving the bank more money in exchange for them lending you less money. But what if the bank actually bought the house outright with $100,000 of its own money and then later sold it to you for $150,000? In that case, the bank would not be exchanging money for money but would be selling you a house that it just bought and allowing you to pay for that house over a period of twenty years in exchange for a markup. As long as the bank buys the house first and then sells it to you with a markup for allowing deferred payment, technically no riba is involved.

This was a huge step toward hacking the law of riba to allow for mortgages, but there were still practical problems. For starters, the hack exposes the bank to a lot of risk; what if the bank buys a house with the intention of selling it to you with a markup and then you change your mind and back out of the deal? The bank would be stuck with the house. The process also puts a huge burden on the bank; it has to negotiate with the original seller, purchase the property, and sign it over to you. That makes the bank not only a lender but also a real-estate agent, real-estate lawyer, and holding company. That is far too much for any one entity, so ulama came up with a modern murabaha contract to get around the problem of riba and to let the bank be simply a moneylender. The modern murabaha contract is the fruition of years upon years of work by hundreds of ulama to bring the economies of Muslim-majority nations in line with both the global financial system and precolonial Islamic law.

In a modern murabaha contract, you, the buyer, will go to the bank to say that you are interested in buying a house. The bank will check your credit score, and if it's acceptable, the bank will then authorize you to buy the house on its behalf. The bank will give you the money to purchase it, and you will buy the house in the bank's name. At that point, the bank has bought the house in its entirety through you as their agent. At the same time that they authorize you to buy the house on their behalf, you sign a deferred-payment contract to purchase the house that the bank will soon own; this contract includes a markup for the privilege of paying for it over a number of years. If you have a good credit score, that markup might be less, and if you have bad credit, it might be more. You then buy the house from the bank, paying both the purchase price and the markup in regular installments over the agreed upon number of years.

That's it. That's the hack. The simple act of having you purchase the property on the bank's behalf while charging you a deferred-payment markup makes the contract legally sound. When central banks lend money or sell securities, they need only say that they are authorizing others to purchase some unnamed commodity on their behalf while charging a deferred-payment markup in the process. The commodity itself isn't important; banks can simply lend out money trusting that a commodity, such as a house or a car, will materialize at some point. Likewise, individuals can purchase securities trusting that the lending bank will use the proceeds to buy and sell some commodity, and then they can buy back the securities at a later date with a markup. Ulama have taken to calling the murabaha contract "sharia compliant," because it ensures that you are not engaging in riba or violating precolonial Islamic law. It's deceptively simple and has transformed sharia-compliant banking into a $2 trillion industry. Approximately 75 percent of all sharia-compliant financial contracts are based on murabaha contracts; without them the system would fail.

If the murabaha hack sounds like a dressed-up interest-bearing loan, that's because it is. There are minor differences between murabaha and traditional interest-bearing loans—for example, one cannot charge interest for late payments and there are different rules in case of default—but they are essentially the same thing. In fact, most Islamic banks expressly use prevailing interest rates to determine the markup that they will charge on a murabaha transaction. The banks neither hide this fact nor pretend that they are doing anything different. The chief executive of the Qatar Islamic Bank, for example, admitted that

> rates of interest are taken into account when the markup on murabaha transactions is determined. This is being practical and facing the facts of life.

Other banks have been similarly forthcoming that murabaha contracts are based on prevailing interest rates.

So, in what sense is the modern murabaha contract sharia compliant? Isn't it just interest by another name? Some have leveled that very criticism, yet sharia-compliant banking charges forward with the blessing of the majority of fiqh-minded Muslims. To understand why, recall that the challenge for ulama was to avoid riba, not to avoid interest-bearing loans; the two are not the same. In precolonial Islamic law, riba was clearly forbidden and was defined as including either (1) any loan that increases debt over time or (2) any transaction in which money is exchanged for money. Whoever avoids those two specific actions is in the clear. Because ulama found a way to allow for interest-bearing loans while avoiding those two actions, they succeeded in their hack, and governments and individuals have an acute economic interest in accepting it as a true reflection of the sharia.

Power Relations and the Future of Hacking

To an outside observer and to many fundamentalists, it might seem like the hacks just described make a mockery of the law and are bald-faced attempts to find loopholes to justify some desired action. The murabaha hack might be seen as violating the spirit of the law, which seems to frown upon interest-bearing loans as a societal ill. Those are perfectly reasonable reactions to Islamic legal hacking, but fiqh-minded ulama do not share that outlook. Historically, legal scholars argued that we never really know the spirit or the intention behind the law. Only God knows why one thing is permitted and another forbidden. Fiqh-minded Muslims are not tasked with figuring out God's reasoning behind the law but with identifying the law and following it.

Why, for instance, is pork forbidden in the Qur'an? One might say that it is because pigs eat dirt, or because they have some special bacteria or worms in their bodies that are harmful to humans. But if one were to feed pigs a diet of exclusively organic fruits and vegetables and get rid of any harmful bacteria or worms, pork would still be forbidden. And if scientists were to create synthetic pig meat made entirely of soybeans but with the exact taste and texture of pork so that no one could tell the difference between the two, the synthetic pork would be permissible and the real pork would still be forbidden; unless, of course, someone devised an ingenious hack to allow for its consumption.

For fiqh-minded Muslims, a thing is permitted or forbidden not because of some identifiable underlying reason but because the law says so. Ultimately, fiqh-minded Muslims hope that by following the letter of the law, they will achieve salvation on the Day of Judgment. That is, they will be able to stand before God and say that they tried to follow the law without any prejudice and that God should look kindly on them for their efforts. By taking out a mortgage through a murabaha contract, then, someone can say to God on the Day of Judgment that she tried to follow Islamic law when purchasing her home. If it turns out that the murabaha contract is an accurate reflection of the sharia, then she gets two rewards. If it turns out that the murabaha contract does not accurately reflect the sharia, then she gets only one reward, and she got to live in a house. Everybody wins.

In this framework, legal hacking is an act of religious devotion that actually honors the rules and strictures of the law by insisting on finding some legal basis before engaging in an action. After all, if one did not care deeply about working within the law, why bother hacking at all? In fact, most Muslims don't. On the whole, Muslims don't seem to care much about Islamic law, whether hacked or not, and don't operate within its confines. For them, the title "Muslim" is an identity marker, and they feel perfectly comfortable calling themselves Muslim while having little to do with Islamic law. Fiqh-minded Muslims, however, are not willing to discard the law when it does not work for them. By hacking Islamic law, they demonstrate their commitment to always work within the law and to not call any action Islamic until there is first a workable hack in place. Those who don't care about the law don't bother hacking it in the first place.

Hacking is a kind of a sacred act, and it should not be seen as profane just because hacks are motivated by political, social, and economic concerns that function within networks of power. Religiosity is always bound up in societal forces, and a person's actions can be political and religious at the same time. For instance, when religious beliefs lead one to boycott a racist company, seek asylum for refugees, or push for human rights, those beliefs are still religious even as they are political. Ulama who hack laws display a commitment to their religion and a sincere belief that Islamic law should reflect the same conceptions of justice and equality that they see so clearly in the Qur'an and in the practice of Muhammad. Hackers are not looking for loopholes; they are seeking divine justice and are trying to implement God's will in different times and places.

In that quest, laws as deeply entrenched as those on slavery, drugs, and interest have been hacked to accommodate Muslims' evolving needs and concerns. The only limit to hacking seems to be the imagination of the hackers involved. Precolonial ulama would be awestruck at the hacks that have been made to accommodate the nation-state, the modern financial system, human rights, gender equality, and any number of other values that Muslims hold dear.

Contemporary Muslim practice has been hacked to the extent that it would be unrecognizable to many precolonial ulama, and I believe that they would approve. Hacking was a central practice for precolonial ulama; through it, they made Islamic law immediately relevant to society and simultaneously linked practitioners to an ancient legal tradition.

No doubt, hacking has always been vital to Islamic legal practice; its scope, however, has changed significantly in the modern day since there are now so many people who are qualified to hack the law. That should lead us to wonder: if there are so many qualified hackers, why do many Muslim countries still enact precolonial Islamic laws? Why can't women in Saudi Arabia travel without a male guardian? Why does the United Arab Emirates resist enacting a domestic-violence law? Why does Brunei allow child marriage? Of course, those governments will say that it is because of sharia. But we have seen that sharia is only a claim-space that is sometimes described using the language of Islamic law, and Islamic law is hacked all the time. In fact, even the aforementioned countries hack laws to suit their populace. Brunei does not require women to travel with a male guardian, Saudi Arabia has a domestic-violence law, and the United Arab Emirates has a minimum marriage age of eighteen. It would seem that countries can hack whatever laws they want, so why do they hack only some laws and not others?

The answer goes back to how we started this chapter: power. Islamic law is always deployed and exploited to serve the interests of power, whether that power is political, economic, or social. Sometimes Islamic law is used to justify tribal practices. Other times it is used to solidify men's power over women. At still other times, it is used to garner support from either conservative or liberal sectors of society. Sometimes Islamic law is used in mass protests to demand better treatment from political and economic elites. In all cases, Islamic legal hacks are either taken up or ignored based on their relationship to power. When hacks serve the interests of the powerful, they are adopted, and when hacks take power away, they are ignored.

It is important to remember here that there are many types of power. There is the soft power of the ulama, the hard power of the political elites, the power of the people, the power of the press, economic power, military power, the power of the international community, and more. Every person has access to power in some part of their lives, even if they are disempowered in other parts. Power comes from citizenship, social networks, education, internet connectivity, employment, and any number of other privileges. Hearteningly, people are beginning to use their newfound power in new and innovative ways, including through Islamic law.

Recall from chapter 3 that there has been an exponential rise in the number of ulama that are qualified to derive and hack laws in the modern period. These include women and racialized minorities, who are using the power of their collective knowledge base to hack precolonial Islamic laws to make power distribution more equitable. Hackers in Senegal and Gambia, for instance, have had great success using Islamic legal arguments to end the practice of female genital cutting. And the new Saudi domestic-violence ban came on the heels of an extensive online campaign in which hackers argued that the sharia does not allow domestic violence.

The new hackers are using their skills and knowledge to come up with sophisticated and pioneering hacks that are in accordance with modern mores while being rooted in the Islamic legal tradition. Their hacks reflect a deep commitment to religious reasoning and a respect for working within the language of Islamic law. Many of these new hackers see no conflict between Islam and human rights, or women's rights, or sexual rights. Not only is there no conflict, but they see Islam and the sharia as championing these values and are increasingly using Islamic legal language to express their beliefs. In their collective efforts, they are flexing their own kind of power and are putting political, social, and economic elites on notice. They are hacking in traditional venues and in more innovative and modern ones, some of which we will see in the next chapter, and their numbers are growing. They will continue hacking the law into the future; many of their hacks will be good, most will be bad, but with such a large cadre of hackers hard at work Islamic law is sure to look different tomorrow than it does today.

.

CHAPTER 7

Where Does Islamic Law Get Hacked?

GOOD HACKS don't get made overnight. They are the result of years upon years of effort from many fiqh-minded ulama working within existing networks of power. Some hacks can take a few years, like the Mamluk slavery hack, and others can take decades, like the Mughal *Fatawa-e-Alamgiri*, the Ottoman *Majalla*, and the Indonesian commentary on *'Uqud al-Lujjayn*. The glacial pace of these latter hacks reflects the stakes involved: since the ulama involved are funded by the state, they must ensure that their hacks advance state interests and do not step on powerful toes.

The Saudi domestic-violence hack seen in chapter 5 took over a year to complete, even though it was a minor change. That was because ulama had to comply with the wording of a royal decree, which outlawed not only physical domestic violence but psychological violence as well. While accommodating the new decree, the ulama had to make sure that their hack aligned with the Islamic legal tradition and with existing Saudi laws. That's a tall order, and it's no wonder that state-sponsored hacks take so long.

Fortunately, most hacks do not occur on the state level. Indeed, most of Islamic law is practiced in the daily lives of fiqh-minded Muslims, beyond the purview of the state. States may try to promote certain practices, values, and cultural norms using the language of Islamic law, but they cannot dictate what Muslims believe about the sharia. Individual Muslims have visions of sharia that are independent of the state, and fiqh-minded Muslims regularly hack the law to reflect those visions, only rarely with help from the state.

Millions of hackers work together in forums unaligned with any state, and they express innumerable visions of sharia in the language of Islamic law. These hackers are not constrained by state interests and are free to be far bolder in their hacks than are state-sponsored ulama. Some hackers are part of structured organizations, but most are freelancers with complex allegiances. They are found throughout the world, serving the growing number of fiqh-minded Muslims who feel underserved by and disaffected from state-sponsored ulama. These hackers now comprise the majority of contemporary ulama, and it is their voices that best represent fiqh-minded Muslims today.

You may not have heard of these legions of hackers. There are two good reasons for that. The first is because of our stereotypical notions of a Muslim scholar. We tend to think of Muslim scholars as bearded, robe-wearing men with some kind of official standing in the community, espousing traditional values in the face of an ever-encroaching modernity. As we saw in chapter 3, though, most Muslims have a low opinion of traditional ulama, especially those with official standing in the community, and ignore their religious opinions. The ulama that are driving the modern hacking conversation, by contrast, often do not look like stereotypical state-sponsored scholars and have little, if any, "official" standing.

The second reason you haven't heard of these hackers is because discretion is part of their work. They must ensure that they do not run afoul of powerful interests, and so they tend to discuss their hacks only among themselves. As if the potential for suppression wasn't enough reason to run a low-key operation, hackers must also work within the running paradox of Islamic law: the law must be ancient and contemporary at the same time. Hackers do not overtly say that they are hacking the law, or they would lose authority among fiqh-minded Muslims.

Despite—or perhaps because of—their need for discretion, these unaffiliated hackers are better able to capture widespread Muslim beliefs than are state-sponsored ulama. Their greater independence allows them to come up with more creative hacks, and as a result, they can more easily express popular Muslim beliefs about the sharia in the language of Islamic law. When they demonstrate that their hacks are based in the Islamic legal tradition, hackers put social pressure on political elites and state-sponsored ulama to reform their laws. As more hackers provide evidence that Islamic law enshrines women's rights, human rights, and representative government—all values held by the majority of Muslims—the fewer excuses powerful interests have to deny those rights. When hacks are intricate and sophisticated, they find their way into state-sponsored conversations, whether explicitly or not.

In this chapter, we will take a look at four groups of nonstate hackers to see where most hacking actually gets done. The first group is composed of organizations that work in Muslim-majority countries but are not aligned with any government. They are known, appropriately enough, as "nongovernmental organizations" (NGOs). The second and third groups exist only in Muslim-minority contexts, and I will refer to them as "umbrella organizations" and "educational institutes." The last group operates all over the world and is made up of loose hacker collectives that congregate online, so I will refer to them as "online hackers."

These groups, despite being unaffiliated with any state, have a powerful influence on the Islamic legal conversation. Their hacks end up driving debate, and they help determine what is possible in Islamic law. In this chapter, I will provide the basic contours of how each group hacks Islamic law, assess their potential and their limitations, examine how they influence the broader Muslim conversation on Islamic law, and explain how interested individuals can get involved with their hacking initiatives.

Nongovernmental Organizations (NGOs)

In most Muslim-majority countries, there are multinational NGOs that are hacking Islamic law. They are usually dedicated to alleviating some endemic problem or promoting particular values or practices. In West Africa, for instance, several NGOs in Gambia and Senegal are using Islamic law to argue that female genital cutting (FGC) has no place in Islam. This is a rather easy religious argument to make since there is no mention of female circumcision either in the Qur'an or in the well-attested hadith and few precolonial Muslim legal scholars condoned it. Still, FGC is a traditional practice in some countries and is sometimes justified using religious language.

Traditions die hard, so anti-FGC NGOs have had to work diligently to convince local religious and tribal leaders to abandon the practice. They found that the most effective way to do this has been to enlist the help of sympathetic Islamic legal scholars to debate local leaders both publicly and privately. This approach has proved quite successful; at the close of 2015, the Gambian president, Yahya Mansa, signed a bill into law banning FGC amid a groundswell of support. Similar efforts by NGOs working in Senegal have also proved highly effective.

The personal approach used by these NGOs, in which Islamic scholars debate with local leaders, has been far more successful than the more detached approach of state-sponsored ulama. In Egypt, for instance, several hundred prominent ulama convened at al-Azhar University in response to the official Egyptian ban on FGC declared in 2006. At that meeting, the participating ulama unreservedly denounced FGC as un-Islamic, yet their condemnation barely made a dent in Egyptian practice. That is because actually changing practice requires buy in from local leaders who are in touch with the populace, as we saw with the Moroccan Family Law

Reforms and the attempt to ban qat in Yemen. Without local buy in, it looks as though the government is trying to impose foreign ideas on the populace, regardless of the religious reasoning they use. Many NGOs, in contrast to government efforts to force decisions from above, put their faith in personal dialogue and debate at the local level, taking the time to walk local leaders through Islamic legal logic.

NGOs that use this approach therefore put a premium on making good hacks that will be palatable to local communities. Take the example of Musawah, an NGO that promotes a vision of sharia in which men and women are treated equally. Musawah enlists sympathetic ulama to describe their vision in Islamic legal language and then educates local leaders and individuals about how Islamic law promotes gender equality. They are open about the fact that the Islamic legal tradition sometimes poses a challenge for gender equity, but rather than discard problematic portions of the tradition, Musawah engages them thoroughly.

When faced with a major challenge in the legal tradition, such as precolonial laws related to *qiwama* and *wilaya*, Musawah convenes groups of Muslim legal scholars to hack these laws in publications and private forums. Over the years, they have produced an impressive body of literature that contains careful scholarly analysis, much of which can be accessed for free online. Musawah follows up these publications with public events in which local scholars are invited to discuss and debate the particulars of Islamic law with Musawah-affiliated ulama. Such forums have taken place in Morocco, Egypt, Malaysia, Sri Lanka, Uganda, and the United Kingdom, among other countries.

Musawah has also taken the important step of holding educational sessions with local community activists in multiple countries. In these sessions, activists are taught about how to use the language of Islamic law to effect local change. They are taught the difference between sharia and fiqh and are taught Islamic legal arguments that

promote gender-equal laws. Once educated, these activists can engage their local leaders in dialogue and debate. Musawah thereby
aims to create a grassroots counternarrative to gender-oppressive
laws that are promulgated in the name of Islam. The idea is to create
a critical mass of educated Muslims who can push back, on Islamic
legal grounds, against patriarchal laws and to give more Muslims a
say in conversations about Islamic law.

In a relatively short time, Musawah has counted many victories
in changing the way Islamic laws are applied in Muslim countries.
They do not publicly discuss these victories, since doing so would
undermine their grassroots work, but their influence is unmistak-
able. Several NGOs, like Muslims for Progressive Values, Karamah,
Sisters in Islam, and Women Living Under Muslim Laws, have
devised similar methodologies, to varied success. Many of these
NGOs begin with local practice and conduct extensive interviews
to determine visions of sharia held by Muslims in different contexts. They then commission scholarly articles that argue, using Islamic legal reasoning, that ideals held by millions of Muslims, such
as gender equality, human rights, and religious freedom, are championed in Islamic law. These NGOs then hold educational events to
disseminate their arguments to the public. Thus far, these have included legal arguments for permitting female-led ritual prayer, outlawing domestic violence, promoting LGBTQ rights, and more.

NGOs like these are using education and local activism to effect
larger legal change in Muslim-majority contexts. Many of them are
highly organized and have a strong volunteer corps. Although it is
easy to get involved in the work of educating local communities and
facilitating dialogue, the actual hacking tends to take place among
scholars and academics. One can teach others about the hacks once
they are made, but hacking under the auspices of an NGO usually requires credentials. This requirement is for organizational and
pragmatic reasons. It would be irresponsible for these organizations
to promote hacks that have not been carefully studied and vetted to

ensure that they are harmonious with the Islamic legal tradition. Moreover, the credentials of their hackers lend weight and respectability to their hacks. These NGOs are doing very serious work, and especially since they operate under intense scrutiny from governments and state-sponsored ulama, they must ensure that their hacks are both meticulous and authoritative.

Umbrella Organizations

NGOs operate primarily in Muslim countries, providing services that states and state-sponsored ulama cannot or will not. They have the ability to work both within and around existing political structures, unconstrained by sharia source laws, and thus they can hack the law in ways that state-sponsored ulama never could. NGOs are therefore invaluable to the state itself; states need NGOs to change social practices that states themselves are incapable of changing due to their own self-imposed constraints and the limitations of state-sponsored ulama. This need is less obvious in Muslim-minority contexts, in which the state does not have an "official" interpretation of sharia, in which there are no state-sponsored ulama, and in which there are no sharia source laws to contend with.

In the absence of state authorities, fiqh-minded groups in Muslim-minority contexts vie with one another, and several claim that they best represent Muslims in their constituencies and that they are best able to define the sharia. The most visible of these groups are known as umbrella organizations. Umbrella organizations are mosque collectives that claim to represent Muslims in a country or region. I say that they "claim to represent Muslims" because they are representing only mosque-going Muslims and because within any country or region there might be several umbrella organizations, each with its own network of affiliated mosques. It is therefore impossible for any single umbrella organization to truly represent all mosque-going Muslims, but they make the claim anyway.

Some umbrella organizations have more affiliate mosques than others in their region, such as the Islamic Society of North America (ISNA), the Muslim Council of Britain, the Federation of Islamic Organizations in Europe (FIOE), and the Muslim Judicial Council (MJC) of South Africa. These umbrella organizations provide social services, mediate mosque disputes, hold conferences that attract tens of thousands of attendees, issue press releases responding to major national and international events, and try to tell Muslims how to best follow the sharia.

This last part is usually accomplished through an internal fiqh department that provides Islamic legal rulings. ISNA, for instance, hosts the Fiqh Council of North America, and the FIOE hosts the European Council for Fatwa and Research. These councils are stocked with Muslim scholars, most of whom were raised outside their countries of residence, who provide opinions on issues that are important to the everyday lives of fiqh-minded Muslims: what foods are halal, when Ramadan begins, how to conduct marriage and funeral services, and so on. The councils also answer personal questions and provide mosques with guidelines on how to best serve their constituents. The councils tend to support more conservative opinions, and they view themselves as bastions of traditional Islam; yet they are adept at hacking Islamic law and producing legal opinions that respond to new situations and evolving sensibilities.

The Fiqh Council of North America, for example, argued that apostasy is not a criminal offense in Islam and that Islam upholds absolute religious freedom. The European Council for Fatwa and Research affirmed women's unequivocal right to initiate a divorce, and it gives religious sanction to divorces executed in secular courts. The MJC, for its part, produced a rather idiosyncratic hack that makes it "un-Islamic" for an imam to be appointed without an election. This is a bold position; precolonial legal texts are explicit about the rules for appointing an imam, and none that I know of mentions elections. Yet the MJC said that appointing an imam without an election is "contrary to the sharia," and it asserted that all community members must have a say in their community's leadership structure.

In general, though, these councils hew closely to the Islamic legal tradition and avoid hacks that would be objectionable to conservative, fiqh-minded Muslims. That is because umbrella organizations claim to represent mosque communities, and mosque communities tend to be more conservative than not. There is a reason for this: mosques in Muslim-minority contexts are usually funded by dedicated community members who feel that a mosque is vital for their social and spiritual well-being. Such individuals tend to lean conservative, and as a result, mosque policies tend toward conservatism.

This puts mosques in a bit of a bind. In order to appeal to the evolving sensibilities of the larger Muslim community and to grow beyond their conservative bases, mosques need to introduce policies that better reflect the beliefs of a wider swath of Muslims. But they cannot upset their base in the process; otherwise they risk driving away a proven source of attendance and revenue. Mosques must hack laws in order to grow, yet they must make only modest hacks if they want to keep the lights on. Mosques therefore tend to be resistant to change, and despite the recent rise of progressive mosques, most accept only hacks that are relatively uncontroversial.

Umbrella organizations and their fiqh councils mirror mosques' balancing act, promoting modest hacks that better reflect contemporary notions of justice but always maintaining traditional ideas that are important to conservative Muslims. For instance, the Fiqh Council of North America devised a hack arguing that mosque spaces should have no physical barriers between men and women and that women should be included at all levels of mosque governance. They made sure, however, not to explicitly permit female-led ritual prayer, which they see as a red line that would galvanize the conservative base in opposition. Many councils have issued edicts tolerating LGBTQ Muslims and Ahmadi Muslims but have stopped short of fully embracing them, again for fear of angering their base.

This concern for the base is reflected in fiqh councils, whose members always have conservative bona fides. Umbrella organizations seek council members who have advanced degrees in Islamic law or who are leaders of prominent mosque communities. Ideally, a fiqh council member would have both an advanced degree and a record of service, but either will suffice. That is because fiqh council members have to be recognized by conservative-leaning mosques as authority figures so that their opinions will be seen as authoritative. This also means that fiqh council members should reflect conservative notions of what a "true" scholar looks like; they tend to be foreign-born males with some traditional training, whereas females, native-born citizens, and youth are notoriously underrepresented.

These dynamics ensure not only that fiqh councils have authority in the eyes of mosque communities but also that their reach is limited to the niche population that regularly attends mosques. In fact, despite having networks of hundreds of affiliated mosques and hosting conventions that pull in tens of thousands of attendees, umbrella organizations have a narrow field of influence that has been waning in recent years.

Their waning influence is partly due to the fact that fiqh-minded Muslims these days are finding less need for mosques to provide community. Social media now provides a virtual community, and large gatherings can be organized entirely online, without any need for mosque publicity. These virtual communities are not only convenient but have the added benefit of attracting only like-minded individuals. Whereas mosques need to balance and represent the various views of their regular attendees, these virtual communities can be formed along ideological, rather than geographical, lines. That means they can cater to the values of their own, amorphous, self-selecting community rather than to the values of a fixed geographical community.

It is very difficult to track and count these virtual communities for a variety of reasons: users are often anonymous, they exist across multiple platforms, and many are joined by invitation only. But some of these virtual communities have developed physical manifestations, the most visible of which are educational institutes that have popped up in the last couple of decades. These institutes use social media as their organizing principle, and they appeal to wide varieties of fiqh-minded Muslims, not least because they are highly adept at hacking Islamic law to be of immediate relevance to their audiences. Since these educational institutes are free from the constraints of mosque communities, their hacks are far more malleable and bold than those of umbrella organizations. Educational institutes have become increasingly prominent in recent years, and it seems that their popularity has not yet peaked.

Educational Institutes

Mosque culture has been increasingly disrupted over the last twenty years by a phenomenon of traveling scholars and pop-up educational institutes. Itinerant scholars like Zakir Naik, Habib Munzir Almusawa, Farhat Hashmi, Habib Ali Jifri, and Amr Khaled have been traveling the world and drawing crowds too large for most mosques. Instead of delivering lectures at mosques, they speak to packed stadiums, convention centers, and lecture halls. These itinerant ulama, apart from being fiqh-minded and mostly male, are quite diverse. They are of different nationalities, have different levels of classical training, preach different messages, and even look different. Some wear traditional robes and have long beards, and others wear business suits and are clean-shaven. But each can draw a crowd.

Their appeal lies in their ability to hack Islamic law so that it is both ancient and relevant to audiences today. They are skilled at demonstrating Islamic law's abiding applicability, although, of course, each has a different idea of what Islamic law actually is. Some emphasize the spirit of the law, while others focus on the pre-

colonial letter. Fiqh-minded Muslims who have a scientific view of
Islamic law might be drawn to Zakir Naik, whereas those who have
a more spiritual approach to law might be drawn to Amr Khaled. In
the age of the internet and satellite television, ulama who are highly
adept at hacking can put their ideas out there, and audiences will
come to them.

Prominent ulama no longer have to conform their message to
the mores of particular mosque communities; now they can craft
their own message online and a community of like-minded individuals will make themselves known, whether physically or virtually. Some ulama, such as the ones just mentioned, are institutions unto themselves, with huge followings and millions of views
on YouTube. It is unclear how they are financed, but they are somehow able to foot the bill for all-day programs in giant venues. There
are relatively few of these superstars, and they are becoming less and
less common.

More niche hackers are now generating sizeable followings by
posting their particular views on Islamic law online. Sometimes
niche hackers who share similar outlooks on Islamic law will join
together to form a collective. This can take the form of an educational institute that hacks Islamic law based more or less on shared
ideals. Just as with the itinerant ulama described earlier, some institutes are more conservative, while others are more liberal; some focus on the spirit of the law, while others focus on the letter.

Different institutes appeal to different demographics among
the fiqh-minded community, and they all compete for fiqh-minded
eyes, minds, and dollars. They also offer different modes of education, with some offering purely online courses, others local pop-up
courses and retreats, others large conferences, and yet others a mix
of all three. For example, fiqh-minded Sunni Muslims who adhere
closely to one of the four Sunni schools of law might be attracted
to an online course offered by Qibla.com. Or, if they prefer a more

personal experience, they might join one of the many global study circles hosted by SeekersHub.

Fiqh-minded Muslims who espouse a more *salafi* approach to Islamic law might gravitate toward the al-Maghrib Institute, which runs weekend courses in different cities. If a weekend course is too much commitment or if one is looking for a mostly inspirational experience rather than an educational one, al-Maghrib hosts all-day revivals called Ilmfests that are held in large convention centers in North America and the United Kingdom.

If one is interested in taking a critical yet respectful look at the tradition, the website of the Rawiya Foundation is the place to go. Rawiya offers online classes and lectures, often taught by classically trained female scholars, that make sure to highlight the views, contributions, and experiences of Muslim women. In addition to online courses, Rawiya hosts an annual Shaykha Fest, which is dedicated to celebrating and encouraging female scholarship.

To learn classical Arabic along with a neotraditional version of Islamic law, one can purchase a subscription to the Bayyinah Institute's trove of online videos, which includes several levels of Arabic instruction. Those who are less comfortable with online instruction can attend one of the institute's pop-up courses at a local mosque or community center. More dedicated students of Arabic can travel to the Bayyinah campus in Irving, Texas, to study full-time in the nine-month Dream program.

Each institute runs on a different financial model; some charge per course, some solicit donations, and others do both. It is difficult to gauge how many people attend these courses and how much revenue they generate, but by their own accounts, these organizations are reaching tens of thousands of students and generating millions of dollars in revenue. Their business models have proved successful precisely because they target only those people who are already interested in their offerings. Whereas mosques must work with their local constituency—whoever they might be—educational institutes are not limited by geography.

Also, in contrast to mosques, institutes have very low overhead. They mostly provide online resources, and they host conferences or pop-up courses only when there is demonstrated demand in the form of ticket sales or prepaid registration fees. The only one of these institutes with a physical campus, the Bayyinah Institute, generates revenue not from its local community but from students who travel to the campus and pay a $7,750 tuition fee for a nine-month course or a $1,200 fee for a one-month course. These fees are comparable to those of major universities and would be unsustainable if the campus served only the local Irving community. Like other educational institutes, its business model requires educating a steady stream of interested individuals and providing services that suit their needs.

This on-demand business model also allows educational institutes to hack Islamic law with much more freedom than mosques and umbrella organizations. They do not need to balance their hacks to appease a diverse constituency, so they can hack the law to be closer to the ideological beliefs of their students. This is certainly freeing; however, the fact that their business models all rely on student satisfaction means that institutes must hack laws with regularity. If institutes want to continually attract students to their events, they have to constantly prove that they are uniquely able to address the evolving challenges facing Muslim communities. If they simply repeated information that people already knew or agreed with, there would be no need for anyone to attend—and pay for—a course.

Thus, institutes offer courses on hot topics that address concerns that fiqh-minded Muslims have today, and they hack laws in a way that demonstrates their immediate relevance to their constituencies. Traditionally trained scholars at the Rawiya Institute, for instance, hacked precolonial laws to show that women can, indeed, lead ritual prayer. A course on SeekersHub teaches students how to invest in the stock market according to Islamic law. Even the conservative-leaning al-Maghrib Institute holds classes like The Fiqh of Chillin' ("debunk the myth that having fun is haraam") and The Fiqh of Love ("for when you've found someone you think you can love forever!") that are in high demand.

Each course hacks Islamic law, showing that it is both ancient and contemporary at the same time, and calls on precolonial scholars to make very modern arguments. The Fiqh of Love, for instance, cites precolonial laws and precolonial scholars to promote Islamic rules on how Muslim men and women should proceed toward marriage if and when they are interested in each other. Precolonial scholars, in their telling, believed that love is something that can be achieved only through hard work in marriage, that infatuation should not muddle a decision to marry, and that an Islamic courting process in which interpersonal contact is minimized and families are privileged should always be followed. Precolonial legal texts are used as the basis for rules of online and in-person conversations and for defining the limits of intermingling. One learns in the course that unmarried men and women should not meet alone, that parents should be consulted, and that marriage is only the beginning of a long journey that ends in love.

All of these rules sound like they could be part of the Islamic legal tradition, except that in the precolonial period, ulama did not consider that young men and women might be meeting one another to decide whether to get married. Rather, it was assumed that parents would make the bulk of that decision for young people and that the prospective bride and groom would have almost no contact, if any at all. Discussions in the precolonial period concerned whether the betrothed may *see* one another before the wedding, not about acceptable public places in which interested parties can meet to discuss life goals in the presence of a chaperone. Love is not a foreign concept in precolonial legal texts, but it is also not the main concern in legal discussions on marriage.

But taking the class would have you believing otherwise. These courses are taught using the commentarial hacking method we saw earlier in this book, and instructors explain what so-and-so precolonial scholar *really* meant and how it applies today. That, in turn, allows fiqh-minded Muslims to feel completely within the contemporary world and completely within their religious legal tradition. Given the reality that fiqh-minded Muslim men and women interact with one another online, at school, and at work, classes like The Fiqh of Love can teach them how to conduct themselves in fidelity with Islamic law as well as with their lived reality. This serves a need in the community and appeals to a certain segment of fiqh-minded Muslims.

What makes a good course—and a good teacher—is the ability to make the precolonial past directly relevant to the present. Institutes boast that their teachers are both learned and down-to-earth, a combination that fully encapsulates hacking culture. These two qualities suggest that institute teachers have roots in the precolonial legal tradition yet can make Islamic law speak to Muslims today. Thus, academic credentials are not as important for educational institutes as they are for fiqh councils, especially when it comes to male teachers, who are socially privileged to more easily pull off the learned-yet-laid-back look. Charisma and inspiration are at a premium, and teachers who hack effectively and draw students can get away with having no formal training at all.

All signs indicate that these institutes are growing and will continue to add teachers—some of whom may have formal training and some of whom may not—to meet the religious and practical needs of their constituencies. Still, amid success and rising prominence, it is important to note their scale. Educational institutes may be collectively reaching hundreds of thousands of Muslims, but that is still a tiny fraction of the fiqh-minded population. Most fiqh-minded Muslims do not attend educational institutes, just as most do not regularly attend mosques. So, if fiqh-minded Muslims are not in the mosques, and they are not taking classes at educational institutes, then where are they?

The short answer is: we don't know. We know that they exist because of polling data, but we don't know who they are and how they practice. The one place that we do find many fiqh-minded Muslims—many more than are found in mosques and institutes—is online. They are found in forums and on message boards and fan sites, but they are not always easy to find. Sometimes they are in obvious places, like Islamic message boards. Other times they are in obscure places, like the Prince of Persia forum of a 1990s-themed gaming website.

It has only gotten harder to track their activity in recent years, as many have created private chat rooms or moved their conversations to instant-messaging platforms like Facebook Messenger and WhatsApp. But when we do see fiqh-minded Muslims gathered in online forums for a sustained period, we find them furiously hacking Islamic law. Their hacks are completely unencumbered by the kinds of political constraints faced by state-sponsored scholars and umbrella organizations, and they are free from the need that educational institutes have to generate revenue. As a result, their hacks are highly creative, pushing Islamic law past pragmatic constraints imposed by the outside world.

I have found the most creative hacks online, whether they are highly conservative or highly liberal. Most online hacks are not entirely thought through, but some are deeply rooted in the Islamic legal tradition and done with great thought and care. Intriguingly, online hacks seem to anticipate conversations in the broader Muslim community. That is, hacks discussed online seem to make their way into larger debates off-line. It is possible that online hacking is somehow driving the off-line Muslim conversations, but it is far more likely that online communities are incubators for innovative hacks that can be called on if and when the community needs them. When popular sentiment shifts in the Muslims community, fiqh-minded Muslims can turn to online forums to find hacks that have already been made and that can be adapted to address community needs. Online communities provide space for fiqh-minded Muslims to try out hacks that would never fly in the mosque today but that might be called on one day to support new visions of sharia using Islamic legal language.

Online Hackers

Online hacker communities have been around for a few decades. In the late 1980s and early 1990s, they were mostly composed of university students, professionals, and tech geeks, who were, after all, the only ones who had regular access to the internet. In the mid-1990s, as internet access expanded and the price of personal computers plummeted, online communities grew exponentially. Hackers were still confined to the popular technologies of their day, especially listservs and bulletin boards, which were imperfect and clunky but exciting in their time.

Listservs are basically group email conversations among people with shared interests. Umbrella organizations and mosques have their own listservs, which are used mostly to post announcements. Other organizations, such as Muslim Student Associations and NGOs, primarily use their listservs as conversation platforms but sometimes use them to hack Islamic law. Muslim graduate students regularly use the Middle Eastern and Islamic Studies Graduate Students (MEISGS) listserv to hack Islamic law, debating legal issues well before they enter the mainstream.

Bulletin boards, the other major means of online hacking in the 1980s and 1990s, allow for wider membership and readership than do listservs and attract a more diverse group of users. In their heyday, bulletin boards such as alt.Muslim brought together tens of thousands of users to share their stories, visions of sharia, and legal hacks that were previously thought to exist only at the margins of Muslim society. What quickly became clear through these listservs and bulletin boards was that fiqh-minded believers had far more diverse and complex ideas about the sharia than those promoted in mosques.

In the late 1990s, technological advances made websites easier to create, servers more readily available, and the internet more widely accessible. Muslim groups and individuals around the world set up websites and online discussion forums dedicated to Islam, some of which were devoted to hacking Islamic law. Millions of Muslims flocked to these discussion forums to share their visions of sharia without fear of retribution. This was a huge leap from listservs and bulletin boards, and it confirmed that views previously thought to be marginal were actually far more mainstream than anyone imagined. It became apparent that fiqh-minded Muslims, whether engineering students in northern Malaysia or bankers in eastern Brazil, espoused visions of sharia that, although traditionally grounded, would be considered invalid by most mosque communities and establishment ulama. But mosque communities and establishment ulama could not dictate the terms of online conversations. Online forums uncovered the diversity of Muslim thought and experience by allowing Muslims from different educational, geographical, and socioeconomic backgrounds to express their views of sharia freely and openly.

Through sustained online conversation and debate, discussion forums facilitated legal hacks that anticipated debates that would arise only years later in Muslim communities. For example, long before the scholar Dr. Amina Wadud led a much-publicized mixed-gender Friday prayer, the MEISGS listserv was debating the permissibility of female-led prayer and the relative virtue of mixed-gender prayers. Many listserv members provided precolonial justifications for female-led prayer and hacked related laws so that female-led prayer fit neatly into the Islamic legal tradition. When Dr. Wadud led the mixed-gender prayer, groups like the Canadian Council for Muslim Women and Women Living Under Muslim Laws mined hacks developed in the listserv to provide ready-made arguments from the precolonial tradition, arguing that Islamic law undoubtedly allows for female-led and mixed-gender prayers.

Members of bulletin boards and listservs also hacked laws related to homosexuality in the early 1990s, well before it became possible to do so in mosque communities. Similarly, the foundational hacks for the 2004 egalitarian "model Muslim-marriage contract" launched by the UK-based Muslim Institute were hashed out through intense online debates in the late 1990s. These and many other hacks continue to be worked out online and are at the ready when new laws are required to meet evolving visions of sharia.

Today, one can find many hacks online that anticipate future shifts in Muslim attitudes. There are hacks supporting the rights of transgender Muslims, hacks for vegans observing the Eid al-Adha sacrifice, and hacks that permit distributing the *zakat* charity to nonprofit groups fighting climate change. Some of these hacks will be adopted, and many will fall by the wayside. The sheer volume of online hacks and the vastly different visions of sharia that they represent are awe-inspiring and almost overwhelming.

The immense volume of online hacks is due partly to the fast flow of information and partly due to scale. Even now, after Facebook and private-chat apps disrupted the centrality of public online forums, public-forum users still number in the tens of millions. Some of these forums are enormous; the preacher Amr Khaled, for instance, runs a forum that counts about one million members. Several forums boast hundreds of thousands of members, and many more have tens of thousands. Forum members come from diverse backgrounds and promote visions of sharia that are sometimes traditional and other times revolutionary. Some forum members are learned scholars, whereas others are weekend warriors who study Islamic law in their spare time. It's hard to know who is who, which means that hackers cannot rely on the force of their personality to make their arguments. Rather, they must ensure that their arguments are of consistently high quality, proving their worth anew with each hack.

Dedicated online hackers develop a mastery of Islamic law and legal argumentation over time and eventually learn to hack at a very high level. When making hacks, they cite texts in Arabic, pull from extensive libraries, and demonstrate facility with Islamic legal theory. By all accounts, these hackers are highly learned and appear to have studied in traditional centers of learning, with access to huge Islamic text repositories. I have found, however, that many elite hackers have no formal training at all, nor connections to Islamic libraries or centers of learning.

Instead, most hackers are self-taught, and there are sufficient—and free—online resources to allow anyone who is interested to gain proficiency in Islamic legal argumentation. When interacting online, it's often hard to tell whether someone is a traditionally trained scholar or entirely self-taught. I experienced this firsthand many years ago when I was an active participant in an online forum on Islamic law. I found myself arguing with a user who was convinced that democracy violated the letter and spirit of Islamic law. At the same time, he insisted that Islam protects individual freedoms and self-determination. He had a strange theory that a top-down theocracy best protects individual freedoms, self-determination, and economic prosperity, and he supported his theory using Islamic legal language. And he wasn't nice about it. He insulted anyone with whom he had even a small difference of opinion, using a mix of precolonial put-downs ("ignorant," "corrupt," "transgressor") and modern ones that I'm not willing to repeat.

He was annoying and cruel, but he was also good at hacking. When I, along with a group of like-minded folks, would respond to him on legal and theological grounds, he held his own, often sending us back into our personal archives to search for better answers. The debate was prolonged and difficult, and, in our minds, the stakes were high. We saw this as part of a larger debate about democracy, in which we were arguing that democracy is fully compatible with Islamic law, and he was arguing the opposite. We were trying to reach not just him but any fiqh-minded Muslims watching our debate who might otherwise be swayed by his arguments.

Neither side ended up "winning," but it bothered me that this guy was out there, perhaps preaching his message to a congregation. I happened to travel to his hometown one weekend and asked to meet up, hoping that I could convince him in person. We met at a halal restaurant, where I found that the scholar with whom I had been carrying on a months-long debate was a nineteen-year old sociology major with multiple piercings and an obsession with punk rock. He had learned classical Arabic through a combination of self-study texts and classes at a local mosque. He owned very few Islamic legal texts but could access precolonial texts from websites.

I should mention here that there are an astounding number of precolonial Arabic legal texts available for download online. The shamela.ws website, for example, allows users to download a computer application that contains over five thousand fully searchable Islamic texts related to theology, law, etiquette, exegesis, hadith, and the like. Similarly, the Indonesian site kitabklasik.net has, in blatant disregard of international copyright law, an online library of over three thousand Islamic books in PDF format, available for anyone to download. From the comfort of his laptop, this young man could conduct research into the Islamic legal tradition and craft intricate arguments from within it. He had no formal training, did not regularly attend a mosque, and was not affiliated with any physical community.

This young hacker embodied for me the complex identities that fiqh-minded Muslims negotiate today with respect to sharia. He was a punk-rocking university student who truly believed that an authoritarian Islamic theocracy would bring about a utopia in which poverty was eradicated and individual freedoms were guaranteed.

He spoke from within the tradition but was neither traditionally trained nor affiliated with a community. His vision of sharia cannot be reduced to caricature; it was carefully—if naively—structured and beautifully expressed in the language of Islamic law. I may not agree with it, but there is no denying that his vision of sharia and his take on Islamic law were deeply rooted in the Islamic legal tradition. The fact that his conclusions have no precedent in classical Islamic thought is somewhat irrelevant; his argument was both ancient and contemporary at the same time, and it was certainly an extension of the Islamic tradition, even if it cannot be found in a precolonial text in so many words.

Hackers accomplish this feat by using the same commentarial hacking method that we have seen throughout this book. They cite precolonial texts and comment on them to describe what the author *really* meant, making an ancient text immediately relevant. But there are two big differences between online hacking and other modes of hacking, besides freedom from political strictures; namely, that online hacking is conversational and it is fast. People come to forums with different visions of sharia and different interpretations of Islamic law. They try out a hack, and other users respond by pointing out related laws that challenge the hack. A determined hacker will then try to comment on all those related laws in a way that maintains a coherent narrative. She will then apply that new narrative to the foundational sources and argue for the superiority of her vision of the sharia. If that vision is compelling, it will be promoted and circulated in different online forums. All of this can be done in a matter of weeks.

A Case Study of Zina Laws

To give you an example of how this works in practice, let's examine a precolonial interpretation of Islamic law that goes against many contemporary visions of the sharia. Specifically, let's look at laws related to *zina*, which is most often translated as "fornication" or "adultery" and which is considered a crime in the precolonial legal tradition. In many Muslim-majority countries, zina is punishable by lashing and, according to some, stoning to death. Most Muslims today, however, believe that adultery is a private act that concerns the individuals involved and no one else. Adultery might be sinful and grounds for divorce, but many believe that it should not be punished by the state, and certainly not by lashing or stoning to death.

Many Muslims today believe that the state has no right to police marital infidelity and that when it comes to sexual relations between adults, the state should be involved only when sexual relations are nonconsensual. Nonconsensual sex, whether within the bonds of marriage or not, is considered immoral and wrong. Consent, then, is now the dividing line between a private matter and a crime requiring state intervention. In the minds of many Muslims around the world, nonconsensual sex, better referred to as rape, is unequivocally prohibited by the sharia and should be subject to punishment. Consensual sex, on the other hand, might or might not be a sin, but either way it is between the consenting adults and God, much like gossiping or smoking.

Despite consent and rape being the primary concerns of most Muslims today when it comes to sexual ethics, states with traditional zina laws make it frustratingly difficult to prosecute rape. Rape victims are saddled with an unreasonable burden of proof, and marital rape is often dismissed altogether as a legal category. Thus, the way that traditional zina laws are interpreted and implemented goes directly against modern conceptions of the sharia. That means that zina laws would need to be hacked to better reflect Muslims' deeply held convictions about sexual justice, and many have tried to do so.

People often go first to the Qur'an and hadith in order to hack this law. The Qur'an condemns zina in no uncertain terms. Beyond moral condemnation, it prescribes physical punishment for those who commit zina, whether male (*zani*) or female (*zaniya*). In Qur'an 24:2, we read,

> The *zani* and the *zaniya*, flog each with one hundred lashes, and do not let pity overtake you when it comes to God's religion, if you truly believe in God and the Last Day. And let a group of believers witness their punishment.

Several hadith, too, condemn zina, with some suggesting that the Prophet ordered people convicted of zina to be stoned. The Qur'an and hadith are so clear about their condemnation of zina that it seems like reinterpretation is virtually impossible. It is fully understandable, then, that reformist ulama have focused on the fact that, although the Qur'an condemns zina, it also presents so many obstacles to prosecuting zina that it should be obvious zina was never meant to be prosecuted.

Some reformist ulama cite the high burden of proof required when prosecuting zina: according to the Qur'an, four witnesses must testify to having seen the accused in the act of coitus. The requirement of four witnesses suggests that zina can be prosecuted only when it occurs somewhat publicly, so contemporary scholars argue that zina is actually about public indecency, not about private infidelity. Other contemporary ulama contend that the punishment for zina is only operational in an ideal society, in which morality reigns, judges are highly competent, and everyone is given what they need to be happy. Zina, in that context, would be unconscionable and would violate the social order that is being created in this perfect society. In that sense, they argue, zina should be thought of as something close to treason, which is subject to corporal punishment. Still other contemporary scholars question the hadiths that prescribe stoning, arguing that they are forgeries and that the Prophet never actually said them. They further contend that the Qur'an meant only to emphasize the enormity of zina by attaching to it a punishment with an extremely high threshold for proof. They point out that in all of the precolonial period, there are only a few reports of people actually being stoned for zina, suggesting that the punishment was meant to be more or less symbolic.

Although these solutions are a step in the right direction, they sidestep the central concern that is driving the hack in the first place. Many Muslims now believe that only nonconsensual sex is a crime that should be prosecuted by the state, whereas sex with consent is a private matter and should not be punished. That means that regardless of whether sex is conducted within the bonds of marriage and regardless of whether it is conducted in public or behind closed doors, a prosecutable crime is committed only if one party was unwilling to participate. In this vision of sharia, consensual adultery might be a sin, but it should not be prosecuted or punished. Thus, the driving concern is not about the burden of proof for prosecution, about whether the act was committed in public or in private, or about whether punishment should be carried out by lashing or stoning or something else. Rather, the driving concern is that consensual sex should not be prosecuted at all, whereas rape, whether within marriage or not, should be punished by the state.

Creating laws to match that vision of sharia might seem like a daunting task given the clear condemnation of zina in the Qur'an and hadith. But as we have seen throughout this book, the Qur'an and hadith are never the problem. They are fully capable of providing guidance for all times and places and, as we will see, can easily be interpreted to safeguard the sexual rights of consenting adults and to categorically prohibit rape. The real root of the problem, and the reason that even the mild reinterpretations mentioned earlier have not enjoyed a warm reception among the fiqh-minded, is that zina is a key concept in the Islamic legal tradition that has to do with much more than marital infidelity.

That is why the laws on zina must be hacked before fiqh-minded

Muslims can reinterpret foundational sources. This requires going through the four steps that we saw in chapter 5.

1. Propose a new law.

2. Identify all related precolonial laws.

3. Reinterpret those precolonial laws so that they create a new, coherent legal narrative that accommodates your proposed law.

4. Reinterpret the foundational sources according to the proposed law.

The laws that need hacking here concern the role of consent in prosecuting sexual relations. Specifically, we need to propose a law that reflects the widespread Muslim belief that consensual relations should not be punished by the state, whereas nonconsensual relations should be prosecuted. Once such a law is proposed, we would need to identify all related precolonial laws. To do that, we would have to examine different precolonial legal discussions on zina, of which there are many.

Zina pops up in multiple places within Islamic legal texts. To see exactly where, you could use a searchable database like the one housed at Shamela.ws, or you could consult an English translation of a precolonial Islamic legal text. Or you could simply pose the question to hackers in an online forum, and you would learn that, in addition to chapters on marriage and divorce, zina comes up in laws on witnessing (whether convicted adulterers can serve as witnesses), custody (who is responsible for a child conceived out of wedlock), inheritance (whether a child born out of wedlock inherits), homosexuality (whether sodomy is the same as zina), coercion, corporal punishment, and a lot more. Legal texts also include sidebars on how to avoid zina—lower the gaze, do not frequent mixed-gender gatherings, avoid physical contact with the opposite gender, dress modestly—and about the evil effects of zina on society. Today, zina appears within a slew of modern laws, including those related to transport, in vitro fertilization, and even texting.

The most in-depth discussions of zina—including descriptions, definitions, and exclusions— are found in chapters or subchapters on corporal punishment. Given that zina is a crime that precolonial scholars assumed would be prosecuted in court, ulama carefully described how zina could be proved, what burden of proof is required, who can serve as a witness, when less than four witnesses will suffice, what the sentencing procedures are, and when a zina conviction should result in corporal punishment and when a lesser punishment will do. Ulama tended to agree that eyewitnesses are inherently unreliable and that when there is any reasonable doubt about any part of the case or even when the accused insist that they thought they were doing nothing wrong, then corporal punishment should be substituted by a fine or jail time.

Ulama meticulously described hypothetical zina trials and came up with numerous laws on prosecuting zina. In the process, they wrangled over many questions. If someone is convicted of zina, for instance, but there is reasonable doubt regarding some aspect of the trial, then how much jail time or how big a fine can be levied? If someone is convicted of zina beyond reasonable doubt, should they be lashed or stoned? If stoned, then who does the stoning, what kind of stones can be used, and for how long should a body be stoned? What is obvious from any reading of these texts is that according to precolonial ulama, zina is undoubtedly a prosecutable offense. The only disagreement that they had was about how to prosecute zina, not whether to prosecute.

If you were to join a forum, then, and argue that zina should not be prosecuted, you would have to somehow explain why precolonial legal scholars discussed laws related to zina in such detail. There is a law, for example, that prohibits those convicted of zina from testifying in court. How does that law make any sense if zina is not prosecuted? What are we to make of the laws of custody and inheritance that pertain to zina? Why is there any discussion of witness reliability in zina trials unless ulama expected there would be zina trials to begin with? These are fair questions, and they point to the challenge involved in hacking Islamic law: to gain authority among the fiqh-minded, hacks must work within existing Islamic laws to create a coherent narrative. Only then will they be accepted as accurate reflections of sharia. This should not be seen as a deterrent; as we have seen many times, a coherent narrative can be achieved through careful hacking.

Online forums accelerate the process, as users from all backgrounds and walks of life challenge proposed hacks whenever they violate existing laws or fail to create coherent narratives. Let me walk you through a few reactions that you might encounter in an online forum to some of the aforementioned attempts to hack zina laws. If you were to argue that, say, zina is supposed to be prosecuted only when committed in public, hackers would cite the famous Mughira b. Shu'ba case, often mentioned in legal texts, in which a companion of the Prophet was tried for zina after the shutters of his bedroom window flew open and people saw him in a compromised position with a woman to whom he was not married. That well-known story suggests that zina should be prosecuted even if it is committed in the privacy of one's home. Hackers would also point out the unintended consequences of encouraging the prosecution of extramarital sex committed in public, especially in the modern day. Using that logic, many thousands of pornographers would need to be prosecuted and potentially stoned for zina.

If you were to take another tack and argue that zina was meant to be prosecuted only in the time of the Prophet, hackers would fire back with legal interpretations of Qur'an 24:2, mentioned earlier, which says, "And do not let pity overtake you when it comes to God's religion." That verse is normally understood to mean that zina must always be punished, regardless of whether you want to or not. If you were to then pivot away from the Qur'an and question the authenticity of the hadith about stoning people convicted of zina, hackers would point out that even if the Prophet didn't prescribe stoning, the Qur'an still prescribes lashing, so a zina conviction would nevertheless result in corporal punishment.

For every attempt to reinterpret the law, hackers will respond with many and varied counterarguments. These should not be seen as conclusive; instead, they are cues that your hack needs more work, that it is incomplete, and that it will not yet enjoy authority among the fiqh-minded. This is, in fact, a huge gift; it is a way to crowdsource the second step in the hacking process: identify all related precolonial laws. Once all or most of the laws related to your hack are identified, you are in a position to create a comprehensive hack that will fit into a legal narrative that accommodates both the precolonial legal tradition and your vision of the sharia.

With the example of zina, if we pay close attention to the legal conversation, we find an entry point for a hack in the very definition that precolonial scholars gave for zina. Zina is defined as the act of coitus between two persons of the opposite sex who are not in a recognized sexual relationship. If four witnesses can be found to testify to an act of zina, then the two accused can be tried in court. If they are found guilty beyond reasonable doubt, then they may be punished with lashing or stoning. If there is a high probability that zina occurred, but there is still reasonable doubt about some aspect of the case, the punishment may be lessened to a fine or jail time.

These zina laws are found in almost every precolonial legal text. And while they define the act of zina in great detail, they rarely discuss issues related to consent or rape. In the uncommon event that scholars did consider consent or rape, they were concerned only with whether coercion is an acceptable excuse for committing zina. That is, if someone claims that they were coerced into committing zina, should they still be prosecuted? Precolonial scholars were mostly agreed that coercion could be used as a valid excuse only when there is danger to life and limb and that those who commit zina cannot reasonably claim to have done so in order to save their lives.

It is no wonder, then, that rape victims have had such a difficult time obtaining justice in sharia courts. Ulama seem to have conflated rape and zina, as though they were simply two different words for the same thing, both requiring punishment from the state. This conflation of rape and zina has wreaked havoc on the lives of rape victims, but it is also an entry point for a hack. We might entertain the idea that the precolonial conflation of zina and rape was actually intentional and that precolonial scholars used the term zina to refer to rape. In that light we might ask, What if precolonial ulama assumed that zina was always coercive and nonconsensual, so that whenever they mentioned zina, they were not talking about consensual sexual relations but only about rape?

That's an intriguing possibility, but to see if it would work for the fiqh-minded, we would have to reread all the laws related to zina (step three in the hacking process) to check whether they form a coherent narrative in this new reading. We saw earlier a law stating that zina is punishable by lashing or stoning when four people testify to having witnessed it. If we define zina as rape, then according to that law, rape is punishable by lashing or stoning when four reliable witnesses testify to having witnessed it. We also saw a law that lessens the punishment of zina to jail time or a fine if there is reasonable doubt about some aspect of the case but still a high probability that zina occurred. When we define zina as rape and we combine this law with the previous one, those laws collectively prescribe sentencing rapists to lashing or stoning when convicted beyond a reasonable doubt and to jail time or a fine whenever there is reasonable doubt about some aspect of the case but still a high probability that the accused committed rape.

Whether or not one agrees with defining zina as rape, those two laws make sense together: rape should be punished by the state, and the extent of the punishment depends on the level of certainty involved in the prosecution. That makes sense and is in accordance with contemporary visions of the sharia, but there are many other laws related to zina that would also have to make sense for the hack to have weight among the fiqh-minded.

This is where online hackers are particularly helpful. They would point out, for example, that there are zina laws related to witnessing; specifically, those convicted of zina must be registered and cannot testify in legal cases. One could answer back that when zina is defined as rape, that law means that convicted rapists must be registered and cannot testify in legal cases. That makes good sense. Online hackers might also point out laws related to custody; namely, that custody of a child of zina goes to the mother. One could answer back that the new reading means that a woman who becomes pregnant after being raped and decides to carry the baby to term retains custody rights. That reading works too. Online hackers might point to the multiple related laws on coercion, and one could answer that those, too, make sense when zina is defined as rape. Recall that under the precolonial system, coercion is not a valid excuse for committing zina. If zina means rape, then that law means an accused rapist cannot be exonerated by claiming that he was coerced into raping someone. That reading also makes sense.

Thus, defining zina as rape works well with many laws, and as it is proven to work with more and more laws, a legal narrative will emerge that can vie for authority among the fiqh-minded. At that point, one can then turn to the scriptures (step four) to provide a reading that aligns with the new legal narrative. Based on the narrative, Qur'an 24:2 now reads:

The rapist, male or female, flog each with one hundred lashes, and do not let pity overtake you when it comes to God's religion, if you truly believe in God and the Last Day. And let a group of believers witness their punishment.

This reading of the Qur'an aligns neatly with the hacked laws and visions of sharia that are animating the hack in the first place; namely, that the state should prosecute only nonconsensual sex. The hadith can be similarly interpreted to argue that whenever Muhammad mentioned zina, he was actually referring to rape. By hacking the laws around zina, a new world of scriptural interpretation is revealed in which consent is at the center and in which rape and rapists are condemned.

One could then use the lens of consent to interpret many other verses of the Qur'an and hadith that are even tangentially related to zina. That, again, is the easy part. The more difficult process involves identifying related laws and creating a narrative for them. That is time-consuming, and it is challenging to craft a narrative that does not end up creating more problems.

Online hackers would point out that although this hack is highly effective in many respects, it is yet incomplete. There is still the matter of children born of zina, who, in the precolonial legal tradition, do not inherit from their birth parents. That law would also have to be hacked. There is still the issue of marital rape, which is not directly addressed by this hack and which would need to be addressed along with hacks to the traditional marriage contract. The zina hack also has the unintended consequence of undermining those who would argue, on Islamic grounds, against capital punishment, and it potentially places the testimony of four witnesses above more certain forms of evidence, like DNA profiling. And whereas the hack works very well within Hanafi and Shafi'i legal texts, it does not fit as well with Maliki texts, which have different thresholds for proving and punishing zina and which would need a unique hack.

Still, the zina hack helps the law reflect widely held beliefs about the sharia much more accurately than it did before. Through further discussion and debate, the hack can be expanded and modified to address all relevant laws in order to provide a fully coherent legal narrative that reflects the widespread belief that the sharia demands consent in sexual relations. It appeals to the many millions of fiqh-minded Muslims who believe that God would never prescribe flogging or stoning for two consenting adults acting on a primal, God-given instinct. And it aligns with the beliefs of many millions of Muslims that rapists must be punished by the state and that God intends legal justice for victims of rape. As the hack becomes more sophisticated and weaves a more compelling legal narrative, it will gain authority among the fiqh-minded and can enter into debate beyond online forums.

This method of proposing, rejecting, and refining hacks is made accessible and speedy through online forums. When millions of hackers are arguing with one another, the refinement process goes much faster than it otherwise might. Once hacks are refined to a high level and gain currency online, we find them voiced by more mainstream figures. As mentioned, homosexuality was being discussed online in the 1990s, and hacks were developed at that time that characterized the Islamic legal tradition as tolerant toward gays and lesbians. About ten years later, mainstream Muslim leaders started preaching tolerance for gay people. And while these public leaders were preaching tolerance, online hackers were hard at work devising arguments that Islamic law not only tolerates gays and lesbians but also celebrates same-sex unions. We are now starting to see books and articles published to that effect, using arguments devised online about ten years ago, and mainstream fiqh-minded leaders are now starting to speak out, albeit slowly, about embracing the LGBTQ community.

It is incredibly simple to get involved with online hacking. One simply joins a forum, of which there are many, and begins commenting on issues that are personally important. People will respond, sometimes encouragingly, sometimes less so. The response you receive will be reflective of the diversity of the fiqh-minded Muslim community. There are fiqh-minded Muslims who believe that the sharia is inherently nonviolent and others who believe that the sharia is a revolutionary manifesto. Some will say that the sharia champions feminism, and others will say that it is irremediably patriarchal. Each position will be expressed in the language of Islamic law, and each will rely on hacking the Islamic legal tradition with the help of like-minded hackers. Working together, hacks will be further researched and refined, and, when they reflect popular sentiments, the best hacks will make their way into the wider world and be promoted as the truest manifestations of the sharia.

Of course, the movement from online to mainstream is not inevitable, and it is not easy. In the online world, one must contend with countless naysayers and doubters along with the requisite misogynists, patriarchs, homophobes, Islamophobes, trolls, and haters who inhabit wide swaths of the internet. Remember the nineteen-year old hacker I mentioned earlier? He was mean. The same freedom that allows online hacks to be so creative also allows people to say horrible things that they would never, one hopes, say off-line. But seasoned hackers can use even vulgar critics to make their hacks sharper and better researched. Over time, hacks are honed and strengthened so that they respond to all manner of criticism, making them more likely to be adopted by fiqh-minded Muslim groups around the world and by umbrella organizations, NGOs, educational institutions, and even states.

I'd like to dwell a bit on this last point about Muslims adopting online hacks. Online hackers always have an eye toward state and mosque communities. Hackers are mindful of the political implications of their hacks, even though they are free to ignore them, because online hacks are useless without communities that might adopt them. But state and mosque communities also need online hackers to make the bold hacks that they cannot. Communities need a place to work out theories without angering their bases and to engage with ideas beyond those held by their geographical constituency. What we see is that each of the four groups discussed in this chapter is incredibly important on its own but that they all work in tandem. State-sponsored ulama need NGOs to do the social and educational work that they cannot; educational institutes rely on mosque and online communities to provide fiqh-minded Muslims with a basic Islamic education; and NGOs need state-sponsored ulama to, if not endorse their work, then at least turn a blind eye to it.

If we study these groups only in isolation, we will get a distorted picture of the fiqh-minded community and the limits of Islamic law. If we look only at umbrella organizations, we might think that Islamic law is restrictive and changes in fits and starts. If we look only at online hacking, we might think that Islamic law is an ever-changing landscape in which anything is possible. When looking at brick-and-mortar communities, we can't help but focus on practical constraints. When looking at online communities, we can't help but imagine the possibilities.

In reality, there is always tension between theory and practice in Islamic legal hacking. This is an abiding problem for any community or legal system; whereas much is possible in theory, change is subject to practical constraints. It is important for us to recognize that this tension is constant, that there are always fiqh-minded Muslims pushing for theoretically sound hacks, and that other fiqh-minded Muslims will always push back based on practical constraints. This constant back-and-forth testifies to the diversity among fiqh-minded Muslims and to the fact that none of the groups mentioned earlier can claim to definitively represent the views of all fiqh-minded Muslims. That means that Islamic law is not the property of state-sponsored ulama, NGOs, umbrella organizations, educational institutes, or online hackers. Instead, Islamic law is negotiated among all of them in a bid to actualize contested visions of sharia in Islamic legal language. In those negotiations, each has a valid claim on sharia and none can claim privileged knowledge over another.

At present, however, the cards are stacked in favor of certain hackers. States, think tanks, media outlets, and prominent individuals are all complicit in granting authority to those hackers who fit stereotypical notions of "real" Muslim legal scholars. Again and again, we see traditionally trained scholars, state-sponsored scholars, and leaders of mosque communities appear on television and on panels as they are asked to speak to huge audiences and advise nations about Islam and Islamic law. But these individuals represent only a percentage of fiqh-minded Muslims and only a tiny sliver of the larger Muslim community. By continually asking these stereotypical scholars to speak for all Muslims and by recognizing only their hacks as legitimate, we end up delegitimizing all other hackers in the eyes of the general public. That makes it infinitely harder for those other hackers to gain legitimacy and be taken seriously in community negotiations. By failing to recognize the validity of their legal visions of sharia, we unwittingly support the status quo.

Fortunately, many institutions and organizations are starting to recognize that hacking legitimately occurs on multiple levels of society. Some prominent online hackers are now employed at think tanks and are funded to hack state laws on blasphemy, apostasy, adultery, free speech, and much more. Fiqh-minded Muslim women, tired of being consistently left out of male-dominated deliberations on the future of the Muslim community, are now forming hacker collectives and are hacking laws among themselves. They, too, are starting to get well-deserved press and recognition for their work.

We are still a long way off from having all—or even most—fiqh-minded Muslims represented in Islamic legal hacking, but the number of hackers seems to be growing exponentially. Fiqh-minded Muslims increasingly feel that their religious beliefs are not being represented, that Islamic law is more expansive than prominent Muslim scholars would have us believe, and that it is unacceptable to let the same tired scholars speak for the majority of Muslims. We are starting to see cracks in the interpretive monopoly that a small cadre of fiqh-minded ulama currently enjoys over the Islamic legal conversation. Breaking that interpretive monopoly is, I believe, inevitable. The era of unrepresentative scholarship will surely prove short-lived; as the Prophet reportedly said, "My community will not agree upon error."

Afterword

I WAS SITTING on a couch the other day reading a book when my partner, herself an Islamic legal scholar, turned to me and asked, "Do you remember when photographs were *haram*?" I sat back, eyes widening: I *did* remember that.

Back in the 1980s, photographs were a perennial topic of debate in the fiqh-minded Muslim community, along with whether hamburgers from McDonald's were *halal* and whether Michael Jackson was Muslim. People held strong opinions on photography and its permissibility in Islam, and they argued about whether, say, photographs could be propped up on desks or hung on walls and about whether some objects, like trees, were okay to photograph, while others, like humans, were prohibited. The debate centered on a series of hadiths prohibiting "image making." This reported ban on image making was likely referring to idol making, but in twentieth-century North America there was a concern that image making might extend to taking photographs. This was serious business, because the hadiths included vivid descriptions of exactly how the image maker would be tortured in hellfire. You didn't want to be an image maker, whatever that was.

So everyone was debating: does the prohibition of image making extend to photographs? A lot of people said yes. I heard microbiologists describe in scientific-sounding language how cameras steal a part of your soul each time you are photographed. I listened to otherwise levelheaded professionals explain why cameras were tools of the anti-Christ. Friends would tell stories of their parents going through religious phases and tearing up all the photographs in their houses. Most families in my community took and displayed photographs, but every once in a while, they would have to explain themselves to more conservative friends and relatives, and heated arguments ensued.

That was then. People don't argue about photographs anymore. Fundamentalist preachers now have websites adorned with their smiling—or scowling—faces. Streaming video poses no legal problem for highly conservative religious scholars. Even jihadist groups that are desperately trying to re-create the time of the Prophet take pride in their Photoshop and video-editing skills. And the selfies; my God, the selfies.

Today, you have to go looking for someone who has a legal problem with photography. Just a few decades ago, they were everywhere. So thoroughly has the law on photography been hacked that younger people are shocked when I tell them that it was ever an issue, let alone a contentious one. The shift in thinking on photography reminds me of Islamic law's malleability. It is ancient, to be sure, but it can pivot on a dime.

We have no idea what Islamic law will look like a few decades from now. Hacks are being circulated today that might seem outlandish or impossible, but it might just be that their time has not yet come. That's the thing about hacks—they are really about the future, and we don't know what the future will look like. Some hacks might look implausible today but be perfectly natural tomorrow. Hacks should be seen in light of Dator's second law, which holds that "any useful statement about the future should at first seem ridiculous."

Who knows what Islamic law will look like ten years from now? Who knows which hacks will soon become common knowledge?

The *murabaha* contract hack that we saw in chapter 5, which serves as the foundation for modern sharia-compliant finance, sat dormant for centuries. Only when the global financial system completely shifted were the circumstances right for it to shine.

There are many such hacks that might seem ridiculous today but might be commonplace tomorrow. In the late-Ottoman period, hackers argued that Muslims observe Ramadan all wrong. Currently, observant Muslims fast every day in the month of Ramadan, unless they are unable to for some reason, in which case they can feed a poor person instead. The late-Ottoman hackers said that it was actually the reverse; they said the Qur'an commands Muslims to feed poor people every day in the month of Ramadan, unless they are unable to for some reason, in which case they can fast instead. Some people today adhere to that hack, but most don't. Maybe that's because most Muslims would never accept a hack like that. Maybe. Or maybe it's just a hack whose time has not yet come.

I'm optimistic about the future of Islamic law. After having had a rough time adjusting to colonialism, nation-states, authoritarianism, and globalization, Islamic law is starting to come into its own. Muslims are beginning to turn to Islamic law as their way of expressing deeply held beliefs about the sharia—beliefs that are different from those of their parents, who themselves have beliefs different from those of their parents.

I have hope in the legions of fifteen-year old fiqh-minded Muslim hackers who have grown up in a hyperconnected, globalized world, who have been raised on a steady diet of human rights and feminism, and who embrace diversity of race, gender, and sexuality. They are the reason why I don't believe traditional scholars when they pronounce with such certainty what can and cannot be considered Islamic. Hackers are the reason why I don't feel restricted by the religious elite's lack of imagination. Hackers are a testament to the fact that Islam is bigger than we will ever know and that Islamic law can accommodate ideas that we cannot yet imagine. Hackers remind me that Islamic law can speak directly to my experience just as it spoke directly to generations before me. That is what makes Islamic law spiritual, that is what makes it religious, and that is what makes me a believer.

Acknowledgments

This project was only possible through a supportive community of friends, family, and colleagues. First and foremost of these is my brilliant partner; I thank you for more than just the time, support, and attention that you poured into this project, but for being my muse, interlocutor, and sparring partner. This book is full of your ideas, shared and debated through endless and joyous conversations, and I can no longer tell where your ideas end and mine begin. I therefore owe you more than I will ever know and am more grateful to you than you will ever know.

I was fortunate to also have institutional support for this project. The early concepts were fleshed out during a research leave made possible by the University of British Columbia's Dean of Arts Faculty Research Award. Special thanks go to Dean Gage Averill and Professor Michael B. Richards for the award. I would like to thank the Stanford Humanities Center at Stanford University for a fellowship year that allowed me to pursue my initial ideas and put them to paper. Special thanks go to Professor Caroline Winterer for giving me the physical and mental space to engage in sustained research and writing.

This work benefitted tremendously from the feedback of friends and colleagues. In 2017, Ayesha S. Chaudhry hosted a symposium on the draft manuscript, an act of generosity that I hope to reciprocate one day. In the symposium, colleagues graciously gave their time and energy to read the book and provide invaluable feedback. Many thanks to Zaid Adhami, Iman Baobeid, Ayesha S. Chaudhry, Sarah Eltantawi, Anver Emon, Ahmed Fekry Ibrahim, Adel Iskander, Shabana Mir, Tamir Moustafa, and Saadia Yacoob; I sincerely appreciate your comments and criticisms. Thank you also to Ziba Mir-Hosseini and Jeff Redding for their written comments, which greatly benefited the manuscript. My thanks to Iqbal Ahmed and Shakeela Begum for their sage advice and close reading of the text. Any errors in this text are my own.

I am grateful to the staff at Stanford University Press for their diligent attention to this book. Special thanks goes to Emily-Jane Cohen, who believed in this project at the outset and patiently guided me through all stages of production.

I want to thank my friends and family for giving me strength and peace during this process. I am grateful for friends like Aysha A. Chowdhry, Zahir Dossa, Youssef Garcia-Bengochea, Susan Hardy, Shenoor Jadavji, al-Husein Madhany, Noor Najeeb, Maher Samra, and William Twaddell. Samira Thomas, you are truly inspiring. I know how rare it is to have a parent who reads, engages with, and appreciates your academic work. Thanks for all the feedback, Dad; it's always a joy, whether we end up agreeing or not. I am grateful for the support of my parents, brothers, in-laws, godchildren, nieces, and nephews. Ibrahim, now this book has your name in it too.

Notes

Chapter 1

from the renowned legal scholar Ibn Taymiyya: *Amr bil maʿruf wa nahy ʿan al-munkar* (Riyadh: Wizarat al-Shuʾun al-Islamiyya, 1418), p. 1:61. **we find the exact opposite:** *Iʿlām al-Muwaqqiʿīn ʿan rabb al-ʿālamīn* (Riyadh: Dar Ibn al-Jawzi, 2002), p. 4:337. **Just to be clear, Ibn al-Qayyim added:** *Ṭurūq al-Ḥukmiyya fī al-Siyāsa al-Sharʿiyya* (Mecca: Dar ʿAlam al-Fawaʾid, 2007), p. 31. **Several polls have been taken:** There are many polls that reflect Muslims' overwhelming preference for both democracy and religious freedom. The most prominent of these is the 2013 Pew poll titled "The World's Muslims: Religion, Politics and Society," which involved over thirty-eight thousand face-to-face interviews with Muslims in thirty-nine countries. Chapter 1 of this document discusses responses to the central question (Q79a) of the poll, "Do you favor or oppose making sharia law, or Islamic law, the official law of the land in your country?" Of course, this is a difficult question to answer, leaving no room for gauging levels of sympathy or even defining what sharia is. Nevertheless, the fact that about 70 percent of respondents answered "favor" is significant; when correcting for the Muslim populations that respondents represent and including separate polling data from India, one could extrapolate from the data to hypothesize that about 60 percent of the world's Muslims would answer "favor." The report notes, however, that there was wide divergence among respondents by country, with Muslims in some countries overwhelmingly opposing sharia and those in other countries overwhelmingly favoring it. Chapter 2 of that report concerns Muslim attitudes toward democracy and religious freedom, noting that strong majorities favor democracy, and over 90 percent favor religious freedom. The report notes the apparent discrepancy between the findings in chapters 1 and 2, explaining that in countries in which there is strong support for sharia, there are also expressed views that sharia should apply only to Muslims. The executive summary concludes, "Overall, the survey finds that most Muslims see no inherent tension between being religiously devout and living in modern society. Nor do they see any conflict between religion and science. Many favor democracy over authoritarian rule, believe that humans and other living things evolved over time and say they personally enjoy Western movies, music and television—even though most think Western popular culture undermines public morality"; The Pew Forum on Religion and Public Life, *The World's Muslims: Religion, Politics and Society* (Washington, DC: Pew Research Center, 2013), p. 10. The Pew poll is supported by polls focusing on specific countries and regions, such as the 2011 Gallup poll of Muslims in India, in which over 80 percent of Muslims surveyed said that if they were asked to draft a constitution, they would include provisions guaranteeing freedom of religion, freedom of speech, and freedom of assembly; Gallup, "Muslims in India: Confident in Democracy Despite Economic and Educational Challenges," accessed August 31, 2017, http://www.gallup.com/poll/157079/muslims-india -confident-democracy-despite-economic-educational-challenges.aspx. See also John Esposito and Dalia Mogahed, *Who Speaks for Islam? What a Billion Muslims Really Think* (New York: Gallup Press, 2007); and M. Steven Fish, *Are Muslims Distinctive? A Look at the Evidence* (New York: Oxford University Press, 2011). **different Muslims have different definitions for and different relationships with sharia:** There are several volumes that highlight multiple and competing visions of sharia within a single volume, such as Anna Korteweg and Jennifer Selby, eds., *Debating Sharia: Islam, Gender Politics and Family Law Arbitration* (Toronto: University of Toronto Press, 2012); M. A. Muqtedar Khan, ed., *Debating Moderate Islam: The Geopolitics of Islam and the West* (Salt Lake City: University of Utah Press, 2007); and I. Nassery, R. Ahmed, and M. Tatari, eds., *The Objectives of Islamic Law: The Promises and Challenges of the Maqāṣid al-Sharīʿa* (Lanham, MD: Lexington Books, 2018) to name a few. **with European colonialism:** Recent books for nonspecialists that clearly and succinctly discuss the colonial intervention in Muslim-majority lands include Roger Crowley, *Conquerors: How Portugal Forged the First Global Empire* (New York: Random House, 2015); Jared Diamond, *Guns, Germs, and Steel* (New York: Norton, 1999); and Norrie Macqueen, *Colonialism* (London: Routledge, 2014). **a single, codified civil law:** Different countries had different paths to codification, and their individual trajectories are documented in works such as Michael R. Anderson, "Islamic Law and the Colonial Encounter in British India," in *Institutions and Ideologies: A SOAS South Asia Reader*, ed. David Arnold and Peter Robb (London: Curzon Press, 1993), pp. 165–85; Penelope Carson, *The East India Company and Religion, 1698–1858* (Suffolk, UK: The Boydell Press, 2012); Sarah Eltantawi, *Shariʿah on Trial: Northern Nigeria's Islamic Revolution* (Berkeley: University of California Press, 2017); Scott A. Kugle, "Framed, Blamed and Renamed: The Recasting of Islamic Jurisprudence in Colonial South Asia," *Modern Asian Studies* 35, no. 2 (2001): 257–313; and several articles in M. Maussen, V. Bader, and A. Moors, eds., *Colonial and Post-Colonial Governance of Islam* (Amsterdam, NL: Amsterdam University Press, 2011). Some recent studies have complicated the notion of how legal codes came to be and what function they served, focusing less on the colonizers and more on the agency of colonized people. Iza R. Hussin's *The Politics of Islamic Law: Local Elites, Colonial Authority, and the Making of the Muslim State* (Chicago: The University of Chicago Press, 2016), for instance, highlights the role of local elites in the formation of legal codes in multiple colonized locales. Similarly, Samera Esmeir's *Juridical Humanity: A Colonial History*

(Stanford, CA: Stanford University Press, 2012) argues that law was seen as a means of expressing humanity and alleviating suffering by colonized Egyptians. These works suggest that, although codification was spearheaded by colonial powers, colonized peoples nonetheless contributed to and found meaning in the process of developing codified laws. **codification was not an entirely colonial invention:** Codification had nascent precursors in texts such as the *Mejelle* and the *Fatawa-e-Alamgiri*, as pointed out by Guy Burak in *The Second Formation of Islamic Law: The Ḥanafī School in the Early Modern Ottoman Empire* (Cambridge, UK: Cambridge University Press, 2015), but there were important differences between precolonial Muslim conceptions and colonial conceptions of codification, as described in detail in part 2 of Wael Hallaq's *An Introduction to Islamic Law* (Cambridge, UK: Cambridge University Press, 2009). Of course, as Cyra A. Choudhury notes, echoing Iza R. Hussin, this was a conversation among local elites that only caught the imagination of lay Muslims much later; "(Mis)Appropriated Liberty: Identity, Gender Justice and Muslim Person Law Reform in India," *Columbia Journal of Gender and Law* 17, no. 45 (2008): 55. **For colonists looking to fill out a legal code:** For a concise overview of how and which texts were used to form hybrid sharia codes in different colonies, see Léon Buskins, "Sharia and the Colonial State," in *The Ashgate Companion to Islamic Law*, ed. Rudolph Peters and Peri Bearman (Burlington, VT: Ashgate, 2014), pp. 216–18. **embraced Malthusian economic theory:** Mike Davis compiled the most comprehensive analysis of the mass death resulting from Malthusian economic practices in his book, *Late Victorian Holocausts: El Niño Famines and the Making of the Third World* (New York: Verso, 2000). More detail on how colonial powers implemented their economic systems and why can be found in David Cannadine, *Ornamentalism: How the British Saw Their Empire* (New York: Oxford University Press, 2002); and Alison Bashford and Joyce E. Chaplin, *Thomas Robert Malthus: Rereading the Principle of Population* (Princeton, NJ: Princeton University Press, 2016). **even many non-Muslim anticolonialists supported sharia:** Interfaith solidarity around sharia popped up in many places; for example, the *Imārat-e-sharīʿa* movement in India, which was led by many prominent Muslim scholars, was premised on Hindu-Muslim unity; Mohammad Sajjad, *Muslim Politics in Bihar: Changing Contours* (Abingdon, UK: Routledge, 2014), p. 320. **two types of constitutional provisions:** For more on sharia source laws, see Clark Lombardi, "Constitutional Provisions Making Sharia 'a' or 'the' Chief Source of Legislation: Where Did They Come From? What Do They Mean? Do They Matter?," *American University International Law Review* 28, no. 3 (2013): 733–74. **When reminded that health care is already free:** Quote taken from Anjem Choudary, who is currently incarcerated for supporting ISIL; cited in Grame Wood, "What ISIS Really Wants," *The Atlantic*, March 2015, accessed August 31, 2017, http://www.theatlantic.com/magazine/archive/2015/03/what-isis-really-wants/384980/. **Anver Emon calls sharia:** For Emon's discussion of sharia as a claim-space, see his *Religious Pluralism and Islamic Law: Dhimmis and Others in the Empire of Law* (Oxford, UK: Oxford University Press, 2012), pp. 15–17. **The distinction is crucial:** The sharia-fiqh dichotomy and its implications are most clearly delineated in a series of scholarly articles in Zainah Anwar, ed., *Wanted: Equality and Justice in the Muslim Family* (Selangor, MY: Musawah, 2009). The text of this volume is available in its entirety at http://www.musawah.org/wanted-equality-and-justice-muslim-family -english. **In the words of Dr. Ziba Mir-Hosseini:** Dr. Mir-Hosseini's quote can be found in her article, "Beyond 'Islam' vs. 'Feminism,'" *IDS Bulletin* 42, no. 1 (January 2011): 71. **Known as Orientalism:** For a description of how Orientalism works with respect to Islamic law, see Ebrahim Moosa, "Colonialism and Islamic Law," in *Islam and Modernity: Key Issues and Debates*, ed. M. K. Masud, A. Salvatore, and M. v. Bruinessen (Edinburgh, UK: University of Edinburgh Press, 2009), pp. 158–81. **In the United States:** Numbers for US mosque attendance are taken from Ihsan Bagby, "The American Mosque 2011: Report Number 1," in *The American Mosque Study* (Washington, DC: CAIR, 2011), p. 7. **Marshall Hodgson called this group:** Hodgson's description of "sharia-minded" Muslims can be found in his book, *The Venture of Islam: Volume I* (Chicago: University of Chicago Press, 1974), pp. 315ff.

Chapter 2
simultaneously static and dynamic: Lena Salaymeh, studying the earliest articulations of Islamic law, describes the tension in these words: "Islamic jurisprudence—like any jurisprudence—is always in a dialogical relationship with contemporaneous and predecessor legal traditions. The logic of Islamic law simultaneously recycles and innovates Islamic traditions within a dynamic normative space"; *The Beginnings of Islamic Law: Late Antique Islamicate Legal Traditions* (Cambridge, UK: Cambridge University Press, 2016). **even Shi'a legal scholars:** The Akhbārī-Uṣūlī divide in Shi'a history has been well documented; to get a sense of the socioeconomic concerns that accompanied the rise of Usulism in the eighteenth century, see Rula Jurdi Abisaab, "The Ulama of Jabal 'Amil in Safavid Iran, 1501–1736: Marginality, Migration and Social Change," *Iranian Studies* 27, nos. 1–4 (1994): 103–22. **scholars, whether Shi'a or Sunni, do not actually use principles:** Many have written about the purported connection and/or disconnect between *uṣūl al-fiqh* and *fiqh*. What is important here is that each claim does political work in defining what Islam, Islamic law, and Muslims are; see Rumee Ahmed, "Islamic Law and Theology," in *The Oxford Handbook on Islamic Law*, ed. A. Emon and R. Ahmed (Oxford, UK: Oxford University Press, 2018). **some of which might have been more accurate and some less so:** The notion that even the most "authentic" *ḥadīth* collections contain dubious *ḥadīth* is not controversial among *ḥadīth* scholars and jurists. The question is not whether collections contain dubious *ḥadīth* but what to do with those dubious *hadith*; see Mohammad Fadel, "Ibn Hajar's Hady al-sārī: A Medieval Interpretation of the Structure of Bukhārī's Jāmi' al-ṣaḥīḥ," *Journal of Near Eastern Studies* 54, no. 3 (1995): 161–97. **A recent document:** The Amman Message can be found, along with its history and signatories, at http://ammanmessage.com. **Hanafis were unequivocal that:** The early Ḥanafī position on reciting the Qur'an in prayer is found in Rumee Ahmed, *Narratives of Islamic Legal Theory* (Oxford, UK: Oxford University Press, 2012), pp. 29ff. For the shifting position on Persian in liturgy and scholarship, see Travis Zadeh, *The Ver-*

nacular Qur'an: Translation and the Rise of Persian Exegesis (Oxford, UK: Oxford University Press, 2012). **A relatively recent example:** The wife-with-a-missing-husband incident is recounted in Muhammad Qasim Zaman, *The Ulama in Contemporary Islam: Custodians of Change* (Princeton, NJ: Princeton University Press, 2002), pp. 26–31. **who himself quoted:** The sixteenth-century scholar to whom Ibn ʿAbidīn referred is Shams al-Dīn Muḥammad al-Qūhistānī (d. ca. 1546), and the entire discussion about changing the Ḥanafī law of divorce can be found in Ibn ʿAbīdīn, *Radd al-Muḥtār Sharḥ Durr al-Mukhtār* (Riyadh: Dar ʿAlim al-Kutub, 2003), pp. 6:460–66. **There's an old saying:** The original statement attributed to ʿAlī b. Abī Ṭālib is, "If our religion was based on opinion, then the bottom of the sock would be wiped prior to the top, yet I saw the Messenger of God wipe the top of his sock." The saying can be found in Abī Dāʾūd, *Kitāb al-Sunan* (Jedda: Dar al-Qibla, 1998), p. 226.

Chapter 3
legal scholars described themselves: al-Sarakhsī explicitly stated that God has given legal scholars a rank equivalent to prophets; see *Kitāb al-Mabsūṭ* (Beirut: Dar al-Maʿrifah, 1989), pp. 1:2–3. **The first story involves:** The story of Sultan Meḥmed al-Fātiḥ and the architect Atik Sinan is widespread throughout Islamic literature. For contextual background to the story, see Selen Bahriye Morkoç, *A Study of Ottoman Narratives on Architecture: Text, Context and Hermeneutics* (Bethesda, MD: Academica Press, 2010), pp. 250ff. **Consider this second story:** Versions of the Sultan Meḥmed IV story can be found in Rudolph Peters, *Crime and Punishment in Islamic Law: Theory and Practice from the Sixteenth to the Twenty-First Century* (Cambridge, UK: Cambridge University Press, 2005), p. 93; and Elyse Semerdjian, *"Off the Straight Path": Illicit Sex, Law, and Community in Ottoman Aleppo* (Syracuse, NY: Syracuse University Press, 2008), p. 129. For a recounting of the story and an in-depth discussion of adultery laws in the Ottoman Empire, see Fariba Zarinebaf, *Crime and Punishment in Istanbul: 1700–1800* (Berkeley: University of California Press, 2010), pp. 86–111 (the Mehmed IV story is on p. 106). **the aforementioned al-Sarakhsi, who wrote:** The quote is from his book, *Uṣūl al-Sarakhsī* (Beirut: Dar al-Kutub al-ʿIlmiyya, 1993), p. 1:9. **The poet and mystic Jalal al-Din al-Rumi:** The Rūmī quote is found in Reynold Nicholson, trans., *The Mathnawi* (Cambridge, UK: E. J. W. Gibb Memorial Trust, 1990), p. 5:3. **do not even mention the towering figure:** On willful omissions of al-Māturīdī in biographical dictionaries, see M. Sait Özervali, "The Authenticity of Māturīdī's Kitāb al-Tawḥīd: A Re-examination," *Isâm Araṣtimalari Derdigi* 1 (1997): 20. **the Hanafi patriarch Muhammad al-Shaybani:** al-Shaybānī is quoted by Shāh Walīullah al-Dihlāwī (d. 1762), along with similar opinions from other scholars, in Marcia Hermensen, trans., *The Conclusive Argument from God: Shāh Walī Ullāh of Delhi's Ḥujjat Allāh al-Bāligha* (Leiden: Brill, 1995), p. 465. Ibn Juzayy's opinion is found in his book *Taqrib al-Wuṣūl ilā ʿIlm al-Uṣūl* (Amman: Dar al-Nafāʾis, 2002), pp. 143–46. **the following four criteria:** The four requirements are distilled from seven well-known stipulations for deriving law regularly cited by jurists; namely, these are knowing (1) about the legal verses of the Qur'an, (2) how to access *ḥadīth* texts,

(3) what issues are agreed to by Consensus, (4) how legal evidence is derived, (5) the Arabic language, (6) the rules of abrogation, and (7) how to determine a *ḥadīth*'s authenticity. For the purpose of brevity, I combined (1) and (2) under one heading and (4), (6), and (7) under one heading, but all seven stipulations are nonetheless represented. For most scholars, these formed the baseline for *ijtihād*; for more detail, see Wael Hallaq, "Was the Gate of Ijtihad Closed?," *International Journal of Middle East Studies* 16, no. 1 (1984): 3–41. **it was a big deal in the precolonial period:** Literacy was seen as a virtue in the precolonial world and as an exceptional academic achievement; Edmund Burke III, "Islam at the Center: Technological Complexes and the Roots of Modernity," *Journal of World History* 20, no. 2 (2009): 178. On literacy rates in Islamicate lands throughout Muslim history, see Francis Robinson, "Technology and Religious Change: Islam and the Impact on Print," *Modern Asian Studies* 27, no. 1 (1993): 234–37; Brian Street, *Literacy in Theory and in Practice* (New York: Cambridge University Press, 1984), p. 179; Nelly Hanna, "Literacy and the 'Great Divide' in the Islamic World, 1300–1800," *Journal of Global History* 2, no. 2 (2007): 184; Adeeb Khalid, *The Politics of Muslim Cultural Reform: Jadidism in Central Asia* (Berkeley: University of California Press, 1998), pp. 24–25; Claude Markovits, *Historie de l'Inde moderne 1480–1950* (Lille, FR: Fayard, 1994), p. 194; Donald Quatert, *The Ottoman Empire, 1700–1922*, 2nd ed. (Cambridge, UK: Cambridge University Press, 2005), p. 169; and Terri DeYoung, "Love, Death, and the Ghost of al-Khansāʾ," in *Tradition, Modernity, and Postmodernity in Arabic Literature*, ed. K. Abdel-Malek and W. Hallaq (Leiden: Brill, 2000), p. 49. **ensured a wide readership:** On the reception of al-Māturīdī's book on theology, *Kitāb al-Tawḥīd*, see Rudolph Ulrich, *al-Māturīdī and the Development of Sunnī Theology in Samarqand* (Leiden: Brill, 2015), pp. 191–93. **for travelers and for residents:** In translating the passage from *al-Zubad*, I strayed slightly from the original Arabic to make it rhyme in English, but the meaning and rulings are the same; Aḥmad ibn al-Ḥusayn ibn Raslān, *Alfiyyah al-Zubad fī Fiqh al-Shāfiʿī* (Beirut: Dar al-Mashariʾ, 2001), p. 16. **al-Ghazali (d. 1111) remarked:** al-Ghazālī's quote is taken from his book, *al-Mustaṣfā min ʿIlm al-Uṣūl*, and the translation was adapted from Abdullah bin Hamid Ali, trans., *al-Ghazali on the Essentials of Interpretative Autonomy (Ijtihād)* (Lamppost Productions, 2013), http://www.lamppostproductions.com /wp-content/uploads/2013/01/Al-Ghazali-on-the-Conditions-of-Ijtihad.pdf. **Gender was the most obvious barrier:** To get a sense of the challenges to women's full participation in knowledge production, see Asma Sayeed, *Women and the Transmission of Religious Knowledge in Islam* (Cambridge, UK: Cambridge University Press, 2013). **Gomaa argued:** Ali Gomaa's fatwa stated, "I greet President Mubarak who offered dialogue and responded to the demands of the people. Going against legitimacy is forbidden (Haram). This is an invitation for chaos. We support stability. What we have now is a blind chaos leading to a civil war. I call on all parents to ask their children to stay home." Cited in "Live Blog Feb 2—Egypt Protests," Al-Jazeera, accessed August 31, 2017, http://www.aljazeera.com/blogs/middleeast/2011/02/3134.html. For a poignant analysis of Gomaa's statement and its reception, see Zareena Grewal, *Islam Is a Foreign Country: American Muslims and the Global Crisis of Authority* (New

Haven, CT: Yale University Press, 2015), pp. 347–50. **The Islamic legal conversation has become richer:** For a detailed discussion on the effect of literacy and connectivity on Islamic legal discourse, see M. Nawawy and S. Khamis, *Islam Dot Com* (New York: Palgrave-MacMillan, 2009), pp. 45ff.

Chapter 4
we will look at three patching methods: For a comprehensive text on patching in theory and in practice, see Ahmed Fekry Ibrahim, *Pragmatism in Islamic Law: A Social and Intellectual History* (Syracuse, NY: Syracuse University Press, 2014). Fekry aptly dubs patching "pragmatic eclecticism," and his typology reflects an exactitude that was not possible in this book. He notes, for instance, that what I call *takhayyur* is more appropriately *tatabbuʿ al-rukhaṣ* in the historical legal tradition. I use the more modern term *takhayyur*, as it is more readily recognized today. **financial transaction known as *riba*:** Technically, *ribā* forbids the sale of "like for like," meaning that one cannot exchange two rotting apples for one fresh apple or one bar of silver for two bars of silver. The exchange must be of different commodities; otherwise, it is *ribā*. Ulama differed on how commodities should differ; for a thorough exposition of classical opinions, see Hiroyuki Yanagihashi, *A History of the Early Islamic Law of Property: Reconstructing the Legal Development, 7th–9th Centuries* (Leiden: Brill, 2004). **Ottoman ulama made them licit:** For more on how Ottoman Ḥanafīs devised cash-based waqfs, see Jon E. Mandaville, "Usurious Piety: The Cash Waqf Controversy in the Ottoman Empire," *International Journal of Middle East Studies* 10, no. 3 (August 1979): 289–308. ***ulama* borrowed from the Hanafi school:** On the Moroccan adoption of Ḥanafī rulings during the *Mudawwana* reforms, see Aïcha El Hajjami, "The Religious Arguments in the Debate on the Reform of the Moroccan Family Code," in *Gender and Equality in Muslim Family Law: Justice and Ethics in the Islamic Tradition*, ed. Ziba Mir-Hosseini et al. (London: I. B. Tauris, 2013), pp. 89–90; and for the difficulties encountered in the process, see Etty Terem, *Old Texts, New Practices: Islamic Reform in Modern Morocco* (Stanford, CA: Stanford University Press, 2014). **Ibn Taymiyya stopped him:** This story is cited in Elyse Semerdjian, *"Off the Straight Path": Illicit Sex, Law, and Community in Ottoman Aleppo* (Syracuse, NY: Syracuse University Press, 2008), p. 135. **non-Muslims must be barred:** The Malaysian fatwa barring non-Muslims from using the name "Allah" was issued by government scholars in the province of Selangor and published under the title *Wajib Pelihara Kesucian Nama Allah Selangor* (Selangor: Majlis Agama Islam Selangor, 2013). The full text can be found here: http://www.mais.gov.my/info-mais/informasi/penerbitan/muat-turun/33-buku-kalimah-allah-full-version-bm/file. **block the means of intermingling:** Ibn al-Qayyim's quote is from his *Ṭurūq al-Ḥukmiyya fī al-Siyāsa al-Sharʿiyya* (Beirut: Maktaba al-Muʾayyad, 1989), p. 239. **istislah was used by banks:** For an overview of how ulama in the early twentieth century used *maṣlaḥa* to overhaul Islamic laws related to banking, see Haider Ala Hamoudi, "Muhammad's Social Justice or Muslim Cant?: Langdellianism and the Failures of Islamic Finance," *Cornell International Law Journal* 40, no. 1 (Winter 2007): 89–133. **in almost every case:** The quote

on *maṣlaḥa*'s function in legitimating regimes and curbing civil rights is taken from Alex Schank, "Constitutional Shariʿa: Authoritarian Experiments with Islamic Judicial Review in Egypt, Iran, and Saudi Arabia," *The Georgetown Law Journal* 102 (2014): 519–50. This is not a new observation; Fazlur Rahman noted the inherent subjectivity of *maṣlaḥa* and its potential for abuse in "Toward Reformulating the Methodology of Islamic Law," *NYU Journal of International Law and Politics* 12 (1979): 219–24. Anver Emon and Felicitas Opwis have more recently argued that this was actually the original intention of the *maṣlaḥa* and the *maqāṣid* as legal tools: they were meant to restrict reforms, not to enable them; see Anver Emon, *Islamic Natural Law Theories* (Oxford, UK: Oxford University Press, 2010); and Felicitas Opwis, *Maṣlaḥa and the Purpose of the Law: Islamic Discourse on Legal Change from the 4th/10th Century to 8th/14th Century* (Leiden: Brill, 2010). For a discussion on the inextricable link between the *maqāṣid* and power, see Rumee Ahmed, "Which Comes First, the *Maqāṣid* or the *Shariʿa*?" and Anver Emon "Epilogue," both in *The Objectives of Islamic Law: The Promises and Challenges of the Maqāṣid al-Shariʿa*, ed. I. Nassery, R. Ahmed, and M. Tatari (Lanham, MD: Lexington Books, 2018). **there should be a moratorium:** The call for a moratorium on the application of Islamic corporal punishments was most prominently made by Tariq Ramadan; see "An International Call for Moratorium on Corporal Punishment, Stoning and the Death Penalty in the Islamic World," accessed August 31, 2017, https://tariqramadan.com/an-international-call-for-moratorium-on-corporal-punishment-stoning-and-the-death-penalty-in-the-islamic-world/.

Chapter 5

cannot say so outright: One of the best documented cases of the balancing act that ulama must perform when changing laws is found in the implementation of Indonesia's 1974 Marriage Act; see M. Cammack, A. Bedner, and S. van Huis, "Democracy, Human Rights, and Islamic Family Law in Post-Soeharto Indonesia," *New Middle Eastern Studies* 5 (2015): 5ff. **How does she know:** For an extensive commentary on the rules for latecomers to congregational prayer, see al-Shurunbulālī, *Marāqī al-Falāḥ Sharḥ Nūr al-Īḍāḥ* (Beirut: Dar al-Kutub al-ʿIlmiyya, 2004), p. 176. **the following report:** The bowing *ḥadīth* was graded "good" (*ḥasan*) by al-Tirmidhī; cited in Khaled Abou El Fadl, *And God Knows the Soldiers: The Authoritative and Authoritarian in Islamic Discourses* (Lanham, MD: University Press of America, 2001), p. 46. Original citation is Muḥammad ʿAbd al-Raḥmān al-Mubārakpūrī, *Tuḥfat al-Aḥwadhī bi Sharḥ Jāmiʿ al-Tirmidhī* (Beirut: Dar al-Kutub al-ʿIlmiyyah, n.d.), pp. 7:425–26. **Muslims overwhelmingly believe:** The claim that Muslims overwhelmingly reject domestic violence is based on the World Values Survey, in which the vast majority of Muslims surveyed stated that it was "never justifiable to hit one's wife" (V208); http://www.worldvaluessurvey.org/WVSOnline.jsp. **others have proposed rereading:** For an exhaustive survey of modern reinterpretations of Qur'an 4:34, see Ayesha S. Chaudhry, *Domestic Violence and the Islamic Tradition* (Oxford, UK: Oxford University Press, 2014), chap. 5. **The resulting decree:** The text of the Saudi domestic-violence law, known as the Law of Protection from Abuse (Royal Decree Ni. M/52),

can be found here: http://www.moh.gov.sa/depts/psychiatric/Depts/Documents/انجليزي
نظام20%الحماية20%من20%الايذاء20%-.pdf. The Saudi emergency conferences were widely
reported and commented on; details can be found at http://www.okaz.com.sa/article
/623524/. **would look something like this:** For a multidisciplinary approach that provides a larger picture of the *qiwāma* and *wilāya* concept map in Muslim family law,
see Z. Mir-Hosseini, M. Al-Sharmani, and J. Rumminger, eds., *Men in Charge? Re-
thinking Authority in Muslim Legal Tradition* (Oxford, UK: Oneworld, 2015). To see
the many manifestations of *qiwāma* in precolonial marriage and divorce laws, see
Kecia Ali, *Marriage and Slavery in Early Islam* (Cambridge, MA: Harvard University Press, 2010). **Some ulama even cited:** The Egyptian Dar al-Ifta at the time cited
maṣlaḥa as the reason for changing the laws on domestic violence; see http://www
.masrawy.com/Islameyat/Fatawa-Nesaa/details/2014/12/1/400823/الصحيح-في-ضرب-الزوجة
-دار-الافتاء-توضح-الحكم-الشرعي-.

Chapter 6

ulama had to adapt: The relationship between the *ulama* and the ruling class in the
Ottoman and Mamluk empires is well documented. See, for instance, Colin Imber,
Ebu's-su'ud: The Islamic Legal Tradition (Stanford, CA: Stanford University Press,
1997); Leslie Peirce, *Morality Tales: Law and Gender in the Ottoman Court of Aintab*
(Berkeley: University of California Press, 2003); Kristen Stilt, *Islamic Law in Action:
Authority, Discretion, and Everyday Experiences in Mamluk Egypt* (Oxford, UK: Oxford University Press, 2011); and Michael Winter, "'Ulama' between State and Society in Pre-Modern Sunni Islam," in *Guardians of the Faith in Modern Times: "Ulama"
in the Middle East*, ed. Meir Hatina (Leiden: Brill, 2009), pp. 21–45. **the law of witnessing:** On the issue of slaves serving as witnesses, there was a difference of opinion. The famous jurist al-Qudūrī (d. 1037), for example, did bar slaves from serving as
arbiters, and he imposed limits on their status as witnesses. His *Mukhtaṣar* inspired
a number of commentaries and was taught in seminaries across the Muslim world. It
is interesting, however, that Mamlūk Ḥanafī scholars such as Badr al-Dīn al-ʿAynī,
Aḥmad al-Sarūjī, Quṭb al-Dīn al-Kākī, Jamāl al-Dīn al-Zaylaʿī, and Aḥkām al-Dīn
al-Bābartī eschewed commenting on al-Qudūrī and in fact mention him much less
frequently than do other Ḥanafīs. Also of note is that later Egyptian Ḥanafīs such
as Ibn Nujaym, al-Ḥaṣkafī, Ibn ʿĀbidīn, and others choose to comment on al-Nasafī
or al-Mawṣilī, both of whom allowed slaves to serve as witnesses, rather than on al-
Qudūrī. That is surely not due only to the latter's views on slavery, but I raise it to
demonstrate that al-Qudūrī's opinion on the matter was not a problem for Mamluk-
era Ḥanafīs. **considered promoting the Hanafi school:** Mamluks were also inclined
toward Ḥanafīs because the latter did not make Qurashī descent a condition for being caliph. The Mamluks ended up getting around this anyway, though, by simply
installing a figurehead caliph who claimed Qurashī descent; Aziz al-Azmeh, *Muslim Kingship: Power and the Sacred in Muslim, Christian, and Pagan Politics* (London:
I. B. Tauris, 2001), p. 176. **Their first attempts were clumsy:** The story of the Cai-
rene chief judge offering to auction off the Mamluks can be found in Sayyid Riz-

wan Ali, *Izz al-Din al-Sulami: His Life and Works* (Islamabad: Islamic Research Institute, 1978), pp. 95ff. To get a sense of the social and religious discrimination that came with being a *mamlūk*, see Koby Yosef, "The Term *Mamlūk* and Slave Status during the Mamluk Sultanate," *Al-Qantara* 34, no. 1 (2013): 7–34. **stipulations that a government official must be:** For a representative list of qualifications for government officials in pre-Mamluk Shāfiʿī thought, see al-Nawawī, *Minhāj al-Ṭālibīn* (Jeddah: Dar al-Minhaj, 2005), p. 557. **easy to miss the move:** To see the subtle shift, compare al-Nawawī's requirements for government officials, particularly judges, with those of Shāfiʿīs commenting on al-Nawawī's work during and after the Mamluk era, such as al-Khaṭīb al-Shirbīnī, *Mughnī al-Muḥtāj* (Beirut: Dar al-Maʿrifa, 1997), p. 4:501; and Zakariyya al-Anṣārī, *Fatḥ al-Wahhāb bi Sharḥ Manhaj al-Ṭullāb* (Beirut: Dar al-Kutub al-ʿIlmiyya, 1997), p. 2:362–63; both clarified that a judge cannot be unfree and interpreted that to mean "not a *raqīq*." The shift continued even well after the Mamluk dynasty, as jurists such as Aḥmad al-Qalyūbī (d. 1659)—who commented on a work of Jalāluddīn al-Maḥallī, who himself commented on the original text of al-Nawawī—isolated the "not a *raqīq*" qualification and highlighted it to the exclusion of anything about being unfree, so that it appears as though al-Nawawī's original text said that judges cannot be *raqīq*s; Shihāb al-Dīn al-Qalyūbī, *Ḥāshiyatān ʿalā Sharḥ Minhāj al-Ṭālibīn* (Egypt: Mustafa Bab al-Halabi, 1956), p. 4:296. **rise of coffeehouses:** For more on the coffee debate in medieval Islamic law, see Ralph S. Hattox, *Coffee and Coffeehouses: The Origins of a Social Beverage in the Medieval Near East* (Seattle: University of Washington Press, 1985) pp. 29–45, 103ff. **economic and agricultural menace:** Statistics on *qat* growth and cultivation in Yemen were taken from C. Ward and P. Gatter, *Qat in Yemen—Towards a Policy and Action Plan* (Washington, DC: The World Bank, 2000), pp. 16–18. **absolutely permitted in Islam:** The 1999 fatwa by the then chief justice of the Yemen Supreme Court permitting qat use can be found here: http://elaph.com/Politics/2004/12/29906.htm. **recent poll in an Ethiopian town:** The poll on attitudes toward qat use in Ethiopia is cited in Lamina Sikiru, "Flower of Paradise (Khat: *Catha edulis*): Psychosocial, Health, and Sports Perspectives," *African Journal of Health Sciences* 22 (2012): 165. **scholars made their hack:** A fatwa describing just how qat must be eaten so as not to invalidate the prayer can be found at http://fatwa.islamweb.net/fatwa/index.php?page=showfatwa &Option=FatwaId&Id=79597. **A minority of Yemeni scholars:** The dissenting ulama had a long and detailed dissent, but their website—olamayemen.com—has been shut down since the early days of the Saudi-Yemen war. A description of dissenting opinions from ulama outside of Yemen can be found at http://yemen-press.com /news15512.html. The recent fatwa in which the Yemen chief justice discouraged but did not condemn qat use can be found at http://fatwa.islamweb.net/fatwa/index .php?page=showfatwa&Option=FatwaId&lang=A&Id=13241. **rise of Islamic finance:** There is no shortage of literature on the foundations and application of Islamic finance, but most of it is written with some form of ideological bent, usually serving the interests of financial institutions, government agencies, or both. It is difficult to find an overview that is both academically rigorous and accessible, but a good place to start is Ibrahim Warde, *Islamic Finance in the Global Economy* (Edinburgh, UK: Edinburgh University Press, 2000). For a more academic approach with specific case studies, see Frank Vogel and Samuel Hayes III, *Islamic Law and Finance: Religion, Risk, and Return* (The Hague: Kluwer Law International, 1998). **Qatar Islamic Bank:** The quote from the chief executive of the Qatar Islamic Bank is found in Quasim M. Quasim, "Islamic Banking: New Opportunities for Cooperation between Western and Islamic Financial Institutions," in *Islamic Banking and Finance* (London: Butterworths, 1986), p. 25. It is cited in Abdullah Saeed, *Islamic Banking and Interest: A Study of the Prohibition of Riba and Its Contemporary Interpretation* (Leiden: Brill, 1999), p. 84.

Chapter 7
barely made a dent: FGC data taken from UNICEF Childinfo, as reported on the World Bank's data aggregator, accessed August 31, 2017, https://data.worldbank.org/indicator/SH.STA.FGMS.ZS?locations=EG. The prevalence of FGC among females in Egypt aged fifteen to forty-nine was 95.5% in 2006, the year of the international conference. Data taken in 2008 suggested that the number was 95.3%. Data taken from studies conducted in 2014 and 2015 reflected a 92.3% and 87.2% prevalence, respectively. **the FIOE hosts:** A recent monograph serves as an introduction to the history of the ECFR and its rulings; Iyad Zahalka, *Shari'a in the Modern Era*, trans. Ohad Stadler and Cecilia Sibony (Cambridge, UK: Cambridge University Press, 2016), pp. 58ff. **The councils tend to:** *Fiqh* councils should not be confused with sharia councils, the latter of which have some measure of state sanction and have rulings that, while not binding, may be admissible in court. For more on sharia councils, see Letizia Ricardi, "Women at a Crossroads between UK Legislation and Sharia Law," *GSTF International Journal of Law and Social Sciences* 3, no. 2 (April 2014): 86–91. **argued that apostasy:** The Fiqh Council of North America's fatwa on absolute religious freedom is found in Jamal Badawi, "Is Apostasy a Capital Crime in Islam?," ISNA, accessed August 31, 2017, http://www.fiqhcouncil.org/node/34. **right to initiate a divorce:** The ECFR's fatwa on a wife's right to a unilateral divorce can be found in Julie MacFarlane, *Islamic Divorce in North America* (New York: Oxford University Press, 2012), p. 235. **appointed without an election:** The MJC's fatwa on appointing imams can be found in Abdulkader Tayob, *Islam in South Africa: Mosques, Imams, and Sermons* (Gainesville, FL: University of Florida Press, 1999), pp. 50–51. **mirror mosques' balancing act:** For a full explanation of the politics of council fatwas, see Alexandre Caeiro, "The Power of European Fatwas: The Minority *Fiqh* Project and the Making of an Islamic Counterpublic," *International Journal of Middle East Studies* 42 (2010): 435–49; and Caeiro, "The Making of the Fatwa: The Production of Islamic Legal Expertise in Europe," *Archives de Sciences Sociales des Religions* 155 (2011): 81–100. **a different financial model:** SeekersHub, for instance, offers free online courses, for which they have a reported thirty-six thousand registrations. They conduct highly efficient fund-raising campaigns (for the latest campaign, see http://seekershub.org/donate/) with targets like $300,000 in thirty days (they raised over $210,000 for that

particular campaign); see "Successful Seekers Ramadan Campaign but Work Remains," SeekersHub, accessed August 31, 2017, http://seekershub.org/blog/2012/09 /successful-seekers-ramadan-campaign-but-work-remains/. A 2016 campaign aimed to have 100,000 donors each donating $50 per month by the end of the year. The al-Maghrib Institute raises funds partly by charging $85 per course and, at the time of this writing, reports having over 120,000 unique students globally (http://www.al-maghrib.org/). In 2015, al-Maghrib reported revenues of $1.5 million and has reported over $1 million in revenues each year since 2011; in that time, they reported profits of just over $1.18 million (https://projects.propublica.org/nonprofits/organiza tions/270091991). Qibla charges about $300 per course, but I do not have reliable numbers for their attendees or financial statements. The Reviving the Islamic Spirit annual conference charges a $55–65 entry fee, with an estimated 20,000 people in attendance each year. They also host a knowledge retreat ($175) at the conference and an appreciation luncheon with the scholars ($120). Also, over 250 vendors rent booths in the Grand Bazaar at a rate of $900 per booth. Bayyinah charges tuition for its courses ($7,750 for an in-residence nine-month course, not including living expenses, and $1,200 for a one-month course) and has an estimated yearly revenue of over $2 million (https://www.dandb.com/businessdirectory/bayyinahllc-irving-tx-88316 93.html). Compared to mosques and umbrella organizations, educational institutes are far more profitable and financially nimble. Consider that the largest North American umbrella organizations, the Islamic Society of North America and the Islamic Circle of North America, run regular deficits, according to ProPublica. The same is true of more advocacy-oriented groups such as the Muslim Public Affairs Council and Muslim Advocates. There are exceptions, such as the Muslim American Society, which reports regular profits, according to ProPublica. **business models all rely:** This dynamic is not limited to mosques and educational institutes but to an industry of Islam- and Muslim-related products and services; see Faegheh Shirazi, *Brand Islam: The Marketing and Commodification of Piety* (Austin: University of Texas Press, 2016). **how to invest:** The SeekersHub course is titled, "Money Matters: Islamic Finance in Everyday Life," SeekersHub, accessed August 31, 2017, http://seekershub.org/home /courses/GEN130. **holds classes like:** al-Maghrib regularly changes the titles and topics of its seminars, so the Fiqh of Chillin' and the Fiqh of Love are no longer on offer. But al-Maghrib produces trailers for many of its seminars, and the trailers can still be viewed for the Fiqh of Chillin' (https://www.youtube.com/watch?v=we1YiA6 xutU) and for the Fiqh of Love (https://www.youtube.com/watch?v=NyY9q8SF7W0). **Most Muslims today, however:** Several polls suggest that most Muslims do not support stoning adulterers. Some polls are very clear about this, such as the 2016 ICM poll in Britain, which showed that only 5% of British Muslims sympathized even a little with stoning, while 79% condemned it (see p. 23 of the ICM data, accessible at https://www.icmunlimited.com/wp-content/uploads/2016/04/Mulims-full-suite -data-plus-topline.pdf). Other polls need a little more scrutiny. A recent Pew poll has been much-cited to suggest that most Muslims support stoning for adultery. There are two problems with the poll, though. The first, mentioned earlier, is that the poll asked only whether respondents "favored" or "opposed" certain ideas, leaving no room for nuance or sympathy. The second, and more germane to the immediate issue, is that the poll asked about people's views on stoning only if they answered "favor" to the question "Do you favor or oppose making sharia law, or Islamic law, the official law of the land of our country?" (See questions 79a and 92c of the poll numbers, found at http://assets.pewresearch.org/wp-content/uploads/sites/11/2013/04/worlds -muslims-religion-politics-society-topline1.pdf.) So, for instance, the adultery poll suggests that 48% of respondents in Indonesia, a country with over 205 million Muslims, favor stoning adulterers. But only 72% of Indonesian respondents said that they favored making sharia law, or Islamic law, the law of the land. So, the poll is actually saying that of the 72% who favored making sharia the law of the land, 48% also supported the stoning of adulterers. That means that, in total, 35% of Indonesians polled supported stoning adulterers, still a worrying number, but 65% of Indonesians polled rejected it. Similarly, the poll suggests that 54% of respondents in Bangladesh, a country of about 150 million Muslims, support stoning adulterers. But only 82% answered "favor" to the question about making sharia the law of the land, which means that 45% of respondents support stoning while 55% reject it. In Nigeria, a country of 80 million Muslims, 37% of respondents approved of stoning adulterers, but since only 71% favored sharia being the law of the land, that means that 26% of Nigerians polled supported stoning adulterers while 74% opposed the practice. Closely scrutinizing these poll numbers demonstrates that (1) most Muslims oppose *zinā* laws as they currently stand and (2) favoring sharia law does not mean that you automatically approve of corporal punishments commonly associated with countries with sharia source laws. **The real root of the problem:** for more on zina laws, both in their historical articulations and their manifestations in contemporary societies, see Hina Azam, *Sexual Violation in Islamic Law: Substance, Evidence, and Procedure* (Cambridge, UK: Cambridge University Press, 2015); and Vanja Hazić and Ziba Mir-Hosseini, *Control and Sexuality: The Revival of Zina Laws in Muslim Contexts* (London: Women Living Under Muslim Laws, 2010).

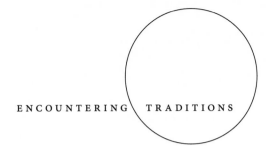

ENCOUNTERING TRADITIONS